Practicing Sabermetrics

Putting the Science of Baseball Statistics to Work

GABRIEL B. COSTA, MICHAEL R. HUBER, *AND* JOHN T. SACCOMAN

McFarland & Company, Inc., Publishers

Jefferson, North Carolina, and London

LIBRARY OF CONGRESS CATALOGUING-IN-PUBLICATION DATA

Costa, Gabriel B.
    Practicing sabermetrics : putting the science of baseball
statistics to work / Gabriel B. Costa, Michael R. Huber, and
John T. Saccoman.
        p.   cm.
    Includes bibliographical references and index.

    ISBN 978-0-7864-4177-8
    softcover : 50# alkaline paper ∞

    1. Baseball — Statistical methods.   2. Baseball —
Mathematical models.   I. Huber, Michael R., 1960–
II. Saccoman, John T., 1964–   III. Title.
    GV877.C68   2009
    796.357 — dc22   2009027463

British Library cataloguing data are available

Cover image ©2009 Shutterstock

Manufactured in the United States of America

McFarland & Company, Inc., Publishers
  Box 611, Jefferson, North Carolina 28640
  www.mcfarlandpub.com

Table of Contents

Preface

Hello, my name is Gabe Costa. My co-authors, Michael R. Huber and John T. Saccoman, and I are grateful that you are looking at this book. *Practicing Sabermetrics* is a follow-up to *Understanding Sabermetrics*, which was published in early 2008 by McFarland.

Mike, John and I are professors of mathematics and life-long fans of the national pastime. We have been fortunate to combine our interests in a singular way: by teaching courses on sabermetrics for over twenty years. The term "sabermetrics" was coined by the noted baseball author and researcher Bill James, who defined it as the search for objective knowledge about baseball (the "saber" part comes from the organization known as the Society for American Baseball Research — SABR — which was established in 1971).

Our purpose for writing *Practicing Sabermetrics* is to give you an opportunity to familiarize yourself with the actual instruments or metrics used in sabermetrics. Our goal has been to make our book as broad as possible and, therefore, to reach as many people as possible. We assume the reader has knowledge of the rules of baseball, is familiar with the fundamentals of algebra and knows a tad about statistics. Chapter 22 is the only place where advanced mathematics is introduced.

With very few exceptions, we have divided our chapters into three main parts: an introduction of the specific concept or concepts; a number of carefully demonstrated problems involving the presented topics; a section where you can actually practice sabermetrics, with the numerical answers provided.

By and large, the chapters are independent. That is, they can be read out of order, so that the professor/teacher/student can "mix and match" — or omit — topics as desired. We have also included a few chapters on advanced sabermetrical themes and have added several pertinent appendices.

We trust our approach will be well received by the serious baseball fan and by students taking courses on both the university and high school levels. Sabermetrics has made serious inroads into academia during the past few decades. The first course ever taught on sabermetrics was at Seton Hall University in 1988. Since then, the United States Military Academy, Bowling Green University, and Quinnipiac University, among other institutions, have offered related courses. We are also aware that the Massachusetts Institute of Technology offers a program to middle school students dealing with the science and mathematics of baseball. It is also our hope that parents and guardians with children, who love baseball but dislike mathematics, would see in our book a vehicle to encourage these children to learn mathematics.

Before I sign off and you hear from Mike and John, I would like to acknowledge the following people to thank them for their support and assistance with respect to this project: Colonel Michael Phillips and my colleagues, the members of the Department of Mathematical Sciences at the United States Military Academy at West Point; the Seton Hall University Priest Community, ministered to by Monsignor James M. Cafone and the administrative leaders of the same institution along with Dr. Joan Guetti and my colleagues of the Department of Mathematics and Computer Science; baseball researcher and historian Bill Jenkinson; Tony Morante of the New York Yankees; and Linda Ruth Tosetti, the granddaughter of George Herman Ruth. Lastly, a note of gratitude must be given to my archbishop, the Most Reverend John J. Myers, J.C.D., D.D. In every sense, his blessing is most appreciated.

* * *

MICHAEL R. HUBER: One of our goals with this work has been to expand the knowledge about the great former players of the national pastime. We have tried to include many of the members of the Baseball Hall of Fame in our examples and problems. The game has been a part of American culture for over a century and a half, and many of the men who put their mark on Major League Baseball did so long before we, the authors, were born. By including mention of them, we hope to preserve their legacy. Many of the measures we use were created to compare the best of the best. Those players are enshrined in Cooperstown, and we felt it appropriate to create problems broadcasting their success. We hope you enjoy the tidbits.

I must thank my co-authors Gabe and John, whose energy and passion for both mathematics and studying baseball is contagious. They have indeed made this a fun project for me. Extraordinary thanks go to Brandon Stern-Charles and Joseph Dyer, two students of mine at Muhlenberg College. Brandon and Joe worked as summer research assistants, helping me collect data and creating and verifying solutions to problems, mostly in the linear weights chapters. They each hit a home run in their efforts.

I also want to thank my family for their support. My father, Erwin Huber, taught me to appreciate the game of baseball when my brothers and I were old enough to wear a glove or throw a ball. He taught me how to read the box scores. He did what many fathers do — took us to practice, coached our teams, helped the Little League organization as an umpire or by selling booster tickets. I tried to pay him back by doing that for my children. Thanks, Dad. I am grateful to my wife, Terry, and our children: Nick, Kirstin, and Steffi. They never said no when asked to go to a baseball museum or attend a game, whether driving a few hours to see an Army game or going to a minor league or major league contest while on vacation, and they know that no one leaves until the last out is made. Finally, I want to thank Father Gabriel Costa again, for baptizing our granddaughter Riley and formally introducing her to baseball with a New York Yankees bib after the ceremony. Grazie!

* * *

JOHN T. SACCOMAN: The baseball and mathematics have been lifelong labors of love, and I am grateful for the opportunities that I have been given to combine them. In particular, I am grateful to Seton Hall University, particularly the Department of Mathematics and Computer Science, for instituting and supporting the course in sabermetrics, and to my coauthors for including me in their various sabermetrics endeavors, as a guest speaker, coauthor, panelist, and team teacher. In addition, I am grateful to my wife, Mary Erin, for putting up with me through it all.

There is a wonderful tradition at the annual SABR meeting. A small group will gather early in the morning and find a park in the city in which to play catch. Playing catch is a pure expression of baseball companionship, and one of life's great pleasures for the baseball fan. I dedicate my efforts here to the four people in my life with whom I most enjoyed playing catch: my father, Dr. John J. Saccoman; my grandfather, Mario Saccoman; my cousin, Anthony Ortega; and my son, Ryan Mario Saccoman.

CHAPTER 1

What Is Sabermetrics and What Does It Do?

Introduction

Baseball is America's game. In spite of the 1919 World Series scandal involving the White Sox (known, thus, as the Black Sox) and the Reds, given the many disgraceful decades when African Americans were barred from playing in the Major Leagues, right up till the present controversies involving steroids, the national pastime has endured. President Franklin D. Roosevelt insisted that the game be played during World War II, so important was baseball to the American spirit.

Throughout the years we have all read novels about the game, watched movies about the game and *everyone* still remember the words and music to the song "Take Me Out to the Ball Game." Baseball is *ingrained* in us.

For the past thirty years or so, however, the game of Baseball has been looked at in new and different ways. When the yearly *Bill James Baseball Abstract* (see our Sources at the back of the book) began to appear, people started to look at the game differently. As was mentioned in the Preface, it was James himself who coined the word "sabermetrics," defining it as "the search for objective knowledge about baseball." By its very nature, this search uses *metrics*; that is, instruments or tools to *measure* performances.

In their book *The Hidden Game of Baseball*, John Thorn and Pete Palmer point out that while one may *love* baseball without numbers, the game itself *cannot be understood* unless we bring numbers into the conversation. Over the past three decades or so, a bevy of talented authors have published in this *broad* area which we call sabermetrics. Writers such as Jim Albert, Jay Bennett, Bill Jenkinson, Michael Lewis and G. Scott Thomas, to name but a few, have looked at the national pastime in a myriad of ways. But they all use *numbers*.

In this book, you will be exposed to many measures. You will review some of the traditional "old-school" statistics, such as Batting Average (*BA*) and Earned Run Average (*ERA*), in addition to seeing newer metrics such as Runs Created (*RC*), Linear Weights (*LWTS*) and the Power Speed Number (*PSN*). By using these measures, it is hoped that a clearer picture emerges with respect to whatever particular question is under discussion.

Let us consider an example. Suppose we want to compare pitchers from two different eras, say the Washington Senators Hall of Famer Walter Johnson and New York Yankees lefthander Whitey Ford. To do a "sabermetrical analysis," we would and could employ certain instruments. But exactly *what* measures should we use? Also, can we *really* compare players from different eras? What about other considerations such as differences in the game due to changes in the rules? How about other historical and contextual aspects, such as the fact that Johnson never played a night game on the West Coast, nor did he ever compete against African American players? Can *these factors* be "measured"?

We will return to these questions. Before we do, however, we must emphasize the following point. We the fans must be made aware of the fact that the degree of certainty in sabermetrics is not on the same order of as that of pure mathematics. *We do not prove theorems in sabermetrics.* After all is said and done, there is almost always a degree of subjectivity involving the interpretation of our conclusions. Care must be exercised in our very choice of measures, how they are applied and what one may derive from their use. In a real sense, sabermetrics is as much of an *art*, as it is a *science*.

However, we can learn *some things* which were previously unclear or unknown. We can gain *some* insights into questions like "Is a walk as good as a hit?," "Should we sacrifice and give up an out in order to get a runner to second base?," and "Was Hall of Famer Ty Cobb really a better all around player than the icon we know as Babe Ruth?"

Let us now return to the Johnson vs. Ford question above. Can we proceed to make such a comparison and is there a *formal* process to follow in answering such questions ... something like an *algorithm*? The answer is *Yes*! The following list of ten suggestions may serve as a *guide*—it is not carved in stone. You can modify this approach as you see fit.

Demonstrating Sabermetrics—10 Point Guide

1. Be careful to *identify* the question or questions under consideration. What *exactly* is being asked or investigated? Can it be *quantified* or it is more *qualitative* in nature? (See #8 below.)

2. Get as much *data* as possible. With the Internet, this is very easy. But be consistent with your sources. There are minor variations among various Web sites due to on-going research by lifelong baseball enthusiasts. For this book, as for our previous book, *Understanding Sabermetrics*, we have used http://www.baseball-reference.com/.

3. Use as many *metrics* as possible. This will only serve to support your approach. On this point, the more *independent* the measures are, the stronger and better the analysis. While it is true that the concept of "independence" can be considered from both statistical and philosophical perspectives, for our purposes it suffices to say that, if possible, the measures should not *overlap*. Let us use slugging percentage (*SLG*), which is reviewed in the next chapter, as an example. Assume that two players, X and Y, have the same number of at-bats (*AB*), and that player X has more total bases (*TB*) than player Y. Then player X will *also* have a higher *SLG* than player Y, since $SLG = \dfrac{TB}{AB}$. Note that no sabermetrical or mathematical errors are introduced by considering *both SLG* and *TB*, but there is a certain element of *redundancy*.

4. Always exercise care with respect to *comparisons*; try not to compare apples with oranges. For example, New York Giants Hall of Famer Mel Ott was a power hitter and clubbed 511 home runs (*HR*) in his career. While playing at home in the Polo Grounds, he hit more than 300 round trippers, while hitting fewer than 200 home runs on the road. But to contrast the "home Mel Ott" with the "away Mel Ott" from a *HR* perspective would be like comparing, well, apples with oranges.

5. Be conscious of the validity and appropriateness of how things are both *predicted* and how they are *measured*. For example, can I really make a *projection* of a player's lifetime *HR* based on his production after one season or do I need more data? In comparing two sets of statistics, am I more interested in *differences* or in *ratios*? Am I *consistent* with and do I understand my *labeling* of measures? For example, slugger Mark McGwire hit 583 career *HR* in 6187 *AB*.

His home run to at-bat ratio is $\dfrac{583}{6187} = .0942$, while his at-bat to home run ratio is $\dfrac{6187}{583} = 10.6123$, to four places. The first ratio can be interpreted as McGwire hitting nearly nine and one-half home runs for every 100 *ABs*, while the second number can be view as McGwire needing a bit more than ten and one-half at-bats for each home run. The numbers tell the same story, but in different ways.

6. The connected concepts of both *relativity* and *normalization* are very

useful when comparing a player of one era to a player in another era. For example, we may ask if Babe Ruth, with 714 *HR*, was a "more dominant" home run hitter than former career leader Hank Aaron (755 *HR*) or the present leader Barry Bonds (762 *HR*). Is there a way to put their respective *HR* totals in a "relative" or "normalized" context which would allow us to answer our question? These closely related topics will be further discussed in the fourth chapter.

7. Does the analysis seem to *converge* to a plausible conclusion? For example, suppose we use ten instruments to compare the following three Hall of Fame rightfielders: Roberto Clemente, Al Kaline and Frank Robinson. Let us further assume that one metric indicates Clemente as the best player of the three, while two statistics point to Kaline as the best of the lot. Can we now conclude that Robinson was the top player of the three, based on the fact that he came out first with regard to the remaining seven measures? Perhaps most people would agree with this deduction, but probably not every fan who saw these three stars while they were active players.

8. Bring into the discussion whatever *non–sabermetrical* factors which are present. This will supplement the analysis. Often, these factors will take the form of marginal comments, and they will almost never be quantitative in nature. However, they will give a fuller picture. For example, baseballs were more often replaced in games played in the 1920s as compared to a decade earlier. So, they were most probably "cleaner," thus easier to see. Were the baseballs of the 1920s "livelier?" Probably. And mentioning these facts this certainly brings something to the table. But, unless we knew the actual *number* of times the baseballs were changed and certain *resiliency* parameters associated with the baseballs, it is difficult to see how these factors could be *measured*, and, hence, what was their actual impact.

9. Always be aware of the possibility of further sabermetrical analysis and the development of new tools and measures. We can always learn more about a situation — we can always expand on our knowledge.

10. Realize that a sabermetrical "proof" is not on the same plane as a mathematical proof. There are always nooks and crannies which can be used, exploited or investigated. Were this not the case, we would all be the poorer, because we would have no need for baseball discussions!

Before we close this chapter, we will leave you with our version of "Twenty Questions." These are typical inquiries, in no particular order, which you will be able to address by using sabermetrics. We suggest that as you read more chapters and familiarize yourself with these metrics, you return to these (or similar) questions and ask yourself how they might be answered, following our ten point guide above. Have fun!

Twenty Questions Using Sabermetrics

• In the 1930s, three American League firstbasemen dominated their league in offensive statistics: Jimmie Foxx, Lou Gehrig and Hank Greenberg. Who was the best of the three?

• Is Yankees pitcher Mike Mussina a better hurler than the Braves' Tom Glavine?

• Should Brooklyn Dodgers legend Gil Hodges be inducted into the Hall of Fame?

• Was Hall of Famer Johnny Bench of the Reds a better catcher than Hall of Famer Mickey Cochrane?

• Is the Stolen Base really that valuable?

• Was Barry Bonds the greatest player ever?

• Which of the following two pitchers was more valuable to his team: Warren Spahn of the Milwaukee Braves or Sandy Koufax of the Los Angeles Dodgers?

• Where does Hall of Famer Ty Cobb rank with the all time great players?

• What is the "most revealing" hitting statistic in the following list: batting average (*BA*), on base average (*OBA,* also abbreviated *OBP*), on base plus slugging (*OPS*), or the total power quotient (*TPQ*)?

• Who was the better defensive centerfielder, Hall of Famer Willie Mays or Hall of Famer Larry Doby?

• What offensive numbers might Red Sox left fielder Ted Williams have accumulated, had his career not been interrupted twice by military obligations?

• How good of a double play combination was the legendary Chicago Cub triumvirate of Joe Tinker, Johnny Evers and Frank Chance?

• Who was the greatest secondbaseman ever?

• Who is the best hitter of the following: Vladimir Guerrero of the Angels, Albert Pujols of the Cardinals or Alex Rodriguez of the Yankees?

• How dominant a player was Hall of Famer Honus Wagner?

• Who would you rather have as a third baseman on your team, George Brett of the Royals or Mike Schmidt of the Phillies?

• Was Christy Mathewson of the New York Giants the greatest pitcher ever?

• Was Hall of Famer Rod Carew a better offensive player than Hall of Famer Charlie Gehringer?

• Who had better power numbers during their careers, Ernie Banks or Eddie Mathews, both of whom were National League All Stars in the 1950s and 1960s?

• How great of a pitcher was Hall of Famer Steve Carlton?

In Summary

Sabermetrics provides us with a lot of information and can assist us in clearing up previously obscure questions. While it very rarely gives us an answer with *absolute* certainty, it quite often gives us very *plausible* conclusions. As we deepen our knowledge of the national pastime because of sabermetrics, we can understand the game all the more. We hope you enjoy our book!

CHAPTER 2

Traditional Offensive Statistics: Hitting and Base-Stealing

Introduction

Certain offensive statistics have been labeled as "traditional," as they have been kept since the early days of Major League Baseball. They include batting average, slugging percentage, and on-base percentage. More recent developments in sabermetrics have led to the creation of other offensive statistics, which are discussed throughout the remainder of this book. Base-stealing statistics were kept beginning in the early 1900s. In this chapter, we are merely concerned with a runner's successful steal percentage (more information on Stolen Base Linear Weights can be found in Chapter 10, while the Power Speed Number is discussed in Chapter 17).

Batting average (BA) is found by dividing the number of base hits (H) by the total number of at-bats (AB):

$$BA = \frac{H}{AB}.$$

A batter's slugging percentage (SLG) is found by dividing the total number of bases (TB) of all base hits by the total number of times at bat:

$$SLG = \frac{TB}{AB}.$$

For example, a single has one total base while a triple has three total bases. A batter's on-base percentage (OBP) is found by dividing the total number of hits plus bases on balls (BB) plus hit by pitch (HBP) by at-bats plus bases on balls plus hit by pitch plus sacrifice flies (SF):

$$OBP = \frac{H + BB + HBP}{AB + BB + HBP + SF}.$$

Recently, a combination of two traditional statistics has become a popular measure of success. The on-base plus slugging (*OPS*) stat combines a batter's on-base percentage and slugging percentage to gauge how effective a batter is in not only getting on base but in driving home other runners. The *OPS* statistic is discussed in detail in Chapter 14.

To determine the successful stolen base percentage, divide the number of stolen bases by the number of attempts (stolen bases (*SB*) plus times caught stealing [*CS*]):

$$SB\% = \frac{SB}{SB + CS}.$$

Unfortunately, caught stealing data is incomplete before 1951. We explain these traditional statistics with an example. In 1941, Joe DiMaggio of the New York Yankees won the league's Most Valuable Player Award. In that season, DiMaggio had his 56-game hitting streak. This means that the "Yankee Clipper" hit safely in 56 consecutive games before finally being retired in every at-bat of a game without getting a base hit. Let's consider the traditional statistics. The streak began on May 15, 1941, with a single in four trips to the plate. For the next two months, through July 16, 1941, Joe got at least one hit in each game. In total, he had 91 base hits in 223 official at-bats. Those hits include 16 doubles, 4 triples, and 15 home runs. That leaves 56 singles. Dividing the number of base hits by at-bats, we see that DiMaggio had a batting average of $BA = \frac{91}{223} = .408$, which is impressive. His slugging percentage for the games in the streak can be calculated as

$$SLG = \frac{(56 \times 1) + (16 \times 2) + (4 \times 3) + (15 \times 4)}{223} = \frac{160}{223} = .717,$$

which is equally impressive. His seasonal statistics were 193 hits (including 43 doubles, 11 triples, and 30 home runs) in 541 at-bats. What were his season average and slugging percentage? We divide his hits and total bases separately by at-bats to find $BA = .357$ and $SLG = .643$.

In addition to the above numbers, Joe had 76 walks and was hit by 4 pitches in 1941. He did not have any sacrifice flies. Therefore, we determine his on-base percentage to be $OBP = \frac{193 + 76 + 4}{541 + 76 + 4 + 0} = .440$.

DiMaggio was known as a great base runner, but in 1941, he only stole four bases, while being caught twice. That gives him a stolen base percentage of 4/6, or 66.7%.

The same traditional statistics can be used to compare teams. For example, in 1966, the Baltimore Orioles put up the following numbers, en route to the World Series: in 160 regular season games, the Orioles amassed 5529 official at-bats, and they stroked 1426 hits, of which 243 were doubles, 35 were triples, and 175 left the yard for home runs. The players on the team had 55 stolen bases but were caught 43 times. In addition to drawing 514 walks, the Orioles players were hit by the pitch 39 times and had 35 sacrifice flies. Using this information, we determine the team batting average to be

$$BA = \frac{1426}{5529} = .258,$$ while their team slugging percentage was

$$SLG = \frac{(973 \times 1) + (243 \times 2) + (35 \times 3) + (175 \times 4)}{5529} = \frac{2264}{5529} = .409.$$ The team on-

base percentage was $$OBP = \frac{1426 + 514 + 39}{5529 + 514 + 39 + 35} = \frac{1979}{6117} = .324.$$ Finally, Bal-

timore had a stolen base percentage of $$SB\% = \frac{55}{55 + 43} = \frac{55}{98} = 56.1\%.$$

Demonstrating Sabermetrics

1. In 1995, Albert Belle had 70 singles and 103 extra-base hits: 52 doubles, 1 triple, and 50 home runs. Given that he had 546 at-bats, what were his batting average and slugging percentage?

Belle had a total of 173 base hits. To find his batting average, we divide his hits by at-bats and see that his $BA = 173/546 = .317$. His slugging percentage is

$$SLG = \frac{(70 \times 1) + (52 \times 2) + (1 \times 3) + (50 \times 4)}{546} = \frac{377}{546} = .690.$$

2. In that same season, Albert Belle had 73 walks (6 times intentionally), was hit by the pitch 6 times, and had 4 sacrifice flies. What was his on-base percentage?

We substitute in the values to find $$OBP = \frac{173 + 73 + 6}{546 + 73 + 6 + 4} = .401.$$

3. In 1945, Snuffy Stirnweiss led the American League in slugging with the lowest slugging percentage since 1908 (.476) and the third lowest percentage ever in the American League. Given that he had 195 hits, of which 32 were doubles, 22 were triples, and 10 were home runs, how many at-bats did Snuffy have?

His at-bat total can be found by dividing his total bases by his slugging percentage. Subtracting his extra-base hits from 195 shows that Snuffy had 131 singles. We calculate $TB = (131 \times 1) + (32 \times 2) + (22 \times 3) + (10 \times 4) = 301$.

Therefore, $$AB = \frac{TB}{SLG} = \frac{301}{.476} = 632.$$

You can go online to verify that Snuffy had 632 at-bats in 1945.

4. Sam Crawford holds the record for most triples in a single season with 26, which he clubbed in 1914 while playing for the Detroit Tigers. In addition, he had 22 doubles, 8 home runs, for a total of 183 hits in 582 at-bats. What was his slugging percentage?

We take the extra-base hits and subtract them from 183, giving 127 singles.

$$\text{Therefore, } SLG = \frac{(127 \times 1) + (22 \times 2) + (26 \times 3) + (8 \times 4)}{582} = \frac{281}{582} = .483.$$

5. Rogers Hornsby led the post–1901 National League in slugging a record six consecutive times, from 1920 through 1925 (he also led the National League in 1917, 1928, and 1929). The batting statistics by season are given in the table below.

Year	AB	H	2B	3B	HR
1920	589	218	44	20	9
1921	592	235	44	18	21
1922	623	250	46	14	42
1923	424	163	32	10	17
1924	536	227	43	14	25
1925	504	203	41	10	39

Calculate Hornsby's slugging percentage for each season and for the entire six-year span.

Before we can determine the slugging percentage, we need to calculate the number of singles in each season. For 1920, we find that he had 218 — (44 + 20 + 9) = 145 singles. So,

$$SLG = \frac{(145 \times 1) + (44 \times 2) + (20 \times 3) + (9 \times 4)}{589} = \frac{329}{589} = .559.$$

Similarly, for 1921, he had 152 singles. Using the same formula, this gave him SLG = .639. In the next year, 1922, Hornsby swatted 148 singles, and his slugging was SLG = .722. For 1923, he had 104 singles and SLG = .627. For 1924, Hornsby again had 145 singles with SLG = .696. In the sixth season, 1925, he only had 113 singles, yet his slugging percentage climbed to SLG = .756.

Over the six-season span, here are his totals:

AB	H	2B	3B	HR
3268	1296	250	86	153

Subtracting the extra-base hits from the total hits gives 807 singles. Substituting into the formula,

$$SLG = \frac{(807 \times 1) + (250 \times 2) + (86 \times 3) + (153 \times 4)}{3268} = \frac{2177}{3268} = .666.$$

Rogers slugged .666 over the 6-year span.

6. In 1922, Hall of Famer Rabbit Maranville came to bat 672 times for the Pittsburgh Pirates, without ever hitting a home run. Of his 198 hits, 26 were doubles and 15 were triples. Further, he had 61 walks, 2 sacrifice flies and 3 times hit by the pitch. Calculate his batting average, slugging percentage, and on-base percentage.

First, we calculate that $BA = \frac{198}{672} = .295$. Next, we determine that Rabbit had 157 singles, which allows us to determine his slugging percentage, which is $SLG = \frac{(157 \times 1) + (26 \times 2) + (15 \times 3) + (0 \times 4)}{672} = \frac{254}{672} = .378$.

Finally, his on-base percentage is $OBP = \frac{198 + 61 + 3}{672 + 61 + 3 + 2} = .355$.

7. The 1927 New York Yankees were known as *Murderer's Row*, with a slugging line-up of Ruth, Gehrig, Lazzeri, Meusel, Combs, ... Given the following table of statistics, calculate the team's slugging percentage.

AB	H	2B	3B	HR
5354	1644	291	103	158

Substituting these numbers into the formula, we find that
$$SLG = \frac{(1092 \times 1) + (291 \times 2) + (103 \times 3) + (158 \times 4)}{5354} = \frac{2615}{5354} = .488.$$
This is the highest team slugging percentage in Major League Baseball history.

8. Brady Anderson has the single season highest stolen base percentage, having swiped 31 of 32 bases for the Baltimore Orioles in 1994. What was his stolen base percentage?

We divide 31 by 32 and find $SB\% = \frac{31}{32} = 96.9\%$.

9. In 1982, Hall of Famer Rickey Henderson set two stolen base records. He stole more bases in a single season than anyone had ever done since 1900, stealing 130 bases. In addition, he was caught more times than anyone else, having been thrown out 42 times while attempting to steal. What was his *SB* percentage?

Using the formula, we determine that $SB\% = \frac{130}{130 + 42} = \frac{130}{172} = 75.6\%$.

10. The 2005 New York Yankees attempted only 111 stolen bases in 162 games, and their players were successful 84 times. Tony Womack led the team

with 27 swipes, Alex Rodriguez had 21, Derek Jeter had 14, and Gary Sheffield had 10, making them the only four Yankees with at least 10 stolen bases that season. What was the team's stolen base percentage?

$$SB\% = \frac{84}{111} = 75.7\%.$$

Practicing Sabermetrics

1. Since 1912, only Frank Robinson and Mark McGwire have led both the American and National Leagues in slugging. In 1966, Frank Robinson won the Triple Crown in batting, while in 1998, Mark McGwire established a new season home run record with 70. Use the information from the following table and determine their respective seasonal slugging percentages.

Year	AB	H	2B	3B	HR
Robinson, NL 1962	609	208	51	2	39
Robinson, AL 1966	576	182	34	2	49
McGwire, AL 1996	423	132	21	0	52
McGwire, NL 1998	509	152	21	0	70

[Answers: Robinson: 1962 — SLG = .624, Robinson: 1966 — SLG = .637, McGwire: 1996 — SLG = .730, McGwire: 1998 — SLG = .752.]

2. In 2004, Seattle Mariners outfielder Ichiro Suzuki set a record for most base hits in a season with 262, breaking the mark held over 70 years by Hack Wilson. These hits consisted of 225 singles, 24 doubles, 5 triples, and 8 home runs. He had 704 at-bats. What were his season batting average and slugging percentage?

[Answers: BA = .372; SLG = .455.]

3. Shawn Green, right fielder for the Los Angeles Dodgers, had a career day at the plate against the Milwaukee Brewers on May 23, 2002. In six at-bats, Green had six hits, scored six runs, and drove in seven runs. His six hits included four home runs and a double. What was his slugging percentage in the game?

[Answer: SLG = 3.167.]

4. Jackie Robinson led the Brooklyn Dodgers and the National League in steals in 1949 with 37. The Dodgers as a team had 117 steals, but they were caught 44 stealing times. What was the Dodgers' stolen base percentage that season?

[Answer: $SB\%$ = 72.%.]

5. Brooks Robinson won the American League Most Valuable Player Award in 1964. His offensive numbers were:

AB	H	2B	3B	HR	BB	HBP	SF
612	194	35	3	28	51	4	10

Determine his batting average, slugging percentage, and on-base percentage. [Answers: *BA* = .317, *SLG* = .521, *OBP* = .368.]

6. Yogi Berra won three American League Most Valuable Player Awards. His seasonal statistics in those three years are shown in the table below. What were his combined batting average and slugging percentage for the three seasons?

Year	AB	H	2B	3B	HR
1951	547	161	19	4	27
1954	584	179	28	6	22
1955	541	147	20	3	27

[Answers: 1951: *BA* = .294; *SLG* = .492,
1954: *BA* = .307; *SLG* = .488,
1955: *BA* = .272; *SLG* = .470.]

7. Lou Brock set a National League record for stolen bases by swiping 118 bases in 1974. He also set a league record by being caught 33 times. What was his stolen base percentage?
[Answer: *SB%* = 78.1%.]

8. Rickey Henderson is considered one of the better lead-off hitters in the last half-century. Given that his career numbers are listed in the table below, calculate his career on-base percentage.

AB	H	2B	3B	HR	BB	HBP	SF
10961	3055	510	66	297	2190	98	67

[Answer: *OBP* = .401.]

9. On May 13, 1958, the San Francisco Giants set a record with five batters who had 4 or more hits in the same game! They beat their rivals, the Los Angeles Dodgers, 16 — 9, in a game where the Giants had 26 hits. Willie Mays went 5 for 5 with two home runs and two triples, while Orlando Cepeda, Daryl Spencer, Bob Schmidt, and Danny O'Connell each collected 4 hits.

Spencer also belted 2 homers and a triple, while Cepeda added a solo round tripper. In 50 at-bats, there were 3 doubles, 3 triples, and 5 home runs. How many total bases did the Giants have and what was the Giants' slugging percentage for the game?

[Answers: TB = 50; SLG = 1.000.]

10. On August 11, 2003, the Kansas City Royals and New York Yankees combined for 19 doubles! The final score was 12 − 9, in favor of the Royals. The hit information is listed in the table below. Determine the slugging percentage for each team in the game, and then determine the overall slugging percentage, combining both teams' numbers.

	AB	H	2B	3B	HR
New York Yankees	38	15	8	0	2
Kansas City Royals	38	14	11	0	0

[Answers: Yankees: SLG = .763, Royals: SLG = .816, Combined: SLG = .789.]

11. Ted Williams holds the post–1900 record for most walks (107) in a season (1939) by a rookie. In that rookie season, the "Splendid Splinter" also had 185 hits and was hit by the pitch twice in 565 at-bats (no record of any sacrifice flies). What was his on-base percentage?

[Answer: OBP = .436.]

12. Through the 2007 season, Carlos Beltran has the highest career stolen base percentage of any Major League player (with a minimum of 100 steals), with 88.0%. He has made 292 attempts, so how many bases has he stolen?

[Answer: 257 stolen bases.]

13. Hall of Famer Eddie Collins stole 6 bases in a game on September 11, 1912, with 3 SB in the 7th inning, and on September 22, 1912, he stole six more bases in the first game of a double-header. Since CS statistics are not available, let's determine his on-base percentage. In 543 at-bats in 1912, Collins had 189 base hits and 101 free passes. He was not hit by the pitch at all that season, nor is he credited with any sacrifice flies. What was his OBP? Incidentally, Eddie Collins stole home *twice* in the same game on September 6, 1913!

[Answer: OBP = .450.]

14. In his rookie season in 1987, Oakland A's first baseman Mark McGwire hit 49 home runs. His 161 hits also consisted of 24 doubles and 4 triples in 557 at-bats. What was *Big Mac's* slugging percentage?

[Answer: SLG = .618.]

15. Hal Trosky set a rookie record with 374 total bases in 1934 while playing for Cleveland. He finished the season with a slugging percentage of .598. Thirty years later, Tony Oliva matched the mark for a rookie with 374 total bases for the Minnesota Twins, slugging a mark of .557. How many at-bats did each slugger have in his rookie season?

[Answers: Trosky *AB* = 625; Oliva *AB* = 672.]

16. The 1957 Washington Senators stole 13 bases — all season! This ranks as the fewest stolen bases by a team in a season since 1886. Their runners were caught stealing 38 times. What was the team's stolen base percentage?

[Answer: *SB%* = 25.5%.]

CHAPTER 3

Traditional Defensive Statistics: Pitching and Fielding

Introduction

In the previous chapter, we saw how to compute some of the traditional offensive statistics. Here, we will discuss how the traditional defensive statistics are computed. While pitching statistics have been fairly effective, the most difficult part of baseball to quantify is the defense. In fact, among all the "traditional" measures, the most discredited has been those for defense.

Many of the "modern" defensive measures require more sophisticated information that is available to the average fan, and thus, those will not be addressed in this book. However, Range Factor is discussed in Chapter 18.

For pitching, the influence of fantasy baseball has seen the rise of the WHIP (Chapter 11) as an accepted measure of pitching effectiveness, while the influence of sabermetrics is seen in Pitching Linear Weights (Chapter 10) and Weighted Pitcher's Rating (Chapter 12).

Pitching

A pitcher's earned run average is the measure of the number of earned runs surrendered per 9 innings, which used to be the number of innings pitchers would hurl per game. It is computed by taking the number of earned runs, allowed, multiplied by 9, and divided by the total number of innings pitched:

$$ERA = \frac{9 \times ER}{IP}.$$

Another measure of pitching effectiveness is the winning percentage. This is computed by taking the total number of wins, divided by the total number of decisions (i.e., wins plus losses):

$$WPCT = \frac{W}{W+L}.$$

The number of complete games and the number of innings per start for a starting pitcher are other measures of effectiveness. The more innings a starter pitches, the fewer innings are pitched by relievers, and when complete games are pitched, no relievers are used. The use of relief pitching has increased since the mid–20th century, until now complete games are a distinct rarity. To see the percentage of games completed, we simply divide complete games (*CG*) by games started (*GS*) and multiply by 100:

$$100 \times \frac{CG}{GS}\%.$$

We compute innings per start simply by dividing innings pitched in starts by games started, $IPS = \frac{IP}{GS}$. Note that this formula will not work for a pitcher who pitches some games as a starter and some games as a reliever. For those pitchers, you would need a breakdown of innings pitched as a starter and innings pitched in relief.

As an example, in 1963, Dodgers' all-time great Sandy Koufax won both the Cy Young Award and National League's Most Valuable Player Award. His statistics line was as follows:

G	GS	CG	IP	ER	K	BB	H	W	L
40	40	20	311	65	306	58	214	25	5

To calculate his ERA, we determine $ERA = \frac{9 \times ER}{IP} = \frac{9 \times 65}{311} = \frac{585}{311} = 1.88$, which led the league that year, as did his strikeouts and innings pitched. His winning percentage was $WPCT = \frac{W}{W+L} = \frac{25}{25+5} = \frac{25}{30} = 0.833$ (always rounded off to the thousandths place), good for second in the league. Teammate Ron Perranoski led the league in winning percentage that year. Koufax completed 20 of his 40 starts, good for a

$$100 \times \frac{CG}{GS}\% = 100 \times \frac{20}{40}\% = 50\%$$

percentage of starts completed. His innings per start was

$$IPS = \frac{IP}{GS} = \frac{311}{40} = 7.775, \text{ or } 7\frac{2}{3}$$

innings, rounded to the nearest third of an inning.

One other measure of a pitcher's effectiveness is the strikeout to walk ratio, *K/BB*. By dividing the number of strikeouts by walks, we can get a sense of a pitcher's effectiveness when a ball is not put into play. In the

National League in 1963, there were a total of 9545 strikeouts and 4560 walks, for a $\frac{9545}{4560} = 2.09$ K/BB. By comparison, Koufax's K/BB was $\frac{306}{58} = 5.28$, which — you guessed it — led the league.

Fielding

The traditional measure of fielding effectiveness has always been the fielding percentage (*FPCT*). Simply put, it is a percentage of successful chances out of all possible chances for a fielder, i.e., putouts plus assists divided by putouts plus assists plus errors:

$$\frac{PO + A}{PO + A + E}.$$

One criticism of the statistic is that it does not take into account when a fielder does not get to a ball that he should have; in other words, if a ball passes a player by, then it counts as a hit, whereas a player with a greater range might have gotten a glove on it, at least. This deficiency is addressed in Chapter 18 (Range Factor). Other non-traditional defensive measures are presented in Chapter 9 (Defensive and Stolen Base Linear Weights), and Chapter 19, (the Hoban Effectiveness Quotient).

Among center fielders, Hall of Famer Willie Mays is acknowledged as one of the best of all time, both offensively and defensively. His defensive prowess was recognized by this selection as a Gold Glove center fielder every year from 1957–1968. In 1955, Mays played 152 (out of the total of 154) games for the New York Giants in center field. He had 407 putouts, 23 (!) assists, and 8 errors. He also participated in 8 double plays. Willie's fielding percentage was $\frac{PO + A}{PO + A + E} = \frac{407 + 23}{407 + 23 + 8} = \frac{430}{438} = 0.982,$ rounded to the nearest thousandth.

While 400 putouts in a season is outstanding, in 1956, Richie Ashburn of the Phillies had 501, to go along with 11 assists, 9 errors, and 4 double plays. His fielding percentage was $\frac{PO + A}{PO + A + E} = \frac{501 + 11}{501 + 11 + 9} = \frac{512}{521} = 0.983.$

It is sometimes convenient to discuss the amount of a particular statistic per 162 games, to get a sense of how a player will perform over the course of a typical season. This is obtained by dividing the number of games played in his career by 162, and then dividing that result by the career number of the statistic in question. For example, Hall of Famer Bill Mazeroski was considered the finest fielding second baseman of all time. In his career, he played 2094 games at the position and participated in 1706 *DP* there. To calculate his DP per 162 games (DP/162),

$$\frac{DP}{162} = \frac{DP}{\frac{G}{162}} = \frac{(DP)(162)}{G} = \frac{(1706)(162)}{(2094)} = 131.98.$$

In the strike-shortened 1994 season, Ivan Rodriguez played 99 of the team's 114 games at catcher, recording 600 *PO*. Since catchers are credited with putouts on most strikeouts, it might be interesting to recalculate his *FPCT* without the strikeouts. Rodriguez caught in 837 of the team's 1023 innings that year. The team recorded 683 strikeouts. To approximate how many strikeouts occurred with "Pudge" behind the plate, we set up a proportion of Pudge's innings behind the plate and team innings, and do the same with strikeouts, solving for the unknown:

$$\frac{\text{Innings}_{\text{Pudge}}}{\text{Innings}_{\text{Rangers}}} = \frac{K_{\text{Pudge}}}{K_{\text{Rangers}}} \rightarrow \frac{837}{1023} = \frac{K_{\text{Pudge}}}{683} \rightarrow (837)(683) = (1023)(K_{\text{Pudge}}) \rightarrow$$

$$\frac{(837)(683)}{1023} = K_{\text{Pudge}} = 559.$$

Thus, approximately 559 of Rodriguez's *PO* might have come from strikeouts. Thus, his "non-strikeout" *PO* total is approximately 600–559 = 41. He also had 44 *A* and committed 5 *E*. His "non-strikeout" *FPCT*, then, is

$$\frac{PO + A}{PO + A + E} = \frac{41 + 44}{41 + 44 + 5} = \frac{85}{90} = 0.944.$$

We remark that we did not count *PO* from dropped third strikes where runners were retired at first base. On the other hand, we also did not subtract out the assists from throwing to first on such plays.

Demonstrating Sabermetrics

1. Pitcher Grover Cleveland Alexander recording 19 consecutive winning seasons in his career, which lasted from 1911 to 1930, with three different National League teams. His win-loss record was 373–208. Calculate his career winning percentage.

$$WPCT = \frac{W}{W + L} = \frac{373}{373 + 208} = \frac{373}{581} = 0.730.$$

2. Alexander also struck out 2198 batters in his career, while walking 951. He completed 437 of his 599 career starts. Calculate his career *CG* percentage and career *K*/*BB*.

$$100 \times \frac{CG}{GS}\% = 100 \times \frac{437}{599}\% = 100 \times 0.729\%, \text{ or roughly 73 percent.}$$

His $K / BB = \frac{2198}{951} = 2.31$.

3. "Ol' Pete," as Alexander was called, yielded 1476 earned runs in a total of 5190 *IP*. Determine his career *ERA*.

$$ERA = \frac{9 \times ER}{IP} = \frac{9 \times 1476}{5190} = \frac{13284}{5190} = 2.56,$$ which ranks in the top 50 all-time

(among pitchers with 1000 or more *IP*).

4. As mentioned above, Sandy Koufax's Dodgers teammate, Ron Perranoski, led the NL in *WPCT* in 1963. His record (in relief!) was 16–3. Find his league-leading winning percentage.

$$WPCT = \frac{W}{W + L} = \frac{16}{16 + 3} = \frac{16}{19} = 0.842.$$

5. All-time great Greg Maddux had one of his best seasons in 1995. He pitched in 28 games, all starts, and completed 10 of them. He amassed 209 innings pitched. Calculate his *IPS* and *CG* percentage.

$$100 \times \frac{CG}{GS}\% = 100 \times \frac{10}{28}\% = 100 \times 0.357\%,$$ or roughly 36 percent of his starts

completed.

$$IPS = \frac{IP}{GS} = \frac{209}{28} = 7.464,$$ or 7⅓ *IP* per start.

6. In 2008, Cleveland pitcher Cliff Lee had 22 wins and a *WPCT* of 0.880. How many losses did Lee have in 2008?

$$WPCT = \frac{22}{22 + L} = 0.880 \rightarrow 22 = (22 + L)(0.880).$$ Solving for *L* yields *L* = 3.

7. In 1951, Phillies' Hall of Fame CF Richie Ashburn played all 154 of the team's games. He had 538 *PO*, 15 *A* (6 for *DP*), and 7 *E*. Calculate his Fielding Percentage.

$$FPCT = \frac{PO + A}{PO + A + E} = \frac{538 + 15}{538 + 15 + 7} = \frac{553}{560} = 0.988.$$

8. In 1981, Steve Garvey of the Dodgers played 110 games at first base in a strike-shortened season. He had 1019 *PO*, 55 *A*, and only 1 *E*. Calculate his *FPCT*.

$$FPCT = \frac{PO + A}{PO + A + E} = \frac{1019 + 55}{1019 + 55 + 1} = \frac{1074}{1075} = 0.999.$$

9. Hall of Fame Cincinnati Reds catcher Johnny Bench won the Rookie of the Year Award in 1968. He had 942 PO, 102 A and 9 E. What was his *FPCT*? Catchers receive credit for a put-out on strikeouts, except in the case where the ball is dropped under certain conditions.

$$FPCT = \frac{PO + A}{PO + A + E} = \frac{942 + 102}{942 + 102 + 9} = \frac{1044}{1053} = 0.991.$$

10. One of the finest-fielding outfielders of all time, Paul Blair, played

31 of the games of his career in left field. He had 15 *PO*, 0 *A* and 0 *E* in those games. What was his career *FPCT* as a left fielder?

$$FPCT = \frac{PO + A}{PO + A + E} = \frac{15 + 0}{15 + 0 + 0} = \frac{15}{15} = 1.000.$$

11. Primarily a CF in his career, Paul Blair also played 62 games in right field. He had 58 putouts, one assist, and a *FPCT* of 0.983. How many of his 54 career outfield errors did Paul Blair record as a right fielder?

$$FPCT = \frac{PO + A}{PO + A + E} \rightarrow \frac{58 + 1}{58 + 1 + E} = \frac{59}{59 + E} = 0.983.$$

Solving for *E* yields *E* = 1.02. Since there was likely some roundoff in calculating his *FPCT*, we can say that he made one error as a right fielder in his career.

12. Hall of Fame outfielder Ed Delahanty started out as a second baseman. He played 56 games at the position in 1888 for the Phillies, making 129 *PO*, 170 *A*, and committing 44 *E*. What was his *FPCT* for that year at second base?

$$FPCT = \frac{PO + A}{PO + A + E} = \frac{129 + 170}{129 + 170 + 44} = \frac{299}{343} = 0.872.$$

13. All-time Yankee great, Hall of Famer Lou Gehrig, played 2137 games at first base in his career, and had 19,510 *PO*. How many putouts did he have per 162 games?

$$\frac{PO}{162} = \frac{P0}{\frac{G}{162}} = \frac{(PO)(162)}{G} = \frac{(19510)(162)}{(2137)} = 1479.$$

14. Mets catcher Jerry Grote had 718 *PO*, 63 *A* and 7 *E* in 1969. He caught 918 of the team's 1468 innings. Met pitchers recorded 1012 strikeouts that year. Estimate the number of strikeouts recorded while Grote was catcher, and estimate his *FPCT* without the strikeouts.

$$\frac{\text{Innings}_{\text{Grote}}}{\text{Innings}_{\text{Mets}}} = \frac{K_{\text{Grote}}}{K_{\text{Mets}}} \rightarrow \frac{918}{1468} = \frac{K_{\text{Grote}}}{1012} \rightarrow (918)(1012) = (1468)(K_{\text{Grote}}) \rightarrow$$

$$\frac{(918)(1012)}{1468} = K_{\text{Grote}} = 663.$$

Thus, Grote had approximately 718 – 633 = 85 "non-strikeout" *PO* that year. His "non-strikeout" *FPCT*, then, is

$$FPCT = \frac{PO + A}{PO + A + E} = \frac{85 + 63}{85 + 63 + 7} = \frac{148}{155} = 0.955.$$

Practicing Sabermetrics

1. In 1956, Don Newcombe won both the MLB Cy Young Award and the NL MVP Award. He started 36 of the 38 games in which he appeared, posted a 27–7 record, with 18 CG. Calculate his *WPCT* and his *CG%*.

[Answer: *WPCT* = 0.794, *CG%* = 50%.]

2. In this remarkable season, Newcombe also pitched 268 innings, gave up 91 earned runs, struck out 139 batters and walked 46. What were his *K/BB* ratio and *ERA*?

[Answer: *K/BB* = 3.02, *ERA* = 3.06.]

3. Rollie Fingers, pitching for the Milwaukee Brewers in the AL in 1981, also won both the MVP and CY Young awards for his league. In 78 *IP*, he surrendered only 9 *ER*. What was his *ERA*?

[Answer: *ERA* = 1.04.]

4. Roger Clemens duplicated this award feat in 1986. Pitching for the Boston Red Sox, he struck out 20 Seattle Mariners in one game. Using this chart, determine his *WPCT*, ERA, IPS, K/BB, and CG%.

G	GS	CG	W	L	IP	ER	K	BB	H
33	33	10	24	4	254	70	238	67	179

[Answer: *WPCT* = 0.857, *ERA* = 2.48, *IPS* = 7⅔, *K/BB* = 3.55, and *CG%* = 30%.]

5. In 1992, Hall of Famer Dennis Eckersley became the fourth pitcher to receive the two awards in the same season. Working as a relief pitcher for the Oakland Athletics, Eckersley had 80 *IP*, 17 *ER*, 93 *K* and 11 *BB*. What were his *K/BB* ratio and *ERA*?

[Answer: *K/BB* = 8.45, *ERA* = 1.91.]

6. As a starting pitcher in 1977, Eckersley appeared in 33 games, all as a starter. He completed 12 of his starts, and pitched 247⅓ innings. What were his *CG%* and *IPS*?

[Answer: *CG%* = 36%, *IPS* = 7.49, or approximately 7⅓.]

The players whose data serve as the basis for Problems 7–14 hold or share the record for most Gold Gloves won at their respective positions.

7. Pitcher Greg Maddux was also known for his fielding. In 1993, he had 30 *PO*, 64 Assists, and 3 Errors. What was his *FPCT*?

[Answer: 0.969.]

8. Keith Hernandez is widely regarded to be the premier fielding first baseman of all time. He played 2014 games at first, amassing 17909 putouts, 1682 assists, and 115 errors. Calculate his *FPCT* and assists per game, and compare these numbers with the Steve Garvey data from Problem 8 of the "Demonstrating Sabermetrics" section above.

[Answer: Hernandez: *FPCT* = 0.994, Assists/Game = 0.835; Garvey: *FPCT* = 0.999, Assists/Game = 0.5.]

9. Roberto Alomar was an excellent second baseman over the course of his 17-year career. In 1991, he had 333 *PO*, 447 *A*, 15 *E*. He also participated in 79 double plays (*DP*) in 160 games played. What was his *FPCT* and double plays per game (*DP/G*)?

[Answer: *FPCT* = 0.981, *DP/G* = 0.49.]

10. Ozzie Smith is widely regarded as the greatest shortstop of all time. He played 2511 games in his Hall of Fame career, all at SS. He totaled 8375 assists. What is his *A*/162?

[Answer: *A*/162 = 540.32, or 540 assists for every 162 games.]

11. Brooks Robinson earned the nickname "The Human Vacuum Cleaner" for his defensive prowess at third base over his 23 season career with the Baltimore Orioles (and outstanding defensive third basemen are typically called "Brooksie" in his honor). In 1973, he recorded 129 *PO*, 354 *A*, and 15 *E*. The league *FPCT* for third basemen that year was 0.950. What was Brooksie's *FPCT* in 1973? How does it relate to the league's *FPCT* for third basemen?

[Answer: Robinson *FPCT* = 0.970; Brooks was 0.020 better than the league at the position.]

12. Over his career, Roberto Clemente set a standard for defensive play in right field against which all future right fielders would be measured. In 2194 games in RF, Clemente had 4270 *PO*, 260 *A*, and committed 125 *E*. What was his career *FPCT*? How many assists per 162 games?

[Answers: *FPCT* = 0.973, *A*/162 = 19.19 or 19 assists for every 162 games.]

13. In 1973, his final season as an active player, Willie Mays played 45 games as a center fielder for the New York Mets. He had a fielding percentage of 0.990, with 103 *PO* and 1 *A*. How many errors did he commit in center field that year?

[Answer: 1 Error.]

14. Through 2008, Ivan "Pudge" Rodriguez had recorded 1097 assists at catcher in 2173 games. How many assists is this per 162 games?

[Answer: $A/162$ = 81.78.]

15. Thurman Munson won the American League Gold Glove Award for his catching prowess in 1975. He recorded 700 PO, 95 A and committed 23 E while catching 1131 of the Yankees 1424 innings. Yankee pitchers struck out 809 batters that season. Approximate how many of Munson's PO were from strikeouts, and estimate his "non-strikeout" PO and "non-strikeout" $FPCT$ for that season.

[Answers: approximately 643 K from PO, 57 "non-strikeout" PO, and 0.869 "non-strikeout" $FPCT$.]

CHAPTER 4

Relativity and Normalization

Introduction

Relativity and *normalization* are closely related approaches which can be used when making comparisons between and among players, teams and eras. The measures which are derived from these techniques can assist us in "leveling the playing field." For example, they can assist us in trying to determined whether it was "more difficult" for someone like the Yankees' Babe Ruth to hit a home run (*HR*) in the 1920s than it was for someone like Sammy Sosa of the Cubs to hit a home run in the 1990s.

When using relativity and normalization, we generally try to transform many of the raw statistics into a new number, usually by the use of simple division, with respect to a certain average. For example, in 1947, Pirates slugger Ralph Kiner hit 51 *HR* in 565 at-bats (*AB*). So his *HR* to *AB* ratio is, $\frac{51}{565} = 0.0903$ rounded off the four decimal places. In a sense, this number represents a normalization, because one can infer from this statistic that Kiner hit about nine *HR* per every 100 *AB*; that is, this is what he would "normally" produce. We will calculate the normalization value to four decimal places.

Let us continue with this example. In that same year, 1947, the total number of *HR* hit by all players on the sixteen teams comprising the Major League players was 1565. Dividing this number by the total number of 84,436 *AB*, gives a *HR* to *AB* ratio of 0.0185. This number can be thought of as the "average" player — including pitchers — "normally" hitting not even two home runs, per 100 *AB*.

Now, what if we compare these two ratios? That is, if we divide 0.0903 by 0.0185 to obtain the number 4.8689, which is sometimes referred to as a *normalization number*. We now ask, "How can we interpret this normalization number, which, in this case, is nothing more than a ratio of ratios? One meaning that can be gleaned from this is that Ralph Kiner was, relatively speaking, almost five times better than the average home run hitter of 1947.

This warrants a remark. From this example, it follows that one can compare home run hitters of different eras and contrast what might be called "degrees of difficulty" with respect to the statistic under discussion. This is especially true if one (or even a few) of the normalized numbers seem to be out of the ordinary; in this case it may very well be that the player has exhibited a pronounced dominance with regard to the particular measure in question. See Problem 9 in the Demonstrating Sabermetrics section.

Demonstrating Sabermetrics

1. In 1928, Hall of Famer Heinie Manush had a slugging percentage (*SLG*) of .575. If the *SLG* of the American League was .397, find Manush's normalized ratio and give an interpretation to this number.

Taking the ratio of the slugging percentages and rounding to four places, we have $\frac{.575}{.397}$ = 1.4484. This normalized number can be interpreted as meaning that, relatively speaking, Manush was nearly 45 percent better than the average American League slugger in 1928.

Generally, any normalized offensive number greater than 1 means that the player was better than the average player, while a number less than 1 means that he performed at a below average level. A ratio of 1 means that the player's statistic was average for that category. Other conventions may hold for pitching statistics (see Problem 7 below).

2. In 1936, outfielder Earl Averill had a batting average (*BA*) of .378, while the American League hit .289. How much better was Averill than the league's average hitter that year?

Since $\frac{.378}{.289}$ = 1.3080, we can say that Averill was almost 31 percent better than the average hitter that year.

3. In 1954, the American League had an on base percentage (*OBP*) of .331. What would the *OBP* of outfielder Minnie Minoso have had to have been to be 25 percent better than the average player?

Solving the equation $\frac{x}{.331}$ = 1.2500 for x, gives x = 0.4138. This means that Minoso's *OBP* would have had to have been .414.

4. Former American League batting champion Pete Runnels played for the National League's Houston Colt 45's in 1963. He had a *SLG* of .332.

Approximate the league's *SLG*, if Runnels was about 9 percent below the average league slugger that year.

If Runnels was about 9 percent below the average slugger, then the normalization ratio is approximately 0.910. Hence, we must solve the equation $\frac{.332}{x} = 0.9100$ for x, where x is the league's slugging average. We find that $x \approx .365$.

5. At the end of the 1959 season, the American League home run (*HR*) leader, Rocky Colavito of the Indians, was traded for the American League batting champion, Harvey Kuenn, of the Detroit Tigers. Compare their relative performances using normalization, given the following information: (1) Kuenn had a *BA* = .353, while the league batted .253, and (2) Colavito had 42 *HR*, in at-bats (*AB*), while the league hit 1091 *HR* in 41,964 *AB*.

For Kuenn, we have $\frac{.353}{.253} = 1.3953$, which means that he was almost 40 percent better than the average hitter. Colavito's *HR* ratio was $\frac{42}{588} = 0.0714$, while the league's corresponding ratio was $\frac{1091}{41,964} = 0.0260$. Dividing 0.0714 by 0.0260 gives a normalization of 2.7462. These normalization numbers is can be interpreted as Colavito being about two and three-quarters times better than the average *HR* hitter.

Care must be exercised when comparing two different statistical categories, such as *BA* and *HR*, especially when percentages are involved. Note that we are *not* saying that if Kuenn was 40 percent better, then Colavito was 275 percent better than the overall average player, we are merely inferring that for these specific measures, our normalization approach can yield these interpretations. See Paragraph 4 in the "10 Point Guide" of Chapter 1.

6. The Yankees dynasty has produced many great teams, four of which were the 1927, 1936, 1961 and 1998 squads. Which team had the best relative *SLG* given the following information:

Year	Team SLG	League SLG
1927	.489	.399
1936	.483	.421
1961	.442	.395
1998	.460	.432

Dividing the numbers in the second column by the numbers in the third column yields the following normalization ratios:

1927 Yankees: 1.2256; 1936 Yankees: 1.1473; 1961 Yankees: 1.1190; 1998 Yankees: 1.0648.

This approach may prove helpful when comparing teams from different eras.

7. Hall of Famers Walter Johnson, Bob Feller, Juan Marichal and Bob Gibson were all right-handed pitching aces for their teams. Compare their relative earned run averages (*ERA*), for the given years, using the statistics below:

Year	Player	ERA	League ERA
1913	Johnson	1.14	2.93
1940	Feller	2.61	4.38
1966	Marichal	2.23	3.60
1968	Gibson	1.12	2.99

Because we are dealing with a measure in which the *lower* number is the *better* number, we can approach this normalization in two ways. If we compare the individual's *ERA* to the corresponding league *ERA*, then the lower ratio is the better ratio. In this case, we have the following results: Johnson (0.3891); Feller (0.5959); Marichal (0.6194); and Gibson (0.3746). Here it is not as intuitively easy to assign a percentage from these ratios.

The other way is to take a reciprocal approach. That is, we divide the league *ERA* by the pitcher's individual *ERA*. This gives us the following ratios: Johnson (2.5702); Feller (1.6782); Marichal (1.6144); and Gibson (2.6696). We can interpret this to mean that Johnson and Gibson were better than two and a half times the average pitcher, and Feller and Marichal were better than one and a half times the average pitcher.

We prefer to utilize this latter approach and will do so for the rest of this chapter.

8. In 1999, Atlanta Braves pitcher Greg Maddux had an *ERA* of 3.57, while the league posted a mark of 4.56. With respect to this statistic, how much better was Maddux than the average pitcher? What would his *ERA* needed to have been if he was twice as good as the league average pitcher?

Dividing the league *ERA* by Maddux's *ERA*, we have $\dfrac{4.56}{3.57} = 1.2773$.

This means that he was about 28 percent better than the average pitcher.

To find the desired *ERA* which would have made him twice as good, we must solve the following equation for *x*: $\dfrac{4.56}{x} = 2.0000$.

This implies that $x = 2.28$, which is the *ERA* figure which Maddux would have had to post.

9. Using normalization numbers, rank the following players with respect

to *HR* percentages (the last two columns are totals for both leagues for each particular season):

Year	Player	Team	HR	AB	ML HR	ML AB
1920	Babe Ruth	Yankees	54	458	630	84176
1932	Jimmie Foxx	Athletics	58	585	1385	87193
1961	Roger Maris	Yankees	61	590	2730	97032
1977	George Foster	Reds	52	615	3644	143974
1998	Mark McGwire	Cardinals	70	509	5061	167034
1985	Barry Bonds	Giants	73	476	5461	166255

For each player, we must first find his *HR* percentage ratio. In Ruth's case we divide 54 by 458 to obtain a ratio of 0.1179. We then compute the *HR* percentage ratio of the Major Leagues for 1920. For this, we divide 630 by 84,176 to obtain a ratio of 0.0075. When we divide the first ratio by the second ratio, we obtain $\frac{0.1179}{0.0075} = 15.7200$.

Continuing in this manner, we obtain the following normalization numbers: Ruth (15.762), Foxx (6.634), Bonds (4.668), McGwire (4.539), Maris (3.674), and Foster (3.341).

It would seem that Ruth's figure of 15.762 is an outlier. This could indicate a real dominance exhibited by Ruth in 1920, and possibly indicate how difficult it was to hit a home run during that year. Comparisons of these six normalization numbers could also shed some light as to contrasting these sluggers from different eras.

Practicing Sabermetrics

1. Ty Cobb, of the Detroit Tigers, had a *BA* of .420 and a *SLG* of .621 in 1911. His team had the same respective percentages of .292 and .388, while the American League batted .273 and slugged .358 that same year. Percentage-wise, how much better was Cobb than his team and his league in 1911?

[Answers: With respect to *BA*, Cobb was 53.8 percent than the league and about 43.8 percent better than his team. Regarding *SLG*, Cobb was 73.4 percent better than the American League and approximately 60 percent better than the Tigers.]

2. San Francisco Giant infielder Orlando Cepeda was the National League's Rookie of the Year in 1958. That year, he batted .312, slugged .522, hit 29 *HR*, all in 603 *AB*. The Giants batted .263, slugged .422 and swatted

170 *HR* in 5318 *AB*. Determine the following: (1) Cepeda's approximate number of home runs per one hundred *AB*; (2b) the Giants' approximate number of *HR* per one hundred *AB*; and (3) how much better Cepeda was than his team regarding batting, slugging and home runs.

[Answers: (1) 4.8 *HR*; (2) 3.2 *HR*; (3) approximately 18.6 percent, 23.7 percent and 50.4 percent, respectively.]

3. In 1958, National League base runners accounted for 5419 runs scored (*R*), given 42,143 *AB*. Find: (1) the average number of runs scored per at-bat; and (2) the average number of *AB* per *R*.

[Answers: (1) 0.1286; (2) 7.7769. Note that these answers are merely the reciprocals of each other.]

4. Referring to Problem 3, how many runs were scored by the "average" team?

[Answer: The average team scored a little over 677 *R* (677.4) that year.]

5. In 1967 Orlando Cepeda played for the World Champion St. Louis Cardinals. Though not known as a prolific base stealer, he had 11 stolen bases (*SB*) in 13 attempts. The entire team had 102 successful stolen bases, while being caught stealing 54 times. Find: (1) Cepeda's *SB* percentage; (2) his team's *SB* percentage; and (3) how much better Cepeda was than his team regarding base stealing.

[Answers: (1) 84.6 percent; (2) 65.4 percent; (3) the ratio of (1) to (2) gives about 29.4 percent. Note that we do not take the difference but the ratio in these comparisons.]

6. In 1998 the San Diego Padres won the National League pennant, yet amassed team statistics in batting average, slugging percentage and on-base percentage (*OBP*) which were all below the league average (see Problem 8 in the Demonstrating Sabermetrics section). How much better than the league was their team *ERA* of 3.63, given that the league posted a figure of 4.42.

[Answer: 21.8 percent.]

7. In Problem 6, what *ERA* would the Padres have had to attain to be 40 percent better than the league?

[Answer: Approximately 3.16.]

8. Referring to Problem 6, in 1998 the Padres posted the following three team numbers: *BA* = .253, *SLG* = .409 and *OBP* = .327, while the National

League averaged *BA* = .262, *SLG* = .410 and *OBP* = .331. Using percentages, how much worse were the Padres regarding these three statistics?

[Answers: 3.4 percent, 0.24 percent, and 1.2 percent, respectively.]

9. In 2005 the National League boasted the following season leaders: Todd Helton of the Colorado Rockies (.445 *OBP* in 509 *AB*), Andruw Jones of the Atlanta Braves (51 *HR* in 586 *AB*), Derrek Lee of the Chicago Cubs (.335 *BA* in 594 *AB*), and Albert Pujols of the St. Louis Cardinals (129 *R* in 591 *AB*). Using normalization numbers, rounded off to four places, rank these four players with respect the corresponding National League averages, given the following league totals: *AB* = 88,120, *R* = 11,535, *HR* = 2580, *BA* = .262, *OBP* = .330. Hint: You must also determine the league *HR* average and *R* average, in addition to these corresponding averages for both Jones and Pujols.

[Answers: In 2005, the National League averaged about 13 runs and almost 3 home runs per 100 at-bats; Pujols averaged almost 22 *R* per 100 *AB* while Jones slugged a bit more than eight-and-a-half *HR* per 100 *AB*. The normalization numbers are: Jones (2.9725), Pujols (1.6675), Helton (1.3485) and Lee (1.2786).

Note the differences between and among these numbers, for example, Jones versus Lee. These are probably to be expected, due to the fact that we are dealing with different measures. Sometimes the data set contains a few observations that are either much smaller or much larger than the bulk of the data; oftentimes, these are labeled as outliers. When outliers appear within the same statistic, there may be a real dominance shown by a particular player with respect to that instrument.]

10. Consider the following table regarding *SB* and time caught stealing (*CS*):

Year	Player	Team	SB	CS	League SB	League CS
1915	Ty Cobb	Tigers	96	38	1443	1051
1962	Maury Wills	Dodgers	104	13	788	409
1982	Rickey Henderson	Athletics	130	42	1394	795
1985	Vince Coleman	Cardinals	110	25	1636	716

For each year, find both the player's and league's *SB* percentage and then rank the four base runners according to his normalization number.

[Answers: In 1915, Cobb's *SB* was 71.6 percent, while the league averaged 57.9 percent; in 1962, Wills' *SB* was 88.9 percent, while the league averaged 65.8 percent; in 1982, Henderson's *SB* was 75.6 percent, while the league averaged

63.7 percent; in 1985 Coleman's *SB* was 81.5 percent, while the league averaged 69.6 percent. The normalization numbers are: Wills (1.3503), Cobb (1.2382), Henderson (1.1865) and Coleman (1.1714). Here Wills has both the best *SB* percentage and the highest normalization number. On the basis of these two measures, it would be difficult not to conclude that Wills had the best year of the four players cited above. Note, also, that he suffered being caught only thirteen times for the entire season; a remarkably low number for anyone with over one hundred pilfered bases.]

CHAPTER 5

Park Factors

Introduction

One of the major characteristics of baseball that separates it from other sports is the fact that not all baseball fields are the same size. Yes, it is always 90 feet between the bases, and 60 feet, 6 inches from the pitcher's mound to home plate, but beyond certain rules governing minimum distances to fences, etc., the other dimensions can and do differ radically from one ballpark to the next. Symmetrical dimensions, asymmetrical dimensions, height of outfield walls, amount of foul territory — all can impact whether a park is more conducive to offensive play or to defensive play.

A study of Park Factors provides and interesting look into how offensive statistics have changed over time as well. But what aspects of a ballpark contribute to its being designated "hitter friendly" or "pitcher friendly"?

The most obvious one is the distance of the fences, as that can seriously impact the number of home runs hit, or not hit. For example, the first incarnation of Comiskey Park in Chicago, home of the White Sox from 1910 to 1990, had a centerfield fence that varied in distance to home plate from a high of 455 feet in the late 1920s to 401 feet in 1983, according to Philip Lowry's wonderful publication *Green Cathedrals.*

The overall amount of foul territory, including the distance from home plate to the backstop, also plays a role in determining a ballpark's skewing towards offense or defense. The greater the amount of foul territory, the better the chances of batters being retired on foul fly balls. Lowry characterizes Comiskey as having had a "large" foul territory, with a distance from home plate to backstop at 98 feet for its first 23 seasons, and closing at 78 feet in 1990.

But when we look at the effects of ballpark on the number of runs scored, we can get a clearer picture of how it should be viewed by computing the

Park Factor. While there are different formulas for Park Factor (*PF*), we will use the basic one:

$$PF = \left(\frac{\left(\dfrac{\text{Runs Scored (Home)} + \text{Runs Allowed (Home)}}{\text{Number of Home Games}} \right)}{\left(\dfrac{\text{Runs Scored (Road)} + \text{Runs Allowed (Road)}}{\text{Number of Road Games}} \right)} \right)$$

Let's denote runs scored as *R*, runs allowed as *RA*, and we will insert home or away into parentheses following *R* or *RA*. This allows us to rewrite the park factor as:

$$PF = \left(\frac{\left(\dfrac{R\,(\text{Home}) + RA\,(\text{Home})}{\text{Games (Home)}} \right)}{\left(\dfrac{R\,(\text{Road}) + RA\,(\text{Road})}{\text{Games (Away)}} \right)} \right).$$

Note that the numerator of the main fraction is the average of runs scored in the team's home games, while the denominator of the main fraction is the average of runs scored in the team's road (away) games. Thus, if more runs are scored on average in the home games than in the road games, the fraction will have a value greater than 1, while if the average runs scored away from home is greater, the fraction will have a value less than 1. This can be figured as a percentage.

In 1959, the "Go-Go" Sox brought Deadball Era "Inside Baseball" to close an otherwise power-laden decade. In that season, the White Sox won the American League pennant with 94 wins, allowing a league-low 588 runs while scoring 669 runs, sixth best in an eight team league. Given those numbers, one would surmise that "Old Comiskey" Park favored pitching. But to what degree?

We compute the Park Factor based on runs. The White Sox played 156 games that year (2 road games ended in a tie). According to www.baseball-reference.com, the team scored an average of 4.01 runs per home game (so 309 runs scored at home) and 4.56 runs per game on the road (360 runs scored on the road), while allowing 3.49 runs per game at home (269 runs allowed at home) and 4.05 on the road (320 runs allowed on the road).

We compute the Park Factor for Comiskey Park, 1959:

$$PF = \left(\frac{\left(\dfrac{R\,(\text{Home}) + RA\,(\text{Home})}{\text{Games (Home)}} \right)}{\left(\dfrac{R\,(\text{Road}) + RA\,(\text{Road})}{\text{Games (Away)}} \right)} \right) = \left(\frac{\left(\dfrac{309 + 269}{77} \right)}{\left(\dfrac{360 + 320}{79} \right)} \right) = 0.872.$$

Since 1 – 0.872 = 0.128, we can conclude that Comiskey Park depressed run production by slightly less than 13 percent.

Let us consider Nellie Fox, the Hall of Fame Chisox shortstop who won the AL MVP in 1959. He scored 84 runs that year. How many would he have scored in a more neutral setting?

Applying the Park Factors to his run total, we consider that teams play half their games at home and half on the road, so we cut the Park Factor in half.

In this way, to compute Park Adjusted Runs *(PAR)*, we take

$PAR = R + (1 - PF) \times \dfrac{R}{2}$, so if a player's Park Factor is higher than 1, we will

obtain a negative value for 1 – *PF*, thus lowering his runs scored figure. If he plays in a pitcher's park, his *PF* will be lower than 1, so 1 – *PF* is a positive number, adjusting his runs total upward. A *PF* equal to 1 indicates a perfectly neutral park; i.e., one that favors neither offense nor defense. Similarly, we can define *PAOR* as the park adjusted factor for opponents' runs, using opponents' runs *(OR)* instead of runs *(R)*.

Thus, the calculation of Fox's *PAR*:

$$PAR = R + (1 - PF) \times \frac{R}{2} = 84 + (1 - 0.872) \times \frac{84}{2} = 89.376,$$

so Fox and his teammates' runs scored could be revised upward.

It is better to use data from several years in order to determine *PF*. Very often, a three- or five-year average is used to dampen the effect of a team's particular strength or weakness in a particular season. So, in an attempt to diminish the effect of one possibly anomalous season, we take a three-year average of *PF*. In other words, to establish a *PF* for a particular season, which we will call *PF* – 3 (*PF* – 3 year average), we add up the *PF* for that season and the two previous ones, and divide by three, i.e.,

$$(PF - 3)_{year} = \frac{PF_{year} + PF_{year-1} + PF_{year-2}}{3}.$$

Thus, for 1959, $(PF - 3)_{1959}$ would take the average of the Park Factors for Comiskey for 1957, 1958, and 1959.

The following chart summarizes the runs splits for those years:

Chisox	*R (Home)*	*RA (Home)*	*R (Away)*	*RA (Away)*
1957	347	263	360	303
1958	318	282	316	333

The computations are

$$PF(1957) = \left(\frac{\left(\dfrac{R\,(\text{Home}) + RA\,(\text{Home})}{\text{Games (Home)}}\right)}{\left(\dfrac{R\,(\text{Road}) + RA\,(\text{Road})}{\text{Games (Away)}}\right)}\right) = \left(\frac{\left(\dfrac{347 + 263}{77}\right)}{\left(\dfrac{363 + 303}{78}\right)}\right) = 0.932.$$

$$PF(1958) = \left(\frac{\left(\dfrac{R\,(\text{Home}) + RA\,(\text{Home})}{\text{Games (Home)}}\right)}{\left(\dfrac{R\,(\text{Road}) + RA\,(\text{Road})}{\text{Games (Away)}}\right)}\right) = \left(\frac{\left(\dfrac{318 + 282}{77}\right)}{\left(\dfrac{316 + 333}{78}\right)}\right) = 0.937.$$

Hence,

$$(PF - 3)_{1959} = \frac{PF_{1959} + PF_{1958} + PF_{1957}}{3} = \frac{0.872 + 0.932 + 0.937}{3} = 0.914.$$

From this, we determine that Comiskey was a pitcher's park all those years, and the average is 0.914, which translates to 1 − 0914 = 0.086, so one can conclude that Comiskey Park depressed run production by slightly less than 9 percent.

Now, applying this technique to Nellie Fox for 1959, let's calculate his *PAR*: $PAR = R + (1 - PF) \times \dfrac{R}{2} = 84 + (1 - 0.914) \times \dfrac{84}{2} = 87.612$, revising his runs total upward, but slightly less than in the single-year calculation.

The Chicago White Sox, as a team, surrendered 588 runs and scored 669 in 1959. If we adjust for Comiskey Park, the runs scored would adjust to $PAR = R + (1 - PF) \times \dfrac{R}{2} = 669 + (1 - 0.872) \times \dfrac{669}{2} = 712.$

For the runs allowed, it would revise upwards as well, to

$$PAOR = OR + (1 - PF) \times \frac{OR}{2} = 588 + (1 - 0.872) \times \frac{588}{2} = 626.$$

Demonstrating Sabermetrics

1. Nellie Fox scored 110 runs for the Sox in 1957. Find his Park Adjusted Runs total for that season.

Recall:

Chisox	R (Home)	RA (Home)	R (Away)	RA (Away)
1957	347	263	360	303

$$PF(1957) = \left| \frac{\left(\frac{R\,(\text{Home}) + RA\,(\text{Home})}{\text{Games}\,(\text{Home})} \right)}{\left(\frac{R\,(\text{Road}) + RA\,(\text{Road})}{\text{Games}\,(\text{Away})} \right)} \right| = \left| \frac{\left(\frac{347 + 263}{77} \right)}{\left(\frac{363 + 303}{78} \right)} \right|.$$

or $PF(1957) = 0.932$. Thus,

$$PAR = R + (1 - PF) \times \frac{R}{2} = 110 + (1 - 0.932) \times \frac{110}{2} = 114, \quad \text{or} \quad 114 \ \text{park adjusted}$$

runs.

2. In 1959, catcher Sherm Lollar led the Sox in *RBI* with 84. Calculate his *PA RBI* and *PA − RBI − 3* for that season.

$$PAR = RBI + (1 - PF) \times \frac{RBI}{2} = 84 + (1 - 0.872) \times \frac{84}{2} = 89.376$$

$$PA - RBI - 3 = RBI + (1 - PF) \times \frac{RBI}{2} = 84 + (1 - 0.914) \times \frac{84}{2} = 87.612.$$

3. The 2006 Dodgers had the following splits:

Dodgers	R (Home)	RA (Home)	R (Away)	RA (Away)
2006	438	365	382	386

Rafael Furcal led the team with 113 runs scored. Find his *PAR*. The Dodgers played 162 games in 2006, 81 at home and 81 on the road.

$$PF = \left| \frac{\left(\frac{R\,(\text{Home}) + RA\,(\text{Home})}{\text{Games}\,(\text{Home})} \right)}{\left(\frac{R\,(\text{Road}) + RA\,(\text{Road})}{\text{Games}\,(\text{Away})} \right)} \right| = \left| \frac{\left(\frac{428 + 365}{81} \right)}{\left(\frac{382 + 386}{81} \right)} \right| = 1.05,$$

making Dodgers Stadium a hitter's park. For Furcal,

$$PAR = R + (1 - PF) \times \frac{R}{2} = 113 + (1 - 1.05) \times \frac{113}{2} = 110, \quad \text{so his runs are adjusted}$$

downward.

4. Given that the Baltimore Orioles Park Factors for 2002, 2003, and 2004 were 0.96, 0.90 and 1.08, respectively, calculate $(PF - 3)_{2004}$.

$$(PF - 3)_{2004} = \frac{PF_{2004} + PF_{2003} + PF_{2002}}{3} = \frac{1.08 + 0.90 + 0.96}{3} = 0.98.$$

For Problems 5 – 11, use the following chart for the data for the Colorado Rockies. The team played 81 home games and 81 road games each year, except in 2007, when they played 82 at home and 81 on the road.

Rockies	R (Home)	RA (Home)	R (Away)	RA (Away)
2004	496	532	337	391
2005	451	447	289	415
2006	456	413	357	399
2007	478	396	382	362
2008	411	420	336	402

5. Calculate the Rockies Park Factor for 2004.

$$PF = \left(\frac{\left(\frac{R(Home) + RA(Home)}{Games(Home)}\right)}{\left(\frac{R(Road) + RA(Road)}{Games(Away)}\right)}\right) = \left(\frac{\left(\frac{496 + 532}{81}\right)}{\left(\frac{337 + 391}{81}\right)}\right) = 1.41,$$

which shows that runs scored were increased by 41 percent (!!!) in Coors Field.

6. Calculate the Rockies Park Factor for 2005.

$$PF = \left(\frac{\left(\frac{R(Home) + RA(Home)}{Games(Home)}\right)}{\left(\frac{R(Road) + RA(Road)}{Games(Away)}\right)}\right) = \left(\frac{\left(\frac{451 + 447}{81}\right)}{\left(\frac{289 + 415}{81}\right)}\right) = 1.28,$$

demonstrating an increase of 28 percent at Coors Field.

7. Calculate the Rockies Park Factor for 2008.

$$PF = \left(\frac{\left(\frac{R(Home) + RA(Home)}{Games(Home)}\right)}{\left(\frac{R(Road) + RA(Road)}{Games(Away)}\right)}\right) = \left(\frac{\left(\frac{411 + 420}{81}\right)}{\left(\frac{336 + 402}{81}\right)}\right) = 1.13,$$

so runs scored were increased by 13 percent in Coors Field.

8. Calculate the Rockies $PF - 3$ for the three-year period ending in 2006, given that the park factor for 2006 was 1.15.

$$(PF - 3)_{2006} = \frac{PF_{2006} + PF_{2005} + PF_{2004}}{3} = \frac{1.15 + 1.28 + 1.41}{3} = 1.28.$$

This shows that runs scored were increased by 28 percent in Coors Field over the three year period ending in 2006.

9. We can calculate the five-year average for a five-year period by taking the average park factor over the five years. Calculate $(PF - 5)_{2008}$.

$$(PF - 5)_{2008} = \frac{PF_{2008} + PF_{2007} + PF_{2006} + PF_{2005} + PF_{2004}}{3} =$$

$$\frac{1.13 + 1.16 + 1.15 + 1.28 + 1.41}{3},$$

which comes to 1.22 (the reader can calculate the park factors for 2006, 2007, and 2008). So, runs scored were increased by 22 percent at the Rockies' home park over the five-year period ending in 2008.

10. The Rockies' pitching staff has often been maligned, but Coors Field obviously plays an important role in pitching performance. In 2006, the Rockies' pitchers surrendered 812 runs. Calculate the *PAOR* for 2006, using the data from problem 9 above.

$$PAOR = OR + (1 - PF) \times \frac{OR}{2} = 812 + (1 - 1.15) \times \frac{812}{2} = 751.$$

The significance of this number is that, at 812 runs allowed, the Rockies were 13th in the 16-team National League, but when adjusted for park, 751 would have tied them for 4th in the league in fewest runs allowed. (Obviously, the other teams' runs allowed would have to be adjusted for park as well.)

11. The Rockies in 2006 scored 813 runs, fifth highest in the National League. Calculate the *PAR* using the 3-year average from Problem 10 above.

$$(PAR - 3)_{2006} = R + (1 - (PF - 3)_{2006}) \times \frac{R}{2} = 813 + (1 - 1.28) \times \frac{813}{2} = 700.$$

The real significance of this number is that, at 700 runs scored, the Rockies would have been 15th in the NL in 2006. (Once again, the other teams' runs allowed would have to be adjusted for park as well.)

Practicing Sabermetrics

For Problems 1–6, use the following chart for the data for the Brooklyn Dodgers, who played their home games in fabled Ebbets Field. It has been asserted that the Dodgers of the 1950s were one of the greatest collections of talent ever assembled, but that their hitters were aided (and their pitchers hurt) by the confines of their home park. We will examine that claim.

Season	Home Games	Away Games	R (Home)	RA (Home)	R (Away)	RA (Away)
1951	78	79	412	316	443	356
1952	78	75	389	322	386	281
1953	77	77	517	333	438	356
1954	77	77	380	393	398	347
1955	77	76	461	318	396	332

1. Calculate the *PF* for the Dodgers for 1951, and state what this means about Ebbets Field for that particular season.

[Answer: *PF* = 0.92, or run production was decreased by 8 percent.]

2. Calculate the *PF* for the Dodgers for 1952, and state what this means about Ebbets Field for that particular season.

[Answer: *PF* = 1.02, or run production was increased by 2 percent.]

3. Calculate the *PF* for the Dodgers for 1955, and state what this means about Ebbets Field for that particular season.

[Answer: *PF* = 1.06, or run production was increased by 6 percent.]

4. Given that Dodgers slugger Gil Hodges scored 118 runs and drove in 103 during the 1951 season, calculate his *PAR* and *PA – RBI* for 1951.

[Answer: Hodges *PAR* = 123, *PA – RBI* = 107.]

5. Calculate the Dodgers $(PF - 3)_{1953}$.

[Answer: $(PF - 3)_{1953}$ = 1.00.]

6. Calculate the Dodgers $(PF - 5)_{1955}$ and use it to adjust the team's runs allowed total for 1955.

[Answer: $(PF - 5)_{1955}$ = 1.02, OR(1955) = 318 + 332 = 650, so $(PAOR - 5)_{1955}$ = 643.]

McAfee Coliseum, home of the Oakland Athletics, has long been considered one of the best pitchers parks in baseball. One of the main reasons is for its large area in play in foul territory. For Problems 7–9, use the following chart for the data for the Oakland Athletics.

Season	Home Games	Away Games	R (Home)	RA (Home)	R (Away)	RA (Away)
2004	81	81	405	367	388	375
2005	81	81	391	345	381	313
2006	81	81	372	346	399	381
2007	81	81	331	350	410	408
2008	81	80	326	317	320	373

7. Calculate the Athletics' *PF* and $(PF - 5)_{2006}$, and comment on the significance of these numbers.

[Answer: *PF* (2006) =0.92, $(PF - 5)_{2006}$ = 1.00; thus, in the 2006 season, McAfee lowered run production by 8 percent, but on the three-year average, it was a neutral park.]

8. The Athletics allowed the 6th fewest runs in the 14-team American League in 2007. Calculate the Athletics' *PF* and *PFOR* for 2007, and, using the chart below, determine where the Athletics' adjusted runs allowed total would rank in the AL that year.

Team	RA
Boston	657
Toronto	699
Cleveland	704
Minnesota	725
LA Angels	731
Oakland	758
NY Yankees	777
Kansas City	778
Detroit	797
Seattle	813
Chi White Sox	839
Texas	844
Baltimore	868
Tampa Bay	944

[Answer: *PF* = 0.83, *PFOR* = 821, good for 11th place (between Seattle and Chicago).]

9. Using the *PF* calculated in Problem 8, adjust the Athletics' runs scored total in a similar way. In the chart below, the Athletics were 11th in the 14-team American league in runs scored. Put them in their new position in the AL using the runs scored chart below.

2007 AL	R
NY Yankees	968
Detroit	887
Boston	867
LA Angels	822
Texas	816
Cleveland	811
Seattle	794
Tampa Bay	782
Baltimore	756
Toronto	753
Oakland	741
Minnesota	718
Kansas City	706
Chi White Sox	693

[Answer: *PFR* = 803, good for 7th place (between Seattle and Cleveland).]

CHAPTER 6

Runs Created

Introduction

Sabermetrician Bill James has shown that runs scored and runs allowed are the greatest predictor of a team's performance. However, runs scored and runs batted in are very situationally dependent. What James attempted to create was a model of the number of runs for which each player was responsible, devoid of the context of his teammates.

This model is called Runs Created, or *RC*. The most basic version of the Runs Created formula is $RC = \dfrac{(H + BB) \times TB}{AB + BB}$. The $H + BB$ part is the "on base" portion, and we will denote it by "A," while the TB is the advancement portion, or "B," and the $AB + BB$ makes up the number of opportunities, or "C." In fact, although it has been revised in different versions, the formula will always take on the basic form of $\dfrac{A \times B}{C}$, where A represents the on base portion, B represents the advancement portion, and C represents opportunities.

This formula can be used to calculate the number of runs a team *should have* scored based on the other elements of the offense. This is fairly accurate, even with just these four terms (H, BB, TB, and AB). Note that, throughout this chapter, we will round all quantities for Runs Created and its components to the nearest whole number.

For example, in 2008, the fourteen teams of the American League scored 10,844 runs. The four elements were

AB	H	BB	TB
78119	20911	7521	32812

Thus, we have $RC = \dfrac{(20911 + 7521) \times 32812}{78119 + 20911} = 10{,}890$, which is within 1 percent of the actual run total for the season! Alternatively, Runs Created can be computed as $OBA \times SLG \times AB$, or $OBA \times TB$.

Consider another example. The 2008 Arizona Diamondbacks scored 720 runs. The club had the following numbers:

AB	H	BB	2B	3B	HR
5409	1355	587	318	47	159

First, we need to calculate the total bases. Since singles are not broken out, we can either add up the doubles, triples and home runs, subtracting them from hits, or we can simply use the formula $TB = H + 2B + 2 \times 3B + 3 \times HR$, or $TB = 1355 + 318 + 2 \times 47 + 3 \times 159 = 2244$. This yields $RC = \dfrac{(H + BB) \times (TB)}{AB + BB} = 727$, which is less than 1 percent more than the actual runs scored.

The 1948 St. Louis Cardinals finished in second place in the National League. Their seasonal data was:

AB	H	BB	TB
5302	1396	594	2,065

which leads to RC $= \dfrac{(H + BB) \times (TB)}{AB + BB} = 697$. However, this differs by more than 6 percent from the team's actual runs scored, 742.

As with any mathematical model, the more data that is put into the model, the more accurate the model represents the actual physical situation. When a team outperforms its Runs Created estimate, it can be interpreted as an efficient offense; the converse holds true as well. In this fashion, there are other aspects of a team's offense that the basic Runs Created formula does not include. For example, throughout baseball history, stolen bases (*SB*), caught stealing (*CS*), and hit by pitch (*HBP*) are sometimes counted and sometimes not.

What James did was to create a different formula for each season or collection of seasons in which certain statistics were included or not. There are now twenty-four versions of the Runs Created formula based largely on the statistics available for a particular season. They are all listed in the *Stats Inc. Handbook*. The Runs Created formula used to this point will be called the Basic Runs Created, and be denoted *BRC*.

In the 1948 season, the basic four offensive elements (*H*, *BB*, *TB*, and *AB*) were known, with the addition of *HBP, K, SB* (but not *CS*), sacrifice hits (*SH*) and *GIDP*. The version of the formula used for 1948 (and, in fact, for all National League seasons from 1940–1950 inclusive) has the acronym *HDG*–21, for "Historical Data Group 21."

Here are the statistics for the 1948 Cardinals:

AB	H	BB	TB	HBP	K	SB	SH	GIDP
5302	1396	594	2,065	22	521	24	76	125

The *HDG*–21 formula has as its components the following:

$A = H + BB + HBP - GIDP$

$B = 1.02\ (TB) + 0.26\ (BB + HBP) + 0.05\ (SB) + 0.5\ (SH) - 0.03\ (SO)$

$C = AB + BB + HBP + SH.$

Applying these components to the '48 Cards, we find

$A = 1396 + 594 + 22 - 125 = 1887,$

$B = 1.02\ (2065) + 0.26\ (594 + 22) + 0.05\ (24) + 0.5\ (76) - 0.03\ (521) = 2290,$ and

$C = 5302 + 594 + 22 + 76 = 5994,$

leading to a Runs Created value of $\dfrac{A \times B}{C} = \dfrac{1887 \times 2290}{5994} = 721$. This is within 3 percent of the actual runs total, 742.

One of the uses for Runs Created is to determine how much of the team offense a player has provided, without the context required in runs scored or runs batted in. In 1948, Hall of Famer Stan Musial won the league MVP Award. His offensive numbers are listed below:

AB	H	BB	TB	HBP	K	SB	SH	GIDP
611	230	79	429	3	34	7	1	18

So, $A = 230 + 79 + 3 - 18 = 294,$

$B = 1.02\ (429) + 0.26\ (79 + 3) + 0.05\ (7) + 0.5\ (1) - 0.03\ (34) = 459,$ and

$C = 611 + 79 + 3 + 1 = 694,$

and $\dfrac{A \times B}{C} = \dfrac{294 \times 459}{694} = 194$. Thus, Stan Musial can be credited with having created $\dfrac{194}{721} = 0.269$, or roughly 27 percent, of the 1948 Cardinals offense. This is indeed MVP caliber.

Individual players can also be evaluated according to how many runs each creates over 27 outs (9 innings at 3 outs per inning gives 27 outs in a regulation game). In other words, how many outs are "spent" in the creation of his runs.

First, we compute the number of outs by $OUTS = AB - H + SH + GIDP$. In seasons with other data available, such as SF or CS, these would also be included. $GIDP$ represents an additional out caused, so it is charged to the batter. For Stan Musial, $OUTS = AB - H + SH + GIDP = 611 - 230 + 1 + 18 = 400$.

Runs Created over 27 outs, identified as $RC/27$, is computed by dividing runs created by the number of 27 out groupings in the player's outs, i.e.,

$$RC/27 = \frac{RC}{\left(\frac{OUTS}{27}\right)}. \text{ For Musial, } RC/27 = \frac{RC}{\left(\frac{OUTS}{27}\right)} = \frac{194}{\left(\frac{400}{27}\right)} = 13.$$

In other words, a team consisting of nine "Stan Musials" batting in the National League in 1948 would average 13 runs scored per game. By comparison, 1948's eight team National League averaged 4.43 runs per game.

Demonstrating Sabermetrics

1. Brooklyn Dodger Hall of Famer Jackie Robinson won the National League's Most Valuable Player Award in 1949. Calculate his BRC given his statistics:

AB	H	BB	TB
593	203	86	313

$$BRC = \frac{(H + BB) \times (TB)}{(AB + BB)} = \frac{(203 + 86) \times (313)}{(593 + 86)} = 133.$$

Problems 2 through 5 will require the use of *HDG*-21, with
$A = H + BB + HBP - GIDP$
$B = 1.02\ (TB) + 0.26\ (BB + HBP) + 0.05\ (SB) + 0.5\ (SH) - 0.03\ (K)$
$C = AB + BB + HBP + SH,$
and this expanded chart of Jackie Robinson's statistics:

AB	H	BB	TB	HBP	K	SB	SH	GIDP
593	203	86	313	8	27	37	17	22

2. Determine the "on base" portion A for Jackie Robinson in 1949.
$A = H + BB + HBP - GIDP = 203 + 86 + 8 - 22 = 275$.

3. Determine the "advancement" portion B for Jackie Robinson in 1949.

$B = 1.02 \ (TB) + 0.26 \ (BB + HBP) + 0.05 \ (SB) + 0.5 \ (SH) - 0.03 \ (K)$
$= 1.02 \ (313) + 0.26 \ (86 + 8) + 0.05 \ (37) + 0.5 \ (17) - 0.03 \ (27) = 353.$

4. Determine the "opportunities" portion C for Jackie Robinson in 1949.
$C = AB + BB + HBP + SH = 593 + 86 + 8 + 17 = 704.$

5. Using $\dfrac{A \times B}{C}$ determined above, find Jackie Robinson's Runs Created using HDG–21.

$$HDG\text{–}21 = \frac{A \times B}{C} = \frac{275 \times 353}{704} = 138.$$

6. Find Robinson's $OUTS$ for 1949, and using the answer to question 5, calculate his $RC/27$.

$OUTS = AB - H + SH + GIDP = 593 - 203 + 17 + 22 = 429.$ Therefore,

$$RC/27 = \frac{RC}{\left(\dfrac{OUTS}{27}\right)} = \frac{138}{\left(\dfrac{429}{27}\right)} = 8.68.$$

(NL average: 4.54 runs per team per game).

HDG–23, used for both AL and NL data between from 1955 to 1988, has the following formula:

$A = H + BB + HBP - CS - GIDP$
$B = TB + 0.29(BB + HBP - IBB) + 0.64(SB) + 0.53(SF + SH) - 0.03(K)$
$C = AB + BB + HBP + SH + SF$

Use the information in the table below to perform the calculations for Dale Murphy, former Atlanta Braves center fielder. (Note: IBB stands for intentional bases on balls, SF denotes sacrifice flies, and CS denotes caught stealing.)

1985	AB	H	BB	2B	3B	HR
	616	185	90	32	2	37

HBP	K	SB	CS	SH	SF	GIDP
1	141	10	3	0	5	14

7. Calculate Dale Murphy's TB for 1985.
$TB = H + 2B + 2\times3B + 3\times HR = 185 + 32 + 2\times2 + 3\times37 = 185 + 32 + 4 + 111$
$= 332$ bases.

8. Calculate BRC for Dale Murphy using the 1985 stats.
$$BRC = \frac{(H + BB) \times (TB)}{(AB + BB)} = \frac{(185 + 90) \times (332)}{(616 + 90)} = 129.$$

9. Determine the "on base" portion A for Dale Murphy in 1985.
$A = H + BB + HBP - CS - GIDP = 185 + 90 + 1 - 3 = 259.$

10. Determine the "advancement" portion B for Dale Murphy in 1985.
$B = 1.02$ (TB) + 0.29 $(BB + HBP - IBB)$ + 0.64 (SB) + 0.53 $(SF + SH)$ − 0.03 (K) = 1.02 (332) + 0.26 (90 + 1 − 15) + 0.64 (10) + 0.53 (0 + 5) − 0.03 (141) = 359.

11. Determine the "opportunities" portion C for Dale Murphy in 1985.
$C = AB + BB + HBP + SH + SF$ = 616 + 90 + 1 + 0 + 5 = 712.

12. Using $\dfrac{A \times B}{C}$, find Dale Murphy's Runs Created using HDG–23.

$$HDG\text{–}23 = \frac{A \times B}{C} = \frac{259 \times 359}{712} = 131.$$

13. Find Murphy's $OUTS$ for 1985, and using the answer to Problem 12, determine Murphy's $RC/27$. Since we have SF data, it should be included, but not CS.
$OUTS = AB - H + SH + SF + GIDP$ = 616 − 185 + 0 + 5 + 14 = 450.

$$RC/27 = \frac{RC}{\left(\dfrac{OUTS}{27}\right)} = \frac{131}{\left(\dfrac{450}{27}\right)} = 7.86.$$

14. In 1985 the National League averaged 4.07 runs per team per game. The Pythagorean Record is $\dfrac{(RS)^x}{(RS)^x + (RA)^x}$, where RS is the number of runs a team has scored and RA is the number that it has allowed, is a projection of a team's winning percentage. The exponent x can be various numbers, but for ease, we will use 2. Using the answer to Problem 13, hypothesize what a team of nine "Dale Murphys" at the bat with National League average defense and pitching would have had as a winning percentage in 1985.

$$\text{Pythagorean Record} = \frac{(RS)^2}{(RS)^2 + (RA)^2} = \frac{(7.86)^2}{(7.86)^2 + (4.07)^2} = 0.789.$$ A winning percentage of 0.789 in 162 games translates to 128 wins.

Practicing Sabermetrics

For Problems 1–8, use the data for the 2008 Arizona Diamondbacks to calculate the Runs Created for each starter at his position. We will use the Runs Created for these players in Chapter 7.

For 2008, we will apply the formula HDG(23, with
$A = H + BB + HBP - CS - GIDP$
$B = TB + 0.29(BB + HBP - IBB) + 0.64(SB) + 0.53(SF + SH) - 0.03(K)$
$C = AB + BB + HBP + SH + SF$
We note that HDG–24 is the formula to be used for seasons since 1988,

but there are elements to the model, such as home runs with men on base and hitting in scoring position, that are not easily accessible.

PLAYER		AB	H	2B	3B	HR	BB	K	SB	CS	GIDP	HBP	SH	SF	IBB
C	Chris Snyder	334	79	22	1	16	56	101	0	0	7	4	5	5	5
1B	Conor Jackson	540	162	31	6	12	59	61	10	2	14	9	1	3	3
2B	Orlando Hudson	407	124	29	3	8	40	62	4	1	18	2	3	3	2
SS	Stephen Drew	611	178	44	11	21	41	109	3	3	5	1	3	7	6
3B	Mark Reynolds	539	129	28	3	28	64	204	4	1	10	3	1	6	0
LF	Eric Byrnes	206	43	13	1	6	16	36	4	4	5	2	0	0	0
CF	Chris Young	625	155	42	7	22	62	165	14	5	10	1	6	5	2
RF	Justin Upton	356	89	19	6	15	54	121	1	4	3	4	0	3	6

[Answers:]

	Player	A	B	C	RC
C	Chris Snyder	132	170	404	56
1B	Conor Jackson	214	268	612	94
2B	Orlando Hudson	147	203	455	66
SS	Stephen Drew	212	323	663	103
3B	Mark Reynolds	185	229	613	81
LF	Eric Byrnes	52	84	224	19
CF	Chris Young	203	307	699	89
RF	Justin Upton	140	178	417	60

9. In 1966, Hall of Famer Frank Robinson had a fine offensive season, winning the Triple Crown. His statistics are shown in this table:

AB	H	BB	TB
576	182	87	367

Calculate his BRC.

[Answer: *BRC* = 149.]

10. Given the table below, determine Frank Robinson's *OUTS* for 1966 and calculate his *RC*/27 (using the *RC* from Problem 9). Incorporate *SF* into his *OUTS*.

AB	H	BB	TB	HBP	K
576	182	87	367	10	90

SB	CS	SH	SF	GIDP
8	5	0	7	24

[Answers: *OUTS* = 425, *RC*/27 = 9.56.]

11. In 1966 the American League averaged 3.89 runs per team per game. Using the *RC/27* from Problem 10 above, calculate Frank Robinson's Pythagorean Record (see Problem 14 above in the Demonstrating Sabermetrics section). To how many wins would this winning percentage translate in a 162-game season?

[Answer: *Pythagorean* = .858, *W* = 139.]

12. Find Frank Robinson's *HDG*–23 for 1966, and use it to recalculate his *RC/27*, his Pythagorean Record, and his projected win total.

[Answers: *A* = 250, *B* = 398, *C* = 620, *HDG*–23 = 146, *Pythagorean* = 0.851, *W* = 138.]

CHAPTER 7

Win Shares

Introduction

Sabermetrics guru Bill James developed a player evaluation system that encompasses all facets of a player's contribution to the team, called Win Shares (*WS*). The Hardball Times (http://hardballtimes.com/) defines Win Shares as "a very complicated statistic that takes all the contributions a player makes toward his team's wins and distills them into a single number that represents the number of wins contributed to the team, times three."

In this section, we will work with the Win Shares statistic and perform some calculations that lead to an understanding of the topic. One of the two methods for computing Win Shares is the so-called "long form," which is fairly involved, involving many calculations and data, some of which is not readily available. The other method is called the "short form" and, while still fairly complicated, it uses data that is easier for the average sabermetrician to obtain. Full explanations for both methods can be found in the 2002 book *Win Shares* by Bill James and Jim Henzler, while an explanation of the "short form" can be found in *Understanding Sabermetrics* by the authors of this book.

According to James, the short form method seems to yield a value very close to that of the long form for years after 1920, and is fairly close to the long form for years prior to 1920. A team's total Win Shares is equal to three times the number of actual wins. The WS are apportioned to each player based on hitting/baserunning (48 percent), fielding (17 percent), and pitching (35 percent) contributions.

Marginal Runs

In conjunction with Win Shares, James developed a concept known as Marginal Runs, another way to predict a team's record, based on the number of runs allowed less than the average and the number of runs scored greater than the league average. Thus, marginal runs are divided into two categories, offensive and defensive. On the offensive side, he defines a marginal run as any run scored by a team in excess of one-half the league average, i.e., team runs minus one-half the league average, or $R - (0.5 \times R_{LGAVG})$. For defense, marginal runs are defined as each run allowed below 1.5 times the league average, or $(1.5 \times RA_{LGAVG}) - RA_{TEAM}$. For leagues with no interleague play, $R_{LGAVG} = RA_{LGAVG}$.

In the National League in 2008, there were 16 teams, 11741 runs scored, and 11976 runs allowed. This leads to an average runs scored of 733.8 and a runs allowed average of 748.5. The Arizona Diamondbacks of 2008 scored 720 runs and allowed 706. The team's Marginal Runs for Offense (*MR-O*) are calculated as $MR\text{-}O = R - (0.5 \times R_{LGAVG}) = 720 - (0.5 \times 733.5) = 353$. The Marginal Runs for Defense (*MR-D*) are calculated as $MR\text{-}D = (1.5 \times R_{LGAVG}) - RA_{TEAM} = (1.5 \times 748.5) - 706 = 417$. For the National League in 2008, we have the following Marginal Runs Calculations and totals:

	G	R	OR	MR-O	MR-D	TOT
ARI	162	720	706	353	417	770
ATL	162	753	778	386	345	731
CHC	161	855	671	488	452	940
CIN	162	704	800	337	323	660
COL	162	747	822	380	301	681
FLA	161	770	767	403	356	759
HOU	161	712	743	345	380	725
LAD	162	700	648	333	475	808
MIL	162	750	689	383	434	817
NYM	162	799	715	432	408	840
PHI	162	799	680	432	443	875
PIT	162	735	884	368	239	607
SDP	162	637	764	270	359	629
SFG	162	640	759	273	364	637
STL	162	779	725	412	398	810
WAS	161	641	825	274	298	572

Marginal Runs produce a prediction for Winning Percentage that is virtually identical to the Pythagorean number. It allows for the Marginal Runs concept to be the foundation for the Wins Shares method.

For the 2008 NL, the marginal runs total is divided by the sum of the league averages in runs scored and runs allowed. This sum is 733.8 + 748.5 = 1482.3, so when Arizona's 770 Marginal Runs is divided by 1482.3, the projected *WPCT* is 0.519. Arizona's actual *WPCT* is 0.506. The rest of the projected winning percentages are in the table below:

NL2008	G	R	OR	WPCT	MR-O	MR-D	TOT	Avg Sum	Proj WPCT
ARI	162	720	706	0.506	353	417	770	1482.3	0.519
ATL	162	753	778	0.444	386	345	731	1482.3	0.493
CHC	161	855	671	0.602	488	452	940	1482.3	0.634
CIN	162	704	800	0.457	337	323	660	1482.3	0.445
COL	162	747	822	0.457	380	301	681	1482.3	0.459
FLA	161	770	767	0.522	403	356	759	1482.3	0.512
HOU	161	712	743	0.534	345	380	725	1482.3	0.489
LAD	162	700	648	0.519	333	475	808	1482.3	0.545
MIL	162	750	689	0.556	383	434	817	1482.3	0.551
NYM	162	799	715	0.549	432	408	840	1482.3	0.567
PHI	162	799	680	0.568	432	443	875	1482.3	0.590
PIT	162	735	884	0.414	368	239	607	1482.3	0.409
SDP	162	637	764	0.389	270	359	629	1482.3	0.424
SFG	162	640	759	0.444	273	364	637	1482.3	0.430
STL	162	779	725	0.531	412	398	810	1482.3	0.546
WAS	161	641	825	0.366	274	298	572	1482.3	0.386

Marginal Runs can be computed for each player using the ratio of marginal runs to wins. The normal ratio is approximately 9 to 1, regardless if the team is a good one or a bad one, although that number can vary.

As stated earlier, the Win Shares calculations are quite involved. We will compute one main aspect for each type of Win Shares. For Win Shares assigned for offensive contribution, Runs Created is the key statistic (see Chapter 6 for a detailed explanation of how to compute Runs Created); for Win Shares assigned for pitching contribution, the so-called "Component ERA" is an important number; for Win Shares assigned for defensive contribution, the difficulty of the position is taken into account.

Win Shares — Offense

Here is how to compute offensive win shares using the short form:
- Compute the Outs Made by *each hitter*
- Divide the Outs by 12
- Subtract from the *RC*
- Divide by 3. If non-negative, then this is *each hitter's batting WS*

For the 2008 Arizona Diamondbacks, third baseman Mark Reynolds had 81 *RC* (as computed in the "Practicing Sabermetrics" section of Chapter 6). He had the following statistics:

AB	H	2B	3B	HR	BB	SO	SB	CS	GIDP	HBP	SH	SF	IBB
539	129	28	3	28	64	204	4	1	10	3	1	6	0

We compute his number of outs to be $OUTS = AB - H + SH + GIDP$ = 539 - 129 + 1 + 10 = 421 outs.

The Offensive Win Shares has the following computation:

$$WS = \frac{RC - \left(\dfrac{OUTS}{12}\right)}{3} = \frac{81 - \left(\dfrac{421}{12}\right)}{3} = 15.31.$$

Win Shares — Pitching

For pitchers, the key idea is the so-called "Component ERA," abbreviated *ERC,* or an estimate of the "Runs Created" versus the pitcher, which can be used to establish a context-free *ERA.*

The *ERC* has a similar setup to Runs Created. There is an *"A"* factor, a *"B"* factor, and a *"C"* factor, and they are combined in the same manner: $\dfrac{A \times B}{C}$, where

$A = H + BB + HBP$

$B = \{[(H - HR) \times 1.255] + [4 \times HR]\} \times 0.89 + \{[BB - IBB] \times 0.56\} + [HBP \times 0.56]$

$C = BFP$ (i.e., batters faced by the pitcher)

We note that, for the seasons *IBB* are not known, the *B* factor becomes $B = \{[(H - HR) \times 1.255] + [4 \times HR]\} \times 0.89 + \{[BB + HBP] \times 0.475\}$.

As an example, in 1903, "Iron Man" Joe McGinnity put up these numbers:

IP	H	R	ER	HR	BB	K	HBP	BFP
434	391	162	117	4	109	171	19	1814

$A = H + BB + HBP = 391 + 109 + 19 = 519.$

$B = \{[(H - HR) \times 1.255] + [4 \times HR]\} \times 0.89 + \{[BB + HBP] \times 0.475\} = \{[(391 - 4) \times 1.255] + [4 \times 4]\} \times 0.89 + \{[109 + 19] \times 0.475\} = 507.3.$ (We note that *IBB* is not available for 1903.)

$C = 1814.$

Therefore, $\dfrac{A \times B}{C} = \dfrac{(519) \times (507.3)}{1814} = 145.1$, a "runs created against" figure. Multiplying this by 9 and dividing by *IP* gives an equivalent *ERA.* Here,

$equivERA = \dfrac{(145.1) \times (9)}{434} = 3.01.$ Then, we subtract 0.56 from this to account for unearned runs, so 3.01 − 0.56 = 2.45. This is a context-free projection of what a pitcher's ERA *should* be for a season, given his walks, hits, hit batsmen and home runs allowed.

Win Shares — Defense

James feels that Win Shares marks a breakthrough in the evaluation of players defensive statistics. Among the factors that go into this analysis are the following:

1. Remove strikeouts from catchers' fielding percentages;

2. First basemens' throwing arms can be evaluating by estimating the number of assists that are not simply 3–1 flips to the pitcher covering first base;

3. Ground balls by a team can be estimated;

4. Team double plays need to be adjusted for ground ball tendency and opponents' runners on base;

5. Putouts by third basemen do not indicate a particular skill level;

6. A bad team will have more outfielder and catcher assists than a good team.

The short form method takes none of these into account. Here is how to determine fielding win shares for position players:

- Catchers get 1 *WS* for every 24 *G*
- 1Bmen get 1 *WS* for every 76 *G*
- 2Bmen get 1 *WS* for every 28 *G*
- 3Bmen get 1 *WS* for every 38 *G*
- SS get 1 *WS* for every 25 *G*
- OFers get 1 *WS* for every 48 *G*

In 1903, Roger Bresnahan played 84 games in the outfield, 13 games at 1B, 11 games at C, and 4 games at 3B. By the short form, this would yield $(11 \times \frac{1}{24}) + (13 \times \frac{1}{76}) + (4 \times \frac{1}{38}) + (84 \times \frac{1}{48}) = 2.255$ defensive Win Shares.

Win Shares Per Game

Consider the 1903 New York Giants. Roger Bresnahan had the highest *WS* of any position player, with 27, according to James and Henzler. He also had 406 *AB*, 142 *H*, and 12 *SH* . Given that this is the only data available to compute the number of outs, he made 406 − 142 + 12 = 276 *OUTS*. Since there are 27 *OUTS* in a game, it is reasonable to compute the number of *WS* for every 27 *OUTS*, or *WS/27*, to put the numbers on a "PER GAME" basis. First, we divide 276 by 27 to obtain 10.22, and we divide *WS* by this to obtain $WS/27 = \frac{27}{10.22} = 2.64$. This provides a measure of efficiency, i.e., how many outs were needed to achieve the given WS total. A higher WS/27 indicates a more efficient player.

Bresnahan's fellow Giants outfielder Sam Mertes had 26 *WS* in 1903. To compute his number of outs, we use the chart

AB	*H*	*SH*
517	145	11

So he had $517 - 145 + 11 = 383$ *OUTS*, and $WS/27 = \dfrac{26}{\left(\dfrac{383}{27}\right)} = 1.83$.

Thus, it would seem that Bresnahan had a more efficient season than Mertes. We note that their *WS* totals include their defensive contributions as well.

For pitchers, to get the numbers into the context of a game, we will divide total *IP* by 9 to put the data on a 9-inning footing. Joe McGinnity pitched in 55 games that season, starting 48 and completing 46 (!) while pitching 434 innings. He is credited with 40 *WS*.

We compute $WS/9 = \dfrac{WS}{\left(\dfrac{IP}{9}\right)} = \dfrac{40}{\left(\dfrac{434}{9}\right)} = 0.83$.

In the same season, Cy Young, pitching for the Boston Americans (of the American League) completed 34 of his 35 starts, pitching 341⅔ innings, and earning 38 Win Shares. His $WS/9 = \dfrac{WS}{\left(\dfrac{IP}{9}\right)} = \dfrac{38}{\left(\dfrac{341\frac{2}{3}}{9}\right)} = 1.00$, a more

efficient season than that of the Iron Man, who earned only two more *WS* while pitching about 100 more innings. Note that the pitchers' *WS* also include their batting and fielding contributions. In fact, pitchers at the turn of the 20th century, because of incredibly high numbers of innings pitched, typically amassed the highest number of Win Shares of any players in any era. Over the course of his career, Young pitched 7354⅔ innings and is credited with 634 *WS*, for a $WS/9 = \dfrac{WS}{\left(\dfrac{IP}{9}\right)} = \dfrac{634}{\left(\dfrac{7354\frac{2}{3}}{9}\right)} = 0.78$.

Demonstrating Sabermetrics

These are the runs scored and runs allowed totals for the 2008 American League that will be used for Problems 1–3.

Team	R	RA
BAL	782	869
BOS	845	694
CHW	811	729
CLE	805	761
DET	821	857
KCR	691	781
LAA	765	697
MIN	829	745
NYY	789	727
OAK	646	690
SEA	671	811
TBR	774	671
TEX	901	967
TOR	714	610

1. Find the average runs scored and runs allowed for the American League in 2008.

$$Avg\ R = \frac{10844}{14} = 774.6,\ Avg\ RA = \frac{10609}{14} = 757.8.$$

2. Find the *MR-O* for the 2008 Texas Rangers.

$$MR\text{-}O = R - (0.5 \times R_{LGAVG}) = 901 - (0.5 \times 774.6) = 513.7.$$

3. Find the *MR-D* for the 2008 Toronto Blue Jays.

$$MR\text{-}D = (1.5 \times RA_{LGAVG}) - RA_{TEAM} = (1.5 \times 757.8) - 610 = 526.7.$$

4. In Chapter 6, Demonstrating Sabermetrics section, we computed Jackie Robinson's 1949 *RC* to be 138 and his *OUTS* to be 429. Use this data to compute his Offensive *WS* using the short form method.

$$WS = \frac{RC - \left(\dfrac{OUTS}{12}\right)}{3} = \frac{138 - \left(\dfrac{429}{12}\right)}{3} = 34.08.$$

5. Jackie Robinson played 156 games at 2B in 1949. Calculate his defensive *WS* using the short form method.

Second basemen get 1 *WS* for every 28 *G*; therefore, Robinson's Defensive $WS = 156 \times \left(\dfrac{1}{28}\right) = 5.57.$

6. Jackie Robinson did not pitch in 1949. Find his total *WS* based on the answers to the previous two Problems.

Offensive *WS* + Defensive *WS* = 34.08 + 5.57 = 39.65. We remark that the actual figure from James and Henzler using the long form is 36, and that our total does not include any adjustments that one would make, including one for ballpark.

7. Using the data from Problems 5 and 6, find Jackie Robinson's *WS/27*.

$$WS/27 = \frac{39.65}{\left(\frac{429}{27}\right)} = 2.50.$$

Problems 8 through 10 lead to the computation of component *ERA* (*ERC*) for Sandy Koufax, 1965. Here are his statistics for that season:

IP	H	R	ER	HR	BB	K	HBP	BFP	IBB
335⅔	216	90	76	26	71	382	5	1297	4

8. Find the "*A*" factor of *ERC*.

$$A = H + BB + HBP = 216 + 71 + 5 = 292.$$

9. Find the "*B*" factor of *ERC*.

$B = \{[(H - HR) \times 1.255] + [4 \times HR]\} \times 0.89 + \{[BB - IBB] \times 0.56\} + [HBP \times 0.56]$
$= \{[(216 - 10) \times 1.255] + [4 \times 10]\} \times 0.89 + \{[71 - 4] \times 0.56\} + [5 \times 0.56] = 345.1.$

10. Find the "*C*" factor of *ERC*, and compute *equivERA* with adjustment for unearned runs using the answers to Problems 9 and 10.

$$C = BFP = 1297; \quad \frac{A \times B}{C} = \frac{(292) \times (345.1)}{1297} = 77.69;$$

$equivERA = \dfrac{(77.69) \times (9)}{335⅔} = 2.08.$ Then, we subtract 0.56 from this to account for unearned runs, so 2.08 − 0.56 = 1.52.

11. For the 1965 season, Koufax is credited with 33 *WS*. Find his *WS/9*.

$$WS/9 = \frac{WS}{\left(\frac{IP}{9}\right)} = \frac{33}{\left(\frac{335⅔}{9}\right)} = 0.885.$$

Practicing Sabermetrics

1. The American League in 1919 scored runs as listed in the table:

Team	R	RA
BOS	564	552
CHW	667	534
CLE	636	537
DET	618	578
NYY	578	506
PHA	457	742
SLB	533	567
WAS	533	570

Find the average runs scored per team. Note that, since there was no regular-season interleague play in 1919, the average runs scored per team and average runs allowed per team are the same , so we will refer to the common value as average runs.

[Answers: Total Runs = 564 + 667 + 636 + 618 + 578 + 457 + 533 + 533 = 4568 runs.

Average Runs per team = $\dfrac{4568}{8}$ = 573.25 runs.]

2. Find the Marginal Runs for Offense (*MR-O*) for the 1919 Chicago White Sox.

[Answer: $MR\text{-}O = R - (0.5 \times R_{LGAVG}) = 667 - (0.5 \times 573.25) = 380.4$.]

3. Find the Marginal Runs for Defense (*MR-D*) for the 1919 Chicago White Sox.

[Answer: $MR\text{-}D = (1.5 \times R_{LGAVG}) - RA_{TEAM} = (1.5 \times 573.25) - 534 = 325.9$.]

4. Find the projected winning percentage for the 1919 White Sox using the marginal runs. The team's actual *WPCT* was 0.629.

[Answer: Projected $WPCT = \dfrac{MR\text{-}O + MR\text{-}D}{2 \times R_{LGAVG}} = \dfrac{380.4 + 325.9}{2 \times 573.25} = 0.616$.]

Problems 5 through 8 use the data in the following chart for the 2008 Arizona Diamondbacks. The table was generated in the problems in Chapter 6.

	Player	AB	H	GIDP	SH	RC
C	Chris Snyder	334	79	7	5	56
1B	Conor Jackson	540	162	14	1	94
2B	Orlando Hudson	407	124	18	3	66
SS	Stephen Drew	611	178	5	3	103
3B	Mark Reynolds	539	129	10	1	81
LF	Eric Byrnes	206	43	5	0	19
CF	Chris Young	625	155	10	6	89
RF	Justin Upton	356	89	3	0	60

5. Calculate the *OUTS* and short-form Offensive *WS* for Conor Jackson.

[Answers: *OUTS* = 393; *WS* = 20.42.]

6. Calculate the *OUTS* and short-form Offensive *WS* for Chris Young.
[Answers: *OUTS* = 486; *WS* = 16.17.]

7. Calculate the *OUTS* and short-form Offensive *WS* for Stephen Drew.

[Answers: *OUTS* = 441; *WS* = 22.08.]

8. Calculate the *OUTS* and short-form Offensive *WS* for Justin Upton.
[Answers: *OUTS* = 270; *WS* = 12.5.]

9. In his career, Pete Rose played the following numbers of games at each position: Outfield: 1327, 1B: 939, 3B: 634, and 2B: 628. Using the short form, find his Defensive Wins Shares for his career.

[Answer: Defensive Wins Shares = 79.11.]

Problems 10 through 12 lead to the computation of component ERA (*ERC*) for Lefty Grove, 1931.

IP	H	R	ER	HR	BB	K	HBP	BFP	IBB
288⅔	249	84	66	10	62	175	1	1160	0

10. Find the "*A*" factor of *ERC*.

[Answer: *A* = 312.]

11. Find the "*B*" factor of *ERC*, noting that the *IBB* data is unavailable for 1931.

[Answer: *B* = 332.5.]

12. Find the "*C*" factor of *ERC*, and compute *equivERA* with adjustment for unearned runs using the answers to questions 12 and 13.

[Answers: $C = 1160$; $= \dfrac{A \times B}{C}$ 89.42; *equivERA* = 2.79; *Unearned Adj* = 2.23.]

CHAPTER 8

Linear Weights Batting Runs

Introduction

In the early 1980s, Pete Palmer and John Thorn developed a statistic based on a formula known as Linear Weights, in order to express an essential relationship between scoring runs and winning games. As a precursor to Thorn and Palmer's Linear Weights statistic, we must mention the works of F. C. Lane and George Lindsey. Well before 1920, Ferdinand Cole Lane conducted a study of exactly 1000 base hits, which occurred in 62 major league games. His sought to assign a value to each hit and then study the probability of each hit producing a run, developing the run value of a particular hit (we'll call it *Lane BR1*):

Runs (*Lane BR1*) = $(0.30 \times 1B) + (0.60 \times 2B) + (0.90 \times 3B) + (1.15 \times HR)$.

A single was worth 30 percent of a run, a double was worth 60 percent of a run, a triple was worth 90 percent of a run, and a home run was worth 115 percent of a run. After several years of continuing this study, Lane changed his coefficients, refining his run production model to (we'll call it *Lane BR2*):

Runs (*Lane BR2*) = $(0.457 \times 1B) + (0.786 \times 2B) + (1.15 \times 3B) + (1.55 \times HR)$.

In 1963, George Lindsey published an article in *Operations Research* entitled "An Investigation of Strategies in Baseball," in which he was assigned run values to various offensive events, if those events led to scoring runs. His approach was to assess batting effectiveness based on three assumptions:

- The batter's ultimate purpose is to cause runs to be scored.
- Batting effectiveness should not be measured for individuals based on situations that faced the batter when he came to the plate (since his batting actions did not create those situations).
- The probability of a batter getting different hits (single, double, etc.) is independent of the situation on the bases.

64

Lindsey accumulated out-versus-base data from 373 major league games played mostly in 1959 and 1960 and determined a value of a hit toward scoring runs based on the 24 different number-of-outs versus occupation-of-the-bases scenarios (no runners on with no outs, runner on first with no outs, bases loaded with two outs, etc.). His formula for runs is (we'll call it *Lindsey BR*):

Runs ($Lindsey\ BR$) = $(0.41 \times 1B) + (0.82 \times 2B) + (1.06 \times 3B) + (1.42 \times HR)$.

Lindsey explained that a home run increases the expected score, on average, by 1.42 runs. Specifically, a double was worth 1.97 as much as a single, a triple was worth 2.56 times as much as a single, and a home run was worth 3.42 times as much.

In 1978, in an effort to understand the value of a run produced, Pete Palmer developed a computer simulation, taking into account *all* major league games played since 1901. The simulation provided run values of each event in terms of net runs produced *above the average amount*. His simulation could compare an *individual* player's performance to an *average* player's performance for a given season. John Thorn then teamed up with Pete Palmer to develop the Linear Weights model for predicting runs produced by a batter. They published *The Hidden Game of Baseball* in 1984, which contained the Linear Weights formula for batting runs (*LW1*):

Batting Runs ($LW1$) = $(0.46 \times 1B) + (0.80 \times 2B) + (1.02 \times 3B) + (1.40 \times HR) + [0.33 \times (BB + HBP)] + (0.30 \times SB) - (0.60 \times CS) - [0.25 \times (AB - H)] - (0.50 \times OOB)$.

As you can see, a home run is worth, on average, 1.40 runs, over the course of an average season, while getting caught stealing loses a hitter 0.60 runs. The last term in this formula is an effort to take outs from plate appearances into account; subtracting hits and walks from plate appearances gives outs, and this term received a negative run weight. Notice also that the coefficients for 1B, 2B, 3B, and *HR* are very close to those proposed by both Lane's second model and Lindsey's model. Further, Thorn and Palmer omit the stealing, caught stealing and outs on base terms when comparing the great players of the past, as data for caught stealing is not known. This gives a condensed form for Linear Weights, given by (*LW2*):

Batting Runs ($LW2$) = $(0.47 \times 1B) + (0.78 \times 2B) + (1.09 \times 3B) + (1.40 \times HR) + [0.33 \times (BB + HBP)] - [0.25 \times (AB - H)]$

Notice that the value of a single is 0.47 runs, and each extra base hit (double, triple, home run) has a value of 0.31 times the number of bases beyond a single. Thorn and Palmer claim that this condensed version is accurate to within a fraction of a run. A batter with a positive Linear Weights run production is above the average player, while a batter with a negative run production would be below average.

In 1984, Thorn and Palmer mention that their Linear Weights statistics "has a 'shadow stat' which tracks its accuracy to a remarkable degree and is a breeze to calculate: *OPS*, or On Base Average Plus Slugging Percentage." They go on to mention that the correlation between Linear Weights and *OPS* over the course of an average team's regular season is at 99.7 percent. *OPS* has become a fixture in measuring the offensive production of a player (for more on *OPS*, see Chapter 14).

The Thorn and Palmer Linear Weights model has been revised a few times since it was first published in the eighties, taking into account changes in the situational values. The coefficients for the values of the various hits (single, doubles, etc.) have been modified to account for actual changes in run production. In the 2006 edition of *Baseball Encyclopedia*, the batting runs formula is listed as (we'll simply call it *BR*):

$$\text{Batting Runs } (BR) = (0.47 \times H) + (0.38 \times 2B) + (0.55 \times 3B) +$$
$$(0.93 \times HR) + \left[0.33 \times (BB + HBP)\right] - \left[ABF \times (AB - H)\right]$$

Stolen base terms are omitted and are now calculated in Stolen Base Runs (see Chapter 10). Notice that the coefficients for the various hits are in some case much less than those in the earlier formulas, as the first term multiplies *hits*, not *singles*. The *ABF* term is a league batting factor term, which scales the value of the average batter to 0, thus refining the previous *LW2* equation. *ABF* is computed according to the following calculation:

$$ABF = \frac{(0.47 \times H) + (0.38 \times 2B) + (0.55 \times 3B) + (0.93 \times HR) + \left[0.33 \times (BB + HBP)\right]}{AB - (LGF \times H)}$$

All of the statistics in the *ABF* equation are league statistics. In addition, the *LGF* term is known as the league factor, and it adjusts for the quality of league play. It is scaled to 1 for American League and National League play, and it equals 0.8 for Union Association play (1884) and 0.9 for Federal League play (1914-1915). With an increase in offensive output in recent years, the *ABF* has increased as well, indicating that an out now may cost a team more potential runs than it in the past.

One more note of interest. These batting run formulas do not take into account any ballpark factors. For more on park factors, see Chapter 5.

Which player is tops according to Linear Weights? In *The Hidden Game of Baseball*, Babe Ruth, not surprisingly, was listed as the hands-down leader in both career and single-season batting runs (Thorn and Palmer calculated their lists through the 1983 seasons). Using the 2006 Linear Weights formula with the *ABF*, let's compare some of the great hitters using one of their premier seasons: Ty Cobb in 1911, Babe Ruth in 1921, Rogers Hornsby in 1925, Lou Gehrig in 1927, Ted Williams in 1941, Stan Musial in 1948, Mickey Mantle in 1957, Frank Robinson in 1966, Barry Bonds in 2001, and Albert Pujols in 2005. Their statistics and associated *BR* values are listed in the following table.

Player	Year	BA	H	1B	2B	3B	HR	BB	HBP	AB	BR
Ty Cobb	1911	0.420	248	169	47	24	8	44	8	591	83.04
Babe Ruth	1921	0.378	204	85	44	16	59	145	4	540	126.32
Rogers Hornsby	1924	0.424	227	145	43	14	25	89	2	536	99.65
Lou Gehrig	1927	0.373	218	101	52	18	47	109	3	584	107.38
Ted Williams	1941	0.406	185	112	33	3	37	147	3	456	109.98
Stan Musial	1948	0.376	230	127	46	18	39	79	3	611	96.70
Mickey Mantle	1957	0.365	173	105	28	6	34	146	0	474	95.29
Frank Robinson	1966	0.316	182	97	34	2	49	87	10	576	80.22
Barry Bonds	2001	0.328	156	49	32	2	73	177	9	476	123.69
Albert Pujols	2005	0.359	212	117	51	1	43	79	10	591	81.67

From this exercise, we see that Babe Ruth's 1921 season leads the way as the best season, edging out Barry Bonds' record-breaking 2001 campaign. The best season listed in Thorn and Palmer's book was Ruth's 1921 season; however, the BR listed above do not take into account stolen base runs (see Chapter 10), which *LW*1 accounts for.

Pete Palmer later wrote that as a rough rule of thumb, each additional ten runs scored (or ten less runs allowed) produced one extra win. If a batter has twenty runs produced by a Linear Weights statistic, this approximately accounts for two wins.

Demonstrating Sabermetrics

Note: In those Problems requiring the *ABF*, see Appendix B.

1. Compare the following players using *Lane BR*1 and *Lane BR*2. Discuss any difference.

Player	Season	AB	H	2B	3B	HR
Ty Cobb	1911	591	248	47	24	8
Lou Gehrig	1931	619	211	31	15	46
Babe Ruth	1921	540	204	44	16	59
Ted Williams	1941	456	185	33	3	37

We calculate *Lane BR*1 first. Starting with the original formula and inserting Cobb's data, we find $BR1 = (0.30 \times 1B) + (0.60 \times 2B) + (0.90 \times 3B) + (1.15 \times HR) = (0.30 \times 169) + (0.60 \times 47) + (0.90 \times 24) + (1.15 \times 8) = 109.70$ runs. Using Lane's second formula, $BR2 = (0.457 \times 1B) + (0.786 \times 2B) + (1.15 \times 3B) + (1.55 \times HR) = (0.457 \times 169) + (0.786 \times 47) + (1.15 \times 24) + (1.55 \times 8) = 154.18$ runs.

For Gehrig, $BR1 = (0.30 \times 119) + (0.60 \times 31) + (0.90 \times 15) + (1.15 \times 46) = 120.70$ runs, and $BR2 = (0.457 \times 119) + (0.786 \times 31) + (1.15 \times 15) + (1.55 \times 46) = 167.30$ runs.

For the Bambino, $BR1 = (0.30 \times 85) + (0.60 \times 44) + (0.90 \times 16) + (1.15 \times 59) = 134.15$ runs, and $BR2 = (0.457 \times 85) + (0.786 \times 44) + (1.15 \times 16) + (1.55 \times 559) = 183.28$ runs.

For Williams, $BR1 = (0.30 \times 112) + (0.60 \times 33) + (0.90 \times 3) + (1.15 \times 37) = 98.65$ runs, and $BR2 = (0.457 \times 112) + (0.786 \times 33) + (1.15 \times 3) + (1.55 \times 37) = 137.92$ runs.

Due to the higher magnitude of the coefficients, these runs values are inflated, compared with the Linear Weights values.

2. In 1983, Baltimore Orioles shortstop Cal Ripken won the American League Most Valuable Player Award over his teammate, first baseman Eddie Murray, in a close contest. Based on the second Linear Weights batting run production (*LW2*), who should have won the award? Here is the data:

Player	*AB*	*H*	*2B*	*3B*	*HR*	*BB*	*HBP*	*SB*	*CS*
Cal Ripken	663	211	47	2	27	58	0	0	4
Eddie Murray	582	178	30	3	33	86	3	5	1

For Ripken, $LW2 = (0.47 \times 1B) + (0.78 \times 2B) + (1.09 \times 3B) + (1.40 \times HR) + [0.33 \times (BB + HBP)] - [0.25 \times (AB - H)] = (0.47 \times 135) + (0.78 \times 47 + (1.09 \times 2) + (1.40 \times 27) + = 0.33 \times 58 - 0.25 \times (663 - 211) = 55.14$ runs.

For Murray, $LW2 = (0.47 \times 1B) + (0.78 \times 2B) + (1.09 \times 3B) + (1.40 \times HR) + [0.33 \times (BB + HBP)] - [0.25 \times (AB - H)] = (0.47 \times 112) + (0.78 \times 30 + (1.09 \times 3) + (1.40 \times 33) + 0.33 \times 89 - 0.25 \times (582 - 178) = 63.68$ runs.

Murray has the higher run production.

3. Barry Bonds won the Most Valuable Player Award in the National League while a member of the Pittsburgh Pirates in 1990, 1992, and 1993. His season statistics are listed below. Calculate his *BR* for each season.

Year	*AB*	*H*	*2B*	*3B*	*HR*	*BB*	*HBP*
1990	519	156	32	3	33	93	3
1992	473	147	36	5	34	127	5
1993	539	181	38	4	46	126	2

For 1990, BR = $(0.47 \times H)$ + $(0.38 \times 2B)$ + $(0.55 \times 3B)$ + $(0.93 \times HR)$ + $[0.33 \times (BB + HBP)]$ − $[ABF \times (AB - H)]$= (0.47×156) + (0.38×32) + (0.55×3) + (0.93×33) + $[0.33 \times (93 + 3)]$ − $[.263 \times (519 - 156)]$ = 54.03 runs.

For 1992, BR = (0.47×147) + (0.38×36) + (0.55×5) + (0.93×34) + $[0.33 \times (127 + 5)]$ − $[.263 \times (473–147)]$ = 78.22 runs.

For 1993, BR = (0.47×181) + (0.38×38) + (0.55×4) + (0.93×46) + $[0.33 \times (126 + 2)]$ − $[.263 \times (539 - 181)]$ = 89.00 runs.

4. Jimmy Rollins won the 2007 National League Most Valuable Player Award with a batting average of .296, the first time since Kevin Mitchell in 1989 that the MVP Award went to a batter with a batting average below .300. The previous year, Rollins' teammate Ryan Howard won the prestigious award. Given their stats, calculate and compare the two Phillies' *BR*.

Player	AB	H	2B	3B	HR	BB	HBP
Rollins, 2007	716	212	38	20	30	49	7
Howard, 2006	581	182	25	1	58	108	9

For Rollins, BR = $(0.47 \times H)$ + $(0.38 \times 2B)$ + $(0.55 \times 3B)$ + $(0.93 \times HR)$ + $[0.33 \times (BB + HBP)]$ − $[ABF \times (AB - H)]$ = (0.47×212) + (0.38×38) + (0.55×20) + (0.93×30) + $[0.33 \times (49 + 7)]$ − $[.263 \times (716 - 212)]$ = 25.86 runs.

For Howard, BR = (0.47×182) + (0.38×25) + (0.55×1) + (0.93×58) + $[0.33 \times (108 + 9)]$ − $[.291 \times (581 - 182$ = 72.03 runs.

Howard's *HR* and *BB* contribute greatly to his high total.

5. In 2004, Seattle Mariners outfielder Ichiro Suzuki set a new record for most hits in a season with 262. What was his *BR*?

AB	H	2B	3B	HR	BB	HBP
704	262	24	5	8	49	4

For Ichiro, BR = $(0.47 \times H)$ + $(0.38 \times 2B)$ + $(0.55 \times 3B)$ + $(0.93 \times HR)$ + $[0.33 \times (BB+HBP)]$ − $[ABF \times (AB - H)]$ = (0.47×262) + (0.38×24) + (0.55×5) + (0.93×8) + $[0.33 \times (49 + 4)]$ − $[.296 \times (704 - 262)]$ = 29.70 runs.

6. The last two players to win baseball's Triple Crown in hitting are the Baltimore Orioles' Frank Robinson in 1966 and the Boston Red Sox' Carl Yastrzemski in 1967. Given their numbers below, compare their *BR*.

Player	AB	H	2B	3B	HR	BB	HBP
Robinson	576	182	34	2	49	87	10
Yastrzemski	579	189	31	4	44	91	4

For Robinson, BR = (0.47 × H) + (0.38 × 2B) + (0.55 × 3B) + (0.93 × HR) + [0.33 × (BB + HBP)] − [ABF × (AB − H)] = (0.47 × 182) + (0.38 × 34) + (0.55 × 2) + (0.93 × 49) + [0.33 × (89 + 10)] − [.263 × (576 − 182)] = 80.22 runs.

For Yastrzemski, BR = (0.47 × 189) + (0.38 × 31) + (0.55 × 4) + (0.93 × 44) + [0.33 × (91 + 4) − [.291 × (579 − 189)] = 82.65 runs.

7. In 1941, two feats occurred that may never be seen again. Ted Williams batted .406 for the entire season, and Joe DiMaggio hit safely in 56 consecutive games. The "Yankee Clipper" beat out the "Splendid Splinter" for the American League's MVP Award. Did he deserve it, based on Linear Weights? Compare their seasons using BR.

Player	AB	H	2B	3B	HR	BB	HBP
Williams	456	185	33	3	37	147	3
DiMaggio	541	193	43	11	30	76	4

For Williams, BR = (0.47 × H) + (0.38 × 2B) + (0.55 × 3B) + (0.93 × HR) + [0.33 × (BB + HBP)] − [ABF × (AB − H)] = (0.47 × 185) + (0.38 × 33) + (0.55 × 3) + (0.93 × 37) + [0.33 × (147 + 3)] − [.277 × (456 − 185)] = 109.98 runs.

For DiMaggio, BR = (0.47 × 193) + (0.38 × 43) + (0.55 × 11) + (0.93 × 30) + [0.33 × (76 + 4) − [.277 × (541 − 193)] = 71.00 runs.

According to BR, Ted Williams produced close to 30 more runs than DiMaggio.

8. Compare the two MVP seasons for Hall of Famer Joe Morgan using BR.

Year	AB	H	2B	3B	HR	BB	HBP
1975	498	163	27	6	17	132	3
1976	472	151	30	5	27	114	1

For 1975, BR = (0.47 × H) + (0.38 × 2B) + (0.55 × 3B) + (0.93 × HR) + [0.33 × (BB + HBP)] − [ABF × (AB − H)] = (0.47 × 113) + (0.38 × 27) + (0.55 × 6) + (0.93 × 17) + [0.33 × (132 + 3)] − [.260 × (498 − 163)]= 63.43 runs.

For 1976, BR = (0.47 × 89) + (0.38 × 30) + (0.55 × 5) + (0.93 × 27) + [0.33 × (114 + 1) − [.252 × (472 − 151)] = 67.29 runs.

Each season had similar statistics, producing a similar number of runs.

9. In 1987, Mark McGwire won the Rookie of the Year Award with Oakland. Compare his $LW2$ and BR.

Year	AB	H	2B	3B	HR	BB	HBP
1987	557	161	28	4	49	71	5

First, we calculate the runs from Linear Weights, *LW2*. *LW2* = (0.47 × 1B) + (0.78 × 2B) + (1.09 × 3B) + (1.40 × HR) + [0.33 × (*BB* + *HBP*)] − [0.25 × (*AB* − *H*)] = (0.47 × 80) + (0.78 × 28 + (1.09 × 4) + (1.40 × 70) + [0.33 × 76] − 0.25 × (557 − 161) = 58.48 runs. Next, we turn to *BR*, where *BR* = (0.47 × *H*) + (0.38 × 2B) + (0.55 × 3B) + (0.93 × *HR*) + [0.33 × (*BB* + *HBP*)] − [*ABF* × (*AB* − *H*)] = (0.47 × 80) + (0.38 × 28 + (0.55 × 4) + (0.93 × 49) + [0.33 × (76)] − [.289 × (557 − 161)] = 44.72 runs.

The higher *ABF* number in *BR* (0.289) reduces the number of runs, compared to a similar 0.25 in *LW2*.

10. Tris Speaker batted .383 in 1912, en route to winning the Most Valuable Player Award. If his *BR* = 43.95 runs, find the value for *z* (the number of walks Speaker had in 1912).

AB	H	2B	3B	HR	BB	HBP
580	222	53	12	10	*z*	6

BR = 43.95 = (0.47 × 222) + (0.38 × 53) + (0.55 × 12) + (0.93 × 10) + [0.33 × (*z* + 6)] − [.252 × (580 − 222)]. Solving for *z*, we find that 79.20 = 52.14 + 0.33*z*, or *z* = 81 walks. In fact, Speaker had 82 walks (some accuracy is lost due to round-off).

Practicing Sabermetrics

Note: In those Problems requiring the *ABF*, see Appendix B.

1. Calculate the batting runs (*BR*) for the top four home run hitters of all time, for the season in which each won his first Most Valuable Player Award: Hank Aaron in 1957, Babe Ruth in 1923, and Willie Mays in 1954. Who contributed the most wins to his own team? Here is the data:

Player	Year	AB	H	2B	3B	HR	BB	HBP
Aaron	1957	615	198	27	6	44	57	0
Mays	1954	565	195	33	13	41	66	12
Ruth	1923	522	205	45	13	41	170	4

[Answers: Aaron: 55.85 runs   6 wins;
            Mays: 77.16 runs   8 wins;
            Ruth: 128.02 runs   13 wins.]

2. Consider the following Hall of Fame catchers, all of whom played before 1930: Roger Bresnahan, Buck Ewing, and Ray Schalk. Who contributed the most runs to his own team (use the condensed form for Linear Weights Batting Runs, *LW2*)? Here is the data:

	AB	H	2B	3B	HR	1B	BB	HBP
Roger Bresnahan	4481	1252	218	71	26	937	714	67
Buck Ewing	5363	1625	250	178	72	1125	392	9
Ray Schalk	5306	1345	199	49	11	1086	638	59

[Answers: Bresnahan: 248.29 runs; Ewing: 458.29 runs; Schalk: 122.05 runs.]

3. Only six players have hit 60 or more doubles in a season (notice in which era they all occurred). They are:

Player	Team	Year	Doubles
Earl Webb	Boston (AL)	1931	67
George Burns	Cleveland (AL)	1926	64
Joe Medwick	St. Louis (NL)	1936	64
Hank Greenberg	Detroit (AL)	1934	63
Paul Waner	Pittsburgh (NL)	1932	62
Charlie Gehringer	Detroit (AL)	1936	60

	AB	H	1B	2B	3B	HR	BB	HBP
Earl Webb	589	196	112	67	3	14	70	0
George Burns	603	216	145	64	3	14	28	8
Joe Medwick	636	223	128	64	13	18	34	4
Hank Greenberg	593	201	105	63	7	26	63	2
Paul Waner	630	215	135	62	10	8	56	2
Charlie Gehringer	641	227	140	60	12	15	83	4

Order these hitters by the runs each contributed (use *LW2*) to his team during the indicated season.

[Answers: Gehringer: 71.89 runs; Greenberg: 65.97 runs;
        Medwick: 58.74 runs; Webb: 52.62 runs;
        Waner: 49.30 runs; Burns: 42.07 runs.]

4. Hall of Famer Jimmie Foxx won back-to-back Most Valuable Player Awards in the American League in 1932 and 1933. Compare his *BR* for the two seasons using the statistics in the table below:

Year	AB	H	2B	3B	HR	BB	HBP
1932	585	213	33	9	58	116	0
1933	573	204	37	9	48	96	1

[Answers: 1932: 103.43 runs; 1933: 88.96 runs.]

5. In 1949, two immortal players led their respective leagues in most offensive categories. In the American League, Ted Williams won the MVP Award, while in the senior circuit, Jackie Robinson won the award. Compare their batting runs (*BR*).

Player	AB	H	2B	3B	HR	BB	HBP
Williams	456	185	33	3	37	147	3
Robinson	541	193	43	11	30	76	4

[Answers: Williams: 96.86 runs; Robinson: 56.27 runs.]

6. Philadelphia Phillies third baseman and Hall of Famer Mike Schmidt won the National League Most Valuable Player Award three times (1981 was a strike-shortened season). Compare his batting runs using *LW2* and *BR* for each season.

Year	AB	H	2B	3B	HR	BB	HBP
1980	548	157	25	8	48	89	2
1981	354	112	19	2	31	73	4
1986	552	160	29	1	37	89	7

[Answers: 1980: *LW2* = 63.42 runs, *BR* = 61.48 runs;
1981: *LW2* = 53.51 runs, *BR* = 53.97 runs;
1986: *LW2* = 52.90 runs, *BR* = 50.16 runs.]

7. In 1980, George Brett batted .390 and slugged .664. Calculate his *BR*.

Year	AB	H	2B	3B	HR	BB	HBP
1980	449	175	33	9	24	58	1

[Answer: *BR* = 65.91 runs.]

8. In 1961, the schedules expanded to 162 games and New York Yankees teammates Mickey Mantle and Roger Maris battled each other in an effort to break Babe Ruth's home run record. Compare their seasons, using *BR*.

Player	AB	H	2B	3B	HR	BB	HBP
Mantle	514	163	16	6	54	126	0
Maris	590	159	16	4	61	94	7

[Answers: Mantle: 81.97 runs; Maris: 55.41 runs.]

9. In 2000, Colorado Rockies star Todd Helton had 405 total bases, mainly due to his 103 extra-base hits. He also had a career high slugging percentage with a .698 mark. How many *AB* did he have if his *BR* = 90.94 runs?

H	2B	3B	HR	BB	HBP
216	59	2	42	103	4

[Answer: *AB* = 580.]

CHAPTER 9

Linear Weights Pitching Runs

Introduction

Hall of Fame manager Earl Weaver said that the key to winning base-ball games is pitching, fundamentals, and three run homers. In Chapter 8 we discussed the Linear Weights formula for batting runs, and in Chapter 10 we will look at defense and stolen bases — fundamentals. In this chapter we summarize the Linear Weights models for pitching.

In *Total Baseball*, Thorn and Palmer wrote that "determining the run contributions of pitchers is much easier than determining those of fielders or batters, though not quite so simple as that of base stealers. Actual runs allowed are known, as are innings pitched." The Linear Weights pitching runs model assumes that pitchers are responsible only for earned runs. The earned run average statistic is an indication of a pitcher's *rate of efficiency*, not an indication of his actual benefit to a team's overall performance. As an example, if a team has two pitchers with identical *ERA*s who are compared against a higher league *ERA*, and pitcher A pitched in twice as many innings as pitcher B, then pitcher A must be worth twice as much as pitcher B to his team. We seek to measure the number of runs, beyond the average, that a pitcher has prevented from scoring. The formula for earned run average is:

$$\text{Earned Run Average}\,(ERA) = \frac{\text{Earned Runs} \times 9}{\text{Innings Pitched}}.$$

What about the average number of runs for a pitcher? This will equate to a pitching runs number of zero. The average number of runs is:

$$\text{Average Runs} = \frac{\text{League } ERA \times \text{Innings Pitched}}{9}.$$

The Linear Weights pitching runs formula (*PR*1) is straightforward and simple:

$$\text{Pitching Runs}\,(PR1) = \text{Innings Pitched} \times \frac{\text{League } ERA}{9} - \text{Earned Runs}.$$

Notice that the last term in the formula is actual earned runs allowed, not the earned run average. Pitching runs provides a difference of earned runs allowed at a league average, for the given number of innings pitched, and actual earned run allowed. There is a second formula for pitching runs (*PR2*) that rearranges terms:

$$\text{Pitching Runs } (PR2) = \frac{\text{Innings Pitched} \times (\text{League } ERA - \text{Pitcher's } ERA)}{9}.$$

This second formula, involving only innings pitched and earned run averages, is best employed when evaluating the performance of pitchers for whom the number of earned runs is not available, but the *ERA* is known. Notice the slight error in the two approaches; round-off error for the two *ERA*s can lead to a slight disagreement in pitching run values.

Efficiency and durability are incorporated into these pitching runs formulas. If a pitcher is consistently better than average, his team will benefit more and his Linear Weights pitching runs value will be higher. For example, if a pitcher is allowing one less earned run per game than the average pitcher, his Pitching Runs (*PR1*) total will increase with more innings pitched.

As an example, consider that in 2001, Roger Clemens won his unprecedented sixth Cy Young Award. The voting was not close. The New York Yankees' Clemens picked up 21 of 28 first-place votes, and his total number of points was twice as much as the next vote-getter, the Oakland Athletics' Mark Mulder. Did Roger win a sixth because he already had five? Was he the best pitcher in the American League, relative to other pitchers? Let's compare the six pitchers who received votes for the AL Cy Young Award in 2001. They are listed in the order of voting points finish in the table below. The league *ERA* was 4.48.

Pitcher	Team	Points	W–L	IP	ERA
Roger Clemens	NYY	122	20–3	220	3.51
Mark Mulder	OAK	60	21–8	229	3.45
Freddy Garcia	SEA	55	18–6	239	3.05
Jamie Moyer	SEA	12	20–6	210	3.43
Mike Mussina	NYY	2	17–11	229	3.15
Tim Hudson	OAK	1	18–9	235	3.37

At first glance, the earned run averages of the six pitchers appear to be comparable, although Freddie Garcia had close to a half run smaller *ERA* than Clemens. Innings pitched (*IP*) are also similar. Clemens' won-lost record was astonishing (almost 87 percent), but Jamie Moyer also had a great season. Using the second pitching runs (*PR2*) formula, we determine the following:

Pitcher	IP	ERA	PR2	Team's W–L
Roger Clemens	220	3.51	23.71	95–65
Mark Mulder	229	3.45	26.21	102–60
Freddy Garcia	239	3.05	37.97	116–46
Jamie Moyer	210	3.43	24.50	116–46
Mike Mussina	229	3.15	33.84	95–65
Tim Hudson	235	3.37	28.98	102–60

Of the six pitchers receiving votes, Clemens has the lowest *PR* value. That equates to the fewest wins afforded to his team. Did his won-lost record push him that far ahead of his rivals? Should he have received the Cy Young Award? Freddie Garcia earned over 14 more pitching runs, which equates to about one and a half more wins for his team. The Mariners sailed to a record 116 victories in 2001.

Let's inspect the data further. Compare Clemens with his teammate Mike Mussina, who had ten more pitching runs. Mussina pitched 8 more innings than Clemens, but he allowed six fewer earned runs. Not shown is the fact that Mussina had four complete games, including three shut-outs, in 2001, while Clemens had none of each. Opponents batted 0.237 against Mussina while hitting 0.246 against Clemens. Clemens did receive a higher run support from the Yankees when he pitched, and Mussina did offer one more win for the Yankees from his pitching runs than did Clemens. The vote has long been in the history books, but the 2001 AL Cy Young Award deserves a discussion.

Demonstrating Sabermetrics

1. "Big Ed" Walsh has the lowest career earned run average in history, with a fourteen-season mark of 1.82. Calculate his *PR*1 and *PR*2 given that *Big Ed* recorded 2964 innings pitched, allowed 598 earned runs against a league ERA of 2.65 (averaged over his career). Explain any difference in the two run values.

We calculate *PR*1 first. Walsh's pitching runs are equal to

$$PR1 = IP \times \frac{\text{League } ERA}{9} - ER = 2964\tfrac{1}{3} \times \frac{2.65}{9} - 598 = 274.82 \text{ runs.}$$

Next, we see that $PR2 = \dfrac{IP \times (\text{League } ERA - ERA)}{9} = \dfrac{2964\tfrac{1}{3} \times (2.65 - 1.82)}{9} = 273.37$ runs. As *PR*1 uses the actual number of earned runs, it is more accurate.

2. For his career, Hall of Famer Addie Joss is second all-time in career *ERA*, with the following statistics: in 2327 *IP*, he allowed 488 runs, finish-

ing with an *ERA* of 1.89 against a League *ERA* of 2.68 (averaged over his career). Calculate his pitching runs using *PR1* and *PR2*.

For Joss, $PR1 = IP \times \dfrac{\text{League } ERA}{9} - ER = 2327 \times \dfrac{2.68}{9} - 488 = 204.93$

runs. Next, we find

$$PR2 = \frac{IP \times (\text{League } ERA - ERA)}{9} = \frac{2327 \times (2.65 - 1.89)}{9} = 204.26$$

runs. These two values differ from each other by less than one-half percent.

3. In 1914, at the age of 22, Hubert "Dutch" Leonard posted the lowest post–1900 single-season *ERA*, with a mark of 0.96 in 224⅔ innings pitched. He allowed only 24 earned runs in a season where the league *ERA* was 2.68. Calculate his pitching runs using *PR1*.

For Leonard, $PR1 = IP \times \dfrac{\text{League } ERA}{9} - ER = 224\tfrac{2}{3} \times \dfrac{2.68}{9} - 24 = 42.91$ runs.

4. The National League's Bob Gibson and the American League's Denny McLain each won both the league Most Valuable Player Award and the Cy Young Award in 1968. McLain grabbed all 20 first-place votes in the AL, while Gibson took 14 of 20 first-place votes in the NL (Pete Rose with an *OPS* of .861 took the other 6). Given the following table with their amazing season statistics, calculate both *PR1* and *PR2* for each pitcher.

Pitcher	IP	ERA	Lg ERA	ER
Gibson	304⅔	1.12	2.90	38
McLain	336	1.96	3.01	73

For Gibson, $PR1 = IP \times \dfrac{\text{League } ERA}{9} - ER = 304\tfrac{2}{3} \times \dfrac{2.90}{9} - 38 = 60.18$

runs. His $PR2 = \dfrac{IP \times (\text{League } ERA - ERA)}{9} = \dfrac{304\tfrac{2}{3} \times (2.90 - 1.12)}{9} = 60.26$

runs. Amazing! For McLain, $PR1 = IP \times \dfrac{\text{League } ERA}{9} - ER$

$= 336 \times \dfrac{3.01}{9} - 73 = 39.37$ runs. His

$$PR2 = \frac{IP \times (\text{League } ERA - ERA)}{9} = \frac{336 \times (3.01 - 1.12)}{9} = 39.20 \text{ runs.}$$

5. Over the course of his great career, Hall of Famer Mordecai "Three-Finger" Brown posted a 2.06 *ERA*, which is sixth best all-time. The right-hander also owns the record for lowest *ERA* in a season by a right-handed pitcher since 1900, with a mark of 1.04 in 1906. Calculate his pitching runs for both 1906 and for his career using *PR1* and *PR2*, using the table below.

	IP	ERA	Lg ERA	ER
1906	277⅓	1.04	2.62	32
Career	3172⅓	2.06	2.85	725

For 1906, $PR1 = IP \times \dfrac{\text{League } ERA}{9} - ER = 277\tfrac{1}{3} \times \dfrac{2.62}{9} - 32 = 48.73$ runs. His

$PR2 = \dfrac{IP \times (\text{League } ERA - ERA)}{9} = \dfrac{277\tfrac{1}{3} \times (2.62 - 1.04)}{9} = 48.68$ runs. For his

career, *Three Finger's* $PR1 = 3172\tfrac{1}{3} \times \dfrac{2.06}{9} - 725 = 279.56$ runs, while his

$PR2 = \dfrac{3172\tfrac{1}{3} \times (2.85 - 2.06)}{9} = 278.46$ runs.

6. Christy Mathewson is considered one of the greatest right-handed pitchers of all time, posting a career *ERA* of 2.13, which is eighth best all-time. In 1909, he established a mark of 1.14, tied with Walter Johnson for the fifth lowest *ERA* ever. Calculate his pitching runs for both 1909 and for his career using *PR1* and *PR2*, using the table below.

	IP	ERA	Lg ERA	ER
1909	275⅓	1.14	2.54	35
Career	4780⅔	2.13	2.89	1133

For 1909, $PR1 = IP \times \dfrac{\text{League } ERA}{9} - ER = 275\tfrac{1}{3} \times \dfrac{2.54}{9} - 35 = 42.70$

runs. His $PR2 = \dfrac{IP \times (\text{League } ERA - ERA)}{9} = \dfrac{275\tfrac{1}{3} \times (2.54 - 1.14)}{9} = 42.82$

runs. For his career, Mathewson's $PR1 = 4780\tfrac{2}{3} \times \dfrac{2.13}{9} - 1133 = 402.14$

runs, while his $PR2 = \dfrac{4780\tfrac{2}{3} \times (2.89 - 2.13)}{9} = 403.70$ runs.

7. The 1971 Baltimore Orioles had a starting rotation of four 20-game winners, in a season where the Birds won 101 games. All four starters — Mike Cuellar, Pat Dobson, Dave McNally, and Hall of Famer Jim Palmer — each recorded at least 20 wins. Determine each pitcher's *PR1* as well as the combined *PR1* for the four starters. Their pitching stats for the year are listed in the table below. The American League *ERA* in 1971 was 3.36.

Pitcher	Record	IP	ERA	ER
Cuellar	20–9	292	3.08	100
Dobson	20–8	282	2.90	91

Pitcher	Record	IP	ERA	ER
McNally	21–5	224	2.89	72
Palmer	20–9	282	2.68	84

For Cuellar, $PR1 = IP \times \dfrac{\text{League } ERA}{9} - ER = 292\frac{1}{3} \times \dfrac{3.36}{9} - 100 = 9.13$

runs. For Dobson, $PR1 = 282\frac{1}{3} \times \dfrac{3.36}{9} - 72 = 14.39$ runs. For McNally, $PR1$

$= 224\frac{1}{3} \times \dfrac{3.36}{9} - 72 = 11.74$ runs. For Palmer, $PR1 = 282$

$\times \dfrac{3.36}{9} - 72 = 21.28$ runs. Finally, the combined team$= 1081$

$\times \dfrac{3.36}{9} - 347 = 56.57$ runs.

8. Steve Carlton is the last pitcher in either league to pitch over 300 innings in a season (he had 304 *IP* in 1980). With an *ERA* of 2.34 against a National League *ERA* of 3.79, what was his season *PR2*?

Carlton's $PR2 = \dfrac{IP \times (\text{League } ERA - ERA)}{9} = \dfrac{304 \times (3.79 - 2.34)}{9} = 48.98$

runs. "Lefty" finished his Hall of Fame career with 5217 innings pitched and an *ERA* of 3.70. Coincidentally, the average League *ERA* over his career was also 3.70. Using the *PR2* formula, this accounts for 0 runs! However, when Carlton's *ERA*, *IP*, and *ER* are used in *PR1*, he accounts for 280.89 career runs, making him an above-average pitcher. So, in the rare instance where a pitcher's *ERA* over his career matches the league's *ERA*, it is advisable to use *PR1*, as long as the number of *ER* are known.

9. Robin Roberts was another Phillies hurler who owns a plaque in the Hall of Fame. He won 20 or more games in six consecutive seasons, 1950 through 1955, and his stats are listed below. Calculate his *PR1* for the first three seasons and his *PR2* for the last three years. Then find Robin's average pitching runs over the 6-year span.

Year	IP	ERA	Lg ERA	ER
1950	304⅓	3.02	4.06	102
1951	315	3.03	3.84	106
1952	330	2.59	3.66	95
1953	346⅔	2.75	4.20	106
1954	336⅔	2.97	4.03	111
1954	305	3.28	3.96	111

For 1950, his $PR1 = IP \times \dfrac{\text{League } ERA}{9} - ER = 304\frac{1}{3} \times \dfrac{4.06}{9} - 102 = 35.27$

runs. For 1951, $PR1 = 28.40$ runs, and for 1952, $PR1 = 39.20$ runs. For 1953,

Roberts' $PR2 = \dfrac{IP \times (\text{League } ERA - ERA)}{9} = \dfrac{346\frac{2}{3} \times (4.20 - 2.75)}{9} = 55.86$

runs. For 1954, $PR2 = 39.66$ runs, and for 1955, $PR2 = 23.04$ runs. The average of these six seasons is 36.91 pitching runs per season.

10. Randy "The Big Unit" Johnson won the Cy Young Award in four consecutive seasons while with the Arizona Diamondbacks, 1999 through 2002. Given his statistics below, determine the $PR1$ for each season as well as the combined $PR1$ for the four years.

Year	IP	ERA	Lg ERA	ER
1999	271⅓	2.48	4.61	75
2000	248⅔	2.64	4.78	73
2001	249⅔	2.49	4.67	69
2002	260	2.32	4.57	67

For 1999, his $PR1 = IP \times \dfrac{\text{League } ERA}{9} - ER = 271\frac{2}{3} \times \dfrac{4.61}{9} - 75 = 64.17$ runs.

For 2000, $PR1 = 59.09$ runs, for 2001, $PR1 = 60.57$ runs, and for 1952, $PR1 = 65.02$ runs. The sum of these four seasons amounts to *The Big Unit* having 249.08 pitching runs.

Practicing Sabermetrics

1. Greg Maddux won the National League Cy Young Award in four consecutive seasons, from 1992 through 1995 (the first with the Chicago Cubs and the last three with the Atlanta Braves). Determine the $PR1$ for each season as well as the average $PR1$ for the four years. Compare his four-year average with Randy Johnson's four-year Cy Young Award average (see Problem 10 in the Demonstrating Sabermetrics section). Note: 1994 was a shortened season due to a strike.

Year	IP	ERA	Lg ERA	ER
1992	268	2.18	3.61	65
1993	267	2.36	4.05	70
1994	202	1.56	4.22	35
1995	209⅔	1.63	4.27	38

[Answers: 1992: *PR*1 = 42.50 runs; 1993: *PR*1 = 50.15 runs;
        1994: *PR*1 = 59.72 runs; 1995: *PR*1 = 61.49 runs.
        Maddux 4-season average: 53.46 runs;
        Johnson 4-season average: 62.21 runs.]

2. In 1978, Ron "Gator" Guidry of the New York Yankees had a phenomenal season, winning the American League Cy Young Award and finishing second in the Most Valuable Player Award voting. His record of 25–3 led the Yankees to a World Championship, despite the fact that the team had three managers (Billy Martin, Dick Howser, and Bob Lemon). Given the stats below, determine Guidry's *PR*1.

IP	ERA	Lg ERA	ER
273⅔	1.74	3.63	53

[Answer: 57.39 runs.]

3. Sandy Koufax is considered one of the greatest pitchers of his era. His career stats are

IP	ERA	Lg ERA
2324⅓	2.76	3.62

Determine his *PR*2 career number.

[Answer: 222.10 runs.]

4. Babe Ruth never had a losing season! His stats as a pitcher for the Boston Red Sox and New York Yankees are listed below. In which year was his *PR*1 the highest? The lowest?

Team	IP	ERA	Lg ERA	ER
1914 Boston	23	3.91	2.68	10
1915 Boston	217⅔	2.44	2.78	59
1916 Boston	323⅔	1.75	2.77	63
1917 Boston	326⅓	2.01	2.58	73
1918 Boston	166⅓	2.22	2.69	41
1919 Boston	133⅓	2.97	3.02	44
1920 New York	4	4.50	3.82	2
1921 New York	9	0.00	4.24	9
1930 New York	9	3.00	4.32	3
1933 New York	9	5.00	3.90	5

[Answers: Highest: 1916, with 36.63 runs. Lowest: 1921, with –4.76 runs.]

5. In 1908, at the age of 41, Cy Young pitched a no-hitter for Boston, won 21 games, and had an amazing 1.26 season *ERA*, compared to a 2.46 Lg *ERA*. Calculate his *PR*1 given that he pitched 299 innings.

[Answer: 39.73 runs.]

6. Atlanta Braves pitcher Phil Niekro led the National League in innings pitched from 1977 through 1979. In 1977 and 1978, the Hall of Famer also led the NL in earned runs allowed. In 5404 career innings (4th all-time), he allowed 2012 earned runs (2nd all-time). Determine his pitching runs using *PR*1 for the 1977 and 1978 campaigns.

Year	IP	ERA	Lg ERA	ER
1977	330	4.03	4.46	148
1978	334	2.88	4.08	107

[Answers: 1977: 15.68 runs; 1978: 44.55 runs. Interestingly, Atlanta lost 101 games in 1977 and 93 in 1978.]

7. In 1977, New York Yankees reliever Sparky Lyle won the Cy Young Award, with the following statistics:

IP	ERA	Lg ERA	ER
137	2.17	3.95	33

Calculate his pitching runs using *PR*2.

[Answer: 27.10 runs.]

8. Livan Hernandez led the National League in 2003, 2004, and 2005 in innings pitched. His statistics are listed in the table below. Compare his pitching runs using *PR*1 and *PR*2 for each season.

Year	IP	ERA	Lg ERA	ER
2003	233	3.20	4.50	83
2004	255	3.60	4.53	102
2005	246	3.98	4.06	109

[Answers: 2003: *PR*1 = 33.65 runs; *PR*2 = 33.70 runs;
        2004: *PR*1 = 26.35 runs; *PR*2 = 26.35 runs;
        2005: *PR*1 = 2.11 runs; *PR*2 = 2.19 runs.]

9. The great Walter "The Big Train" Johnson won 33 games in 1912 and 36 in 1913. Given the table below, find the values for *x* and *y*.

Year	IP	ERA	Lg ERA	ER	PR1
1912	369	1.39	3.37	x	81.17
1913	346	1.14	y	44	69.80

[Answers: x = 57; y = 2.96.]

10. Bob "Rapid Robert" Feller holds the record for most complete games in a season since 1921, with 36 *CG* in 1946. In that season, Hall of Famer Feller allowed 90 earned runs in 371 innings, in a season where the Lg *ERA* was 3.33. What was Feller's *ERA*, if he had 47.44 *PR2* pitching runs?

[Answer: *ERA* = 2.18.]

CHAPTER 10

Linear Weights Fielding and Base-Stealing Runs

Introduction

Back to Earl Weaver's theorem for winning ballgames. After good pitching, a team should be able to execute the fundamentals of the game. Part of that involves defense. Weaver's Baltimore Orioles teams always had players winning the Gold Glove Awards for best at their respective defensive positions. He and other managers would sacrifice a good bat for a good glove, especially for middle infielders. Weaver's Gold Glove players included second basemen Davey Johnson (3 Gold Gloves) and Bobby Grich (4), shortstop Mark Belanger (8), third baseman Brooks Robinson (a record 16), center fielder Paul Blair (8), and pitcher Jim Palmer (4). Hall of Famer Luis Aparicio won three of his eight Gold Gloves playing shortstop for the Orioles before Belanger came along. How does effective defense transform into runs? Thorn and Palmer also developed a fielding runs formula, based on Linear Weights.

The Linear Weights Fielding Runs formula for second basemen, shortstops and third basemen involves calculating a league average for each position, followed by a rating for the team in question at each position. The Average Position relative to the League (APL) is given by

$$APL = \frac{0.20 \times \left[PO + (2 \times A) - E + DP \right] \text{league at position}}{PO \text{ league total} - K \text{ league total}}.$$

where PO = putouts, A = assists, E = errors, DP = double plays, and K = strikeouts. Then the team rating for fielding runs (FR) is given by

Team FR per position = $0.20 \times [PO + (2 \times A) - E + DP]$ team at position –

$APL \times$ (team PO – team K).

This data can be found online at www.retrosheet.org, by first selecting the season of interest and then scrolling down past the standings to "ML

Team Totals." The league batting, pitching and defense by position data are presented. To calculate career *FR* involves combining the data for all seasons involved.

The coefficient for assists is 2; assists are doubly weighted because more skill is required to get an assist than to record a putout. Individual players are evaluated by prorating the putouts. In 1971, Brooks Robinson played all but four games at third base in a 158-game season for Baltimore. The Orioles as a team recorded 138 putouts at the 3B position. Brooks gets credit for 131/138 = 94.9 percent of the putouts made at third. Here is the data for third basemen in 1971 (position data is first, followed by total American League numbers in the last two columns):

	PO	A	E	DP	Total PO	Total K
AL	1655	4191	266	400	51823	10414
Orioles	138	362	17	37	4236	793

Using the formulas above, we first calculate the Orioles 3B *APL* in 1971. This is given by

$$APL = \frac{0.20 \times [1655 + (2 \times 4191) - 266 + 400]}{51823 - 10414} = 0.0491,$$

so the Team *FR* = 0.20 × [138 + (2 × 362) –17 + 86] – 0.0491 × (4236 – 793) = 7.26 runs, and Hall of Famer Brooks Robinson gets credit for 0.949 × 7.26 = 6.90 runs.

For catchers, the Fielding Runs is modified in that strikeouts are removed from the catchers' putouts. For first basemen, double plays and putouts were taken away, as they require much less fielding skill except in an occasional instance. This leaves only 0.20 × (2 *A* – *E*) in the formula's numerator. For outfielders, the formula for *FR* is 0.20 × (*PO* + 4 *A* – *E* + 2 *DP*). Thorn and Palmer conjectured that the "weighting for assists was boosted here because a good outfielder can prevent runs through the threat of assists that are never made; for outfielders, the assist is essentially an elective play." However, there might be a source of error in the calculations, as late-inning substitutes for outfielders makes it difficult to estimate the exact number of innings a player plays.

For fielding runs for pitchers, the innings are known and no problem arises. For pitchers, the outfielder's formula is modified to subtract individual pitcher strikeouts from the total number of potential outs (to help great strikeout pitchers like Nolan Ryan or Randy Johnson). Further, pitchers' chances are weighted less than infielders' assists, which might account for the difference between fly ball and ground ball pitchers. Thus the formula for pitchers is 0.10 × (*PO* + 2 *A* – *E* + *DP*).

Let's look at an outfielder example. Oscar "Happy" Felsch holds the record for most double plays by an outfielder in a single season, taking part in 19 *DP* in 1919, while playing 135 games at center field for the Chicago White Sox (known as the infamous Chicago "Black Sox"). In addition, he made 360 putouts and had 32 assists. Here are the pertinent numbers for his team and the league.

	PO	*A*	*E*	*DP*	*Total PO*	*Total K*
AL	7154	441	330	116	30107	3577
White Sox	922	81	46	28	3722	468

How many fielding runs did Happy have in 1919? Remembering to modify the coefficients for *PO* and *DP*, we first find the *APL* as

$$APL = \frac{0.20 \times \left[7154 + (4 \times 441) - 330 + (2 \times 116)\right]}{30107 - 3577} = 0.0665.$$

The Team *FR* = 0.20 × [922 + (4 × 81) − 46 + (2 × 28)] − 0.0665 × (3722 − 468) = 34.84 runs. Since Happy had 360/922 = 39.0 percent of the team's putouts, he gets credit for 0.390 × 34.84 = 13.60 fielding runs.

We now turn our attention to base stealing runs. Recall the formula for batting runs, *LW*1. There are two terms that deal with stolen bases. Is the player who steals the most bases the best thief? What about the number of times a player has been thrown out while trying to steal a base? Is he hurting his team?

Thorn and Palmer developed a "pleasingly simple" method, which they labeled as stealer's runs. We will determine base stealing runs (*BSR*) by multiplying a stolen base (*SB*) by 0.3 and a caught stealing (*CS*) by 0.6 and adding the two products:

$$BSR = 0.3 \, SB - 0.6 \, CS.$$

This really penalizes a player for getting thrown out while attempting to steal a base. Does he run himself and his team out of an inning?

We offer a well-known example. In 1982 Rickey Henderson set a modern record with 130 stolen bases. However, he was also caught 42 times! Therefore his *BSR* = 0.3 (130) − 0.6 (42) = 13.8 runs. Because of the penalty for getting caught, Thorn and Palmer state that "the stolen base is at best a dubious method of increasing a team's run production." In addition, caught stealing data is often incomplete before 1920.

Finally, as with Batting Runs and Pitching Runs, each additional ten runs accounted for produced one extra win. Had Rickey not been caught in 1982, he would have accounted for about 4 wins, but his 42 times caught stealing takes away over 2 wins.

Demonstrating Sabermetrics

1. In 1999, Rafael Palmiero of the Texas Rangers won his third Gold Glove Award as a first baseman. Interestingly, he only played 28 games at first base (he played 135 games as a designated hitter), making 261 putouts. Given the data below for 1999 first basemen, calculate his fielding runs.

	PO	A	E	Total PO	Total K
AL	19807	1375	161	60234	13913
Rangers	1533	75	9	4039	969

With first basemen, we are only concerned with assists and errors. Therefore, the $APL = \dfrac{0.20 \times \left[(2 \times A) - E \right]}{PO - K} = \dfrac{0.20 \times (2 \times 1375 - 161)}{60234 - 13913} = 0.0112$.
The team FR is $FR = 0.20 \, [(2 \times A) - E] - APL \, (PO - K) = 0.20 \, (2 \times 75 - 9) - 0.0112 \, (4039 - 969) = -6.12$ runs. Palmiero gets credit for 261/1533 = 17.0 percent, or -1.04 runs. In 1991, he was a better asset to the Rangers as a designated hitter.

2. Eddie Murray is the only first baseman to win multiple Gold Glove Awards in the American League and be elected into the Hall of Fame. Compare the fielding runs of the players who have won seven or more Gold Glove Awards. Each is listed below with a season in which his fielding percentage was highest. Compare the fielding runs to each player's batting runs for the season.

	PO	A	E	Total PO	Total K
Keith Hernandez	1310	139	4		
NYM Team Data	1412	150	5	4463	1039
NL Data, 1985	18155	1371	141	52400	10674
Don Mattingly	1258	84	3		
NYY Team Data	1639	102	7	4313	899
AL Data, 1993	19870	1623	160	60665	12952
George Scott	1388	118	9		
MIL Team Data	1479	123	9	4365	671
AL Data, 1973	17803	1254	160	52206	9851
Vic Power	1177	145	5		
CLE Team Data	1259	156	7	4153	771
AL Data, 1960	10961	838	112	33251	5993
Bill White	1513	101	6		
STL Team Data	1548	101	6	4332	877
NL Data, 1964	15063	1099	164	43557	9256

Again, this is a problem comparing first basemen, so we only need to use the assists and errors in the *FR* calculations. The putouts will help give us the ratio of runs each first baseman earned.

For Hernandez, the

$$APL = \frac{0.20 \times \left[(2 \times A) - E \right]}{PO - K} = \frac{0.20 \times (2 \times 1371 - 141)}{52400 - 10674} = 0.0125.$$

The Mets' team FR is

$FR = 0.20[(2 \times A) - E] - APL(PO - K) = 0.20(2 \times 150 - 5) - 0.0125(4463 - 1039)$
$= 16.31$ runs. Hernandez gets credit for $1310/1412 = 92.8$ percent, or 15.13 runs.

For Mattingly, the

$$APL = \frac{0.20 \times \left[(2 \times A) - E \right]}{PO - K} = \frac{0.20 \times (2 \times 1623 - 160)}{60665 - 12952} = 0.0129.$$

The Yankees' team FR is

$FR = 0.20[(2 \times A) - E] - APL(PO - K) = 0.20(2 \times 102 - 7) - 0.0129(4313 - 899)$
$= -4.76$ runs. "Donny Baseball" gets credit for $1258/1639 = 76.8$ percent, or -3.66 runs.

For Scott, the

$$APL = \frac{0.20 \times \left[(2 \times A) - E \right]}{PO - K} = \frac{0.20 \times (2 \times 1254 - 160)}{52206 - 9851} = 0.0111.$$

The Brewers' team FR is

$FR = 0.20[(2 \times A) - E] - APL(PO - K) = 0.20(2 \times 123 - 9) - 0.0111(4365 - 671)$
$= 6.44$ runs. Scott gets credit for $1388/1479 = 93.8$ percent, or 6.05 runs.

For Power, the

$$APL = \frac{0.20 \times \left[(2 \times A) - E \right]}{PO - K} = \frac{0.20 \times (2 \times 838 - 112)}{33251 - 5993} = 0.0115.$$

The Indians' team FR is

$FR = 0.20[(2 \times A) - E] - APL(PO - K) = 0.20(2 \times 156 - 7) - 0.0115(4153 - 771)$
$= 22.19$ runs. Power gets credit for $1177/1259 = 93.5$ percent, or 20.74 runs.

For White, the

$$APL = \frac{0.20 \times \left[(2 \times A) - E \right]}{PO - K} = \frac{0.20 \times (2 \times 1099 - 164)}{43557 - 9256} = 0.0119.$$

The Cardinals' team FR is

$FR = 0.20[(2 \times A) - E] - APL(PO - K) = 0.20(2 \times 101 - 6) - 0.0119(4332 - 877)$
$= -1.78$ runs. White gets credit for $1513/1548 = 97.7$ percent, or -1.74 runs.

By comparison, even though Mattingly had the fewest errors, he also played in a season with the highest *APL*, so Vic Power comes away with the highest *FR* for the particular season.

3. Baltimore Orioles legend Brooks Robinson sported a 0.971 career fielding percentage in 2870 games at third base (2nd all-time). He sits behind Mike Lowell, who is still active, as of the 2008 season. Lowell's best defen-

sive season was in 2005, while playing for the Marlins. That season, he led the NL in fielding percentage and double plays, and he accounted for 107 putouts.

	PO	A	E	DP	Total PO	Total K
NL	1932	5163	315	494	69133	16830
Marlins	140	306	9	40	4324	1125

Determine Lowell's 2005 fielding runs.

We first calculate the Red Sox 3B *APL* for 2005. This is given by

$$APL = \frac{0.20 \times \left[1932 + (2 \times 5163) - 315 + 494\right]}{69133 - 16830} = 0.0476,$$

so the Team *FR* = $0.20 \times [140 + (2 \times 306) - 9 + 40] - 0.0476 \times (4324 - 1125)$ = 4.46 runs. Lowell had 107/140 = 76.4 percent of the Marlins' putouts at third base, so he gets credit for credit for 0.764 × 4.46 = 3.41 runs. This is just under half of Brooks Robinson's fielding runs total for 1971, as explained in the Introduction section.

4. Willie Mays, with his 7095 career putouts, leads all outfielders in putouts. In 1954, the "Say Hey Kid" had 9 double plays as a center fielder (the other seven NL teams' center fielders combined for only 12 double plays)! Given the data below, and knowing that Mays had 448 putouts in the outfield, calculate his 1954 fielding runs.

	PO	A	E	DP	Total PO	Total K
NL	3375	92	61	21	33015	5086
Giants	461	13	7	9	4168	692

We modify the coefficients for *FR*, as in the Introduction section example. We first find that $APL = \dfrac{0.20 \times \left[3375 + (4 \times 92) - 61 + (2 \times 21)\right]}{33015 - 5086} = 0.0267.$
The Giants' team
$FR = 0.20 \times [461 + (4 \times 13) - 7 + (2 \times 9)] - 0.0267 \times (4168 - 692) = 12.10$ runs, and since Mays had 448/461 = 97.2 percent of the team's putouts, he gets credit for 0.972 × 12.10 = 11.76 fielding runs.

5. Bid McPhee participated in nine triple plays, all as a second baseman, in his 18 years with the Cincinnati Red Stockings. Bid was also involved in three triple plays as a runner! He was inducted into the Hall of Fame in 2000. Determine his fielding runs for 1896, which was probably his best defensive season. He made 297 putouts that year.

	PO	A	E	DP	Total PO	Total K
NL	3851	4901	564	659	41218	3523
Reds	322	408	21	62	3320	219

We use the same formula as for third basemen in Problem 3. The *APL* is given by

$$APL = \frac{0.20 \times \left[3851 + (2 \times 4901) - 564 + 659\right]}{41218 - 3523} = 0.0729,$$

so the Team *FR* = $0.20 \times [322 + (2 \times 408) - 21 + 62] - 0.0729 \times (3320 - 219) = 9.60$ runs. McPhee had 297/322 = 92.2 percent of the Red Stockings' putouts at second base in 1896, so he gets credit for credit for $0.922 \times 9.60 = 8.86$ runs.

6. Eric Young stole six bases for the Colorado Rockies in a game on June 30th, 1996. He ended the season with 53 successful swipes out of 72 chances. How many base stealing runs did Young have?

Young's *BSR* = 0.3 *SB* – 0.6 *CS* = 0.3 (53) – 0.6 (19) = 4.5 runs.

7. In an American League Championship Series game contested between Cleveland and Baltimore on October 11, 1997, the Indians' Marquis Grissom stole home in the bottom of the 12th inning to end the game. For his career, Grissom stole 429 bases and was caught 116 times. Determine his base stealing runs.

Grissom's *BSR* = 0.3 *SB* – 0.6 *CS* = 0.3 (429) – 0.6 (116) = 59.1 runs.

8. Compare the *BSR* for Vince Coleman and Juan Samuel in their rookie seasons. In 1985, the Cardinals' Coleman stole 110 bases and was caught 25 times, en route to Rookie of the Year honors. Samuel, in 1984, stole 72 bases for the Phillies and was caught 15 times, and he finished second in the Rookie of the Year voting (to Dwight Gooden).

Coleman's *BSR* = 0.3 *SB* – 0.6 *CS* = 0.3 (110) – 0.6 (25) = 18.0 runs, while Samuel's *BSR* = 0.3 *SB* – 0.6 *CS* = 0.3 (72) – 0.6 (15) = 12.6 runs.

Practicing Sabermetrics

1. Hall of Famer Ryne Sandberg holds the best mark for career fielding percentage by a second baseman (0.989). How many fielding runs did he account for in 1991, when he had 267 putouts and only 4 errors?

	PO	A	E	DP	Total PO	Total K
NL	4149	5786	185	1047	52163	11446
Cubs	287	557	6	71	4370	927

[Answer: 11.86 runs.]

2. In 1984, Steve Garvey became the only first baseman ever to have a 1.000 fielding percentage in a season (considering players with a minimum of 125 games in a season). This means he did not commit any errors while playing first base. How many fielding runs did Garvey have in 1984, when he accounted for 1232 putouts?

	PO	A	E	DP	Total PO	Total K
NL	17768	1320	156	1556	52288	10929
Padres	1356	93	0	133	4379	812

[Answer: −5.13 runs. His low number of assists did not help his *FR*.]

3. Boston Red Sox third baseman Butch Hobson made 43 errors in 1978, setting an unenviable record. Given that he made 122 putouts at third, calculate his fielding runs and comment on the answer.

	PO	A	E	DP	Total PO	Total K
AL	1862	4869	321	444	60493	10153
Red Sox	157	326	46	31	4416	706

[Answer: −10.87 runs, due to all of the errors.]

4. Hall of Famer Cal Ripken made only 3 errors in 1990 at shortstop, giving him a 0.9956 fielding percentage (considering players with a minimum of 125 games in a season). This is best among all shortstops in a single season. The rest of the American League shortstops made 277 errors. How many fielding runs did Cal have that year, considering he made 242 of 248 putouts for the Orioles that year?

	PO	A	E	DP	Total PO	Total K
AL	3800	6824	300	1511	60541	12689
Orioles	248	447	3	98	4307	776

[Answer: −27.29 runs. This is difficult to comprehend, given Ripken's great fielding percentage. However, his assists and putouts, relative to the league's other shortstops, are very small, and they contribute to a high *APL*, forcing the *FR* below zero.]

5. In 1927, Hall of Famer Frankie "the Forham Flash" Frisch had 641 assists and 396 putouts at second base for the St. Louis Cardinals. Given the stats below, how many fielding runs did he have?

	PO	A	E	DP	Total PO	Total K
NL	2982	4330	261	728	32997	3496
Giants	399	643	22	105	4103	394

[Answer: 48.75 runs.]

6. Pittsburgh's Max Carey was successful on 51 of 53 stolen base attempts in the 1922 season, becoming the only player before 1951 to have a *SB*% higher than 92 percent (Carey's was 96.2 percent). Determine his stolen base runs for the season.

[Answer: 14.1 runs.]

7. On June 5, 1918, the Giants' Jim Thorpe stole home off of the Pirates' Wilbur Cooper to win the game for New York. He would only have 3 *SB* for the entire season. For his career, Thorpe swiped 29 bases and was caught only twice (the *CS* data is incomplete). Based on the numbers given, calculate his base stealing runs.

[Answer: 7.5 runs.]

CHAPTER 11

WHIP and Similar Statistics

Introduction

Teams win games by scoring more than their opponents. From a pitcher's point of view, however, teams win games by giving up fewer runs than their own teams score. A team needs base runners to score runs. Walks and hits lead to base runners. So, the *WHIP*, or walks plus hits per inning pitched, was developed as a measure of how many (or how few) base runners a pitcher allows per inning pitched. As a note, batters who reach base by error, fielder's choice, or other method are not counted in this statistic. The lower the value of the *WHIP*, the more effective a pitcher is in not allowing base runners, and more importantly, the better he gives his team a chance of winning the game. There appears to be a strong correlation between a low *WHIP* and a high chance to win games. Six of the top seven career *WHIP* statistics belong to members of the Hall of Fame.

The *WHIP* is a simple statistic in terms of its calculation. Simply add up a pitcher's walk and hit totals and divide by the number of innings pitched. For example, on October 28, 2007, the Boston Red Sox beat the Colorado Rockies 4–3 to win the World Series. The winning pitcher of that game was Jon Lester, who also pitched the first no-hitter of 2008. His line score was as follows: 5⅔ innings pitched (*IP*), no runs (*R*), no earned runs (*ER*), 3 hits (*H*), and 3 walks (*BB*). In those innings, he gave up a total of 6 walks and hits, so the *WHIP* is

$$WHIP = \frac{BB + H}{IP} = \frac{3 + 3}{5\frac{2}{3}} = 1.0588.$$

Incidentally, the losing pitcher in that deciding game was Aaron Cook. He pitched 6.0 innings, allowed 6 hits and no walks. His *WHIP* was 1.0000, which was less than Lester's, but Cook was tagged for 3 *ER*, which was instrumental in the loss.

Christy Mathewson holds the National League record for highest career winning percentage (with a minimum of 200 wins) at .665 (he won 373 games while losing 188). His *WHIP* is fifth best all-time. In 4780⅔ innings, Christy allowed 4218 hits and walked 844 batters. To calculate his *WHIP*, we add the hits and walks to get 5062, and divide this value by 4780⅔, giving him a career *WHIP* of 1.0588.

The *WHIP* statistic can also be used for teams, although the correlation to runs scored is now dependent on other factors, such as how many pitchers pitch in the same inning, inherited runners, etc. To calculate a team's *WHIP*, use the same formula, dividing the total number of walks plus hits by the total number of innings pitched by a team's pitching staff. By convention, the *WHIP* stat is carried to four decimal places.

Consider the 2001 Oakland Athletics, who had a pitching staff featuring Barry Zito, Tim Hudson, and Mark Mulder. That trio won 56 games for the A's, each pitched at least 200 innings, and each sported an *ERA* under 3.50. The team *ERA* was 3.59. In 1463⅓ innings, the entire Oakland pitching staff allowed 1384 hits and issued 440 walks. Thus, the team

$$WHIP = \frac{BB + H}{IP} = \frac{1384 + 440}{1463\frac{1}{3}} = 1.2465.$$

In addition to the *WHIP*, there are similar statistics that measure a pitcher's effectiveness regarding base runners. They include the opponents' batting average and the strikeout-to-walk ratio (*K/BB*). The opponents' batting average (or, batting average against, *BAA*) is given by:

$$BAA = \frac{H}{BF - BB - HBP - SH - SF - CINT},$$

where *BF* is batters faced, *SH* is sacrifice hits, *SF* is sacrifice flies, and *CINT* is catcher's interference. These are all tracked in recent years. However, *SH*, *SF*, and *CINT* data is hard to find for pitchers. More researchers use the *WHIP* as an effective measure.

The strikeout-to-walk ratio (*K/BB*) is a measure of control, really of a pitcher's strikes to balls. For example, in 2001, Randy Johnson had 372 strikeouts in 249⅔ innings pitched. In addition, he allowed 71 walks. So, his

$$K/BB = \frac{372}{71} = 5.24.$$

Demonstrating Sabermetrics

1. On August 1, 1941, Lefty Gomez of the New York Yankees allowed 11 walks in a complete-game shut-out victory against St. Louis. The score was 9–0, and Gomez allowed only 5 hits. What was his *WHIP* for the game?

In 9 innings, Gomez allowed 11 walks and 5 hits. Therefore his

$$WHIP = \frac{11+5}{9} = \frac{16}{9} = 1.7778.$$

2. In recent history, A. J. Burnett of the Florida Marlins allowed 9 walks in a complete-game no-hit 3–0 victory over San Diego. The game took place on May 12, 2001. What was his *WHIP* for the game?

By allowing 9 walks and no hits in 9 innings, Burnett's *WHIP* = 1.000.

3. Hall-of-Fame pitcher Whitey Ford holds the record for highest winning percentage (with a minimum of 200 victories). His career record of 236–106 gives him a winning percentage of .690. In 3170⅓ innings, Whitey allowed 2766 hits and walked 1086 batters. What was his *WHIP*?

Whitey's *WHIP* can be determined as

$$WHIP = \frac{1086 + 2766}{3170\frac{1}{3}} = \frac{3852}{3170\frac{1}{3}} = 1.2150.$$

4. Hoyt Wilhelm was a knuckleball pitcher who had appeared in a record 1070 games (since broken by Dennis Eckersley). In 2254⅓ innings, Hall-of-Famer Wilhelm gave up 1757 hits and allowed 778 free passes. What was his career *WHIP*?

Hoyt's walks plus hits total 2535. Dividing that by 2254⅓ innings, we see that his $WHIP = \dfrac{2535}{2254\frac{1}{3}} = 1.1245.$

5. The 1971 Baltimore Orioles featured four 20-game winners in its pitching rotation that took the Orioles to the World Series against Pittsburgh: Mike Cuellar, Pat Dobson, Dave McNally, and Jim Palmer. Their pitching stats for the year are listed in the table below. Calculate each pitcher's *WHIP*, as well as the *WHIP* for the entire rotation.

Pitcher	Record	IP	H	BB
Cuellar	20–9	292⅓	250	78
Dobson	20–8	282⅓	248	63
McNally	21–5	224⅓	188	58
Palmer	20–9	282	231	106

We will determine each pitcher in the order in which they are listed. First, Mike Cuellar allowed 250 + 78 = 328 total walks and hits. Therefore, his $WHIP = \dfrac{328}{292\frac{1}{3}} = 1.1220.$ Next, Pat Dobson allowed 248 + 63 = 311 walks and hits. Therefore, his $WHIP = \dfrac{311}{282\frac{1}{3}} = 1.1015.$

Next, Dave McNally allowed 188 + 58 = 246 walks and hits. Therefore, his

$WHIP = \dfrac{246}{224\frac{1}{3}} = 1.0966$. Finally, Jim Palmer allowed 231 + 106 = 337 walks

and hits. Therefore, his $WHIP = \dfrac{337}{282} = 1.1950$. Furthermore, the four Baltimore starters allowed a total of 305 walks and 917 base hits, in a total of 1081 innings. Their combined $WHIP = \dfrac{1222}{1081} = 1.1304$.

6. On June 11, 2003, in an inter-league game, the Houston Astros used a record six pitchers to *no-no-no-no-no-no-hit* the New York Yankees. Roy Oswalt, Peter Munro, Kirk Saarloos, Brad Lidge, Octavio Dotel, and Billy Wagner combined to blank the Yanks. Munro walked three batters and the six hurlers struck out a total of 13 Yankees batter. Determine the Astros' strike-out-to-walk ratio for the no-hitter.

For the game, the team $K/BB = \dfrac{13}{3} = 4.33$.

7. The Philadelphia Athletics' pitching staff issued 827 walks during the 1915 season, the most walks allowed by a major league team since 1901. This amounted to an average of 5.4 walks per game! In 1348 innings, the last-place A's pitchers also gave up 1358 hits, an average of 8.8 hits per game. What was the team *WHIP*?

Philadelphia's walks plus hits total 2185. Dividing that by 1348 innings, we see that the team $WHIP = \dfrac{2185}{1348} = 1.6209$.

8. The 1968 Cleveland Indians' hurlers, led by 21-game winner Luis Tiant, allowed only 1087 hits during the entire season, a record for the 162-game season. Only 98 of those hits went for home runs. In addition, in 1464 innings, the Indian pitchers allowed 540 walks. What was the team *WHIP*?

The Indians' pitchers gave up a combination of 1627 walks and hits. Dividing that by 1464 innings, we see that the team $WHIP = \dfrac{1627}{1464} = 1.1113$.

9. The date was May 31, 1964. The San Francisco Giants and New York Mets played a double-header in which their pitchers pitched a record 32 innings. Hall of Famer Juan Marichal pitched a complete game for the Giants in the opener, as the Giants won, 5–3. He gave up 8 hits but did not walk any Mets batters. The Giants also took the second game, 8–6, but it was a 23-inning affair. Six San Francisco hurlers faced 85 batters, giving up 20 hits and allowing 3 walks in the 7-hour, 23-minute game. They also struck out 22 New York batters. Interestingly, Hall of Famer Gaylord Perry came on in relief for the Giants and pitched 10 innings, picking up the win. What was the total *WHIP* for the historic double-header?

In the 32 innings, the seven Giants pitchers gave up 28 hits and walked only 3. So, for the double-header, the team $WHIP = \dfrac{31}{32} = 0.9688$.

10. Babe Ruth was a premier pitcher for the Boston Red Sox, before becoming the greatest slugger of all time. Used primarily as a starting pitcher from 1914 to 1919, he stingily allowed 934 hits and 425 walks in 158 games and 1190⅓ innings. He also only dished up 9 home runs to opposing batters, and when he was traded to the Yankees, his record was 89–46. His pitching efforts for the Sox would probably have gained him entrance into Cooperstown. What was the Bambino's $WHIP$?

The former Red Sox ace had a $WHIP$ of $\dfrac{1359}{1190⅓} = 1.1417$.

Incidentally, combining his pitching stats for the Red Sox and Yankees, Babe Ruth's $WHIP$ was 1.1586, which turns out to be 70th best, all-time.

11. Bret Saberhagen has the highest single-season strikeout-to-walk ratio. In 1994, he fanned 143 batters while walking only 13 in 177⅓ IP. Determine his K/BB.

Saberhagen's $K/BB = \dfrac{143}{13} = 11.00$.

Practicing Sabermetrics

1. "Big Ed" Walsh holds the record for the most innings pitched in a single season (since 1900), with 464 IP in 1908, while pitching for the Chicago White Sox. In 1908, Big Ed also led the American League in appearances (66), starts (49), complete games (42), shut-outs (11), saves(6), hits allowed (343), strike-outs (269), and wins (40). His numbers for 1908 and his career are listed in the table below. Calculate his $WHIP$ for 1908 and his career $WHIP$.

	IP	H	BB
1908	464	343	56
Career	2964⅓	2346	617

Walsh's career $WHIP$ is second all-time to Addie Joss. Walsh later umpired and then managed in the Major Leagues. His son, also named Ed Walsh, played for the Chicago White Sox from 1928 to 1932.

[Answers: 1908: $WHIP$ = 0.8599, Career: $WHIP$ = 0.9996.]

2. Phil Niekro led the National League in losses for four consecutive seasons, 1977 through 1980, while a pitcher for the Atlanta Braves. Although he won 71 games in that span, he lost 76 decisions. Despite this, he was still elected into the Baseball Hall of Fame. His numbers for those four seasons are listed in the table below. In addition he had 55 wild pitches, and he ended his 26-year career with 226 wild pitches. Calculate his *WHIP* for each season and the cumulative *WHIP* for the four-year period.

Year	IP	H	BB	W	L
1977	330⅓	315	164	16	20
1978	334⅓	295	102	19	18
1979	342	311	113	21	20
1980	275	256	85	15	18

[Answers: 1977: *WHIP* = 1.4501, 1978: *WHIP* = 1.1874,
1979: *WHIP* = 1.2398, 1980: *WHIP* = 1.2400,
4-Year Period: *WHIP* = 1.2804.]

3. The 2001 Seattle Mariners had the highest winning percentage of any team when they won 116 regular season games while dropping only 46 (a winning percentage of .716). Their pitching staff had an *ERA* of 3.54. More importantly, in 1465 innings, they issued 465 walks and allowed 1293 hits. What was the team *WHIP* for the 2001 Mariners?

[Answer: *WHIP* = 1.2000.]

4. The 2002 San Diego Padres had 37 pitchers on their roster through the course of the season. Of those, 15 were starting pitchers. Those starters served up 1108 hits and 379 walks to opposing batters in a total of 1031 innings. What was the *WHIP* for 2002 Padres starting pitchers?

[Answer: *WHIP* = 1.4423.]

5. The 1930 Philadelphia Phillies allowed 1993 hits in their 52–102 season, an unattractive record. What was their team *WHIP* if they also allowed 543 walks in 1372 innings?

[Answer: *WHIP* = 1.8484.]

6. Johan Santana, while with the Minnesota Twins, led the American League in *WHIP* in four consecutive years, from 2004 though 2007. His numbers for those four seasons are listed in the table below. Calculate his *WHIP* for each season and the cumulative *WHIP* for the four-year period.

Year	IP	H	BB
2004	228	156	54
2005	231⅓	180	45
2006	233⅔	186	47
2007	219	183	52

[Answers: 2004: *WHIP* = 0.9211, 2005: *WHIP* = 0.9712,
      2006: *WHIP* = 0.9971, 2007: *WHIP* = 1.0731,
      4-Year Period: *WHIP* = 0.9898.]

7. Through the 2007 season, Trevor Hoffman holds the record for most saves, with 539. In 942⅔ innings, Hoffman has allowed 724 base hits and has issued 265 bases on balls. What is his *WHIP*?

[Answer: *WHIP* = 1.0492. This value would rank fifth best all-time, if he would qualify with 1000 IP and 100 decisions.]

8. In 1938, Hall of Famer Bob Feller set a modern record by giving up 208 walks in a single season, the most allowed by a pitcher since 1900. In 277⅔ innings of work, Feller also was tagged for 225 hits. Calculate his 1938 *WHIP*.

[Answer: *WHIP* = 1.5594.]

9. Nolan Ryan holds a plethora of pitching records, to include: most career walks (2795), most strikeouts (5714), fewest hits allowed per 9 innings pitched (6.555), and most no-hitters (7). The "Ryan Express" pitched 5386 innings in his Hall of Fame career. Calculate his *WHIP*.

[Answer: *WHIP* = 1.2473.]

10. Oakland Athletics pitcher Vida Blue won both the MVP and Cy Young Awards in 1971. Determine his strikeout-to-walk ratio (*K/BB*) if he allowed 88 walks and struck out 301 batters in 312 *IP*.

[Answer: *K/BB* = 3.42.]

CHAPTER 12

Weighted Pitcher's Rating

Introduction

In the mid–1940s, an individual by the name of Ted Oliver self published a booklet titled *Kings of the Mound: A Pitchers' Rating Manual.* In this publication, he devised a "weighted rating system" (see the remark below). Using a modification of his system, we define a measure which we call the Weighted Pitcher's Rating (*WPR*), which is as follows:

$$WPR = \left(\frac{W}{W+L} - \frac{W_t}{W_t + L_t} \right)(IP).$$

In this formula, W and L represent the pitcher's numbers of games won and lost, respectively; and represent his team's numbers of games won and lost *not including the individual pitcher's record*, respectively; and IP represents the number of innings pitched by the pitcher.

Instead of using IP, Oliver replaced this factor by $W + L$, that is, the pitcher's total number of decisions. We have chosen to IP because we feel that this statistic can reflect a "durability factor" on the part of the pitcher, hence providing more of a "comparable weighted factor" with respect to the rest of the team's pitching staff.

Before commenting on our formula, let us consider an example. In 1961, Yankee Hall of Famer Whitey Ford pitched 283 innings, winning 25 games while losing 4. The Yankees, as a team that season, won 109 games while dropping 53. So our formula takes on the following values:

$$W = 25,\ L = 4,\ W_t = 109 - 25 = 84,\ L_t = 53 - 4 = 49,\ IP = 283.$$

Therefore, Ford's *WPR* for 1961 becomes:

$$WPR = \left(\frac{25}{25+4} - \frac{84}{84+49} \right)(283) = 65.23.$$

We will always round off to the nearest hundredth when considering the *WPR*.

By the way, if we had used Oliver's approach, we would have replaced the 283 *IP* by 25 + 4 = 29 decisions. In this case, Ford's weighted rating would have become 6.68.

A few observations are in order. Intuitively, we understand that the higher the *WPR* , the "better" the pitcher. But to get a sense of the *meaning* of this number, we would have to *compare* it to the *WPRs* of other pitchers. Experience seems to indicate that a *WPR* greater than 50.00 reflects a superior season on the part of the pitcher in question. We also note that the *WPR* need not be a *positive* number; if the following inequality consisting of the two ratios holds

$$\frac{W}{W+L} < \frac{W_t}{W_t + L_t}$$

then the *WPR* will be a *negative* number. Likewise, if the two ratios are equal, then the *WPR* will be *zero*. Finally, we point out that the *IP* factor gives the "weight" to the rating. That is, the more innings pitched, the greater the impact, positively or negatively. This is true, unless the *WPR* is zero, in which case the amount of *IP* has no effect on the *WPR* (the team is just as good with or without the pitcher in question).

Another remark is in order here. Almost always compute a pitcher's *WPR* *relative to his team*. However, we can use this approach relative to his league, or to both leagues, as well. See Problem 8 in the Demonstrating Sabermetrics section.

Demonstrating Sabermetrics

1. In 1939, the Cincinnati Reds won the National League pennant with a won-loss record of 97–57. Right-hander Bucky Walters won 27 games for them while losing 11. Find the Reds won-loss record not counting Walters' decisions. That is, compute W_t and L_t.

Since the Reds won 97 games and Walters won 27 games, W_t=97–27=70. Due to the fact that the Reds lost 57 games, with Walters losing 11 of them, L_t = 57 – 11 = 46.

2. Referring to Problem 1, compute the *WPR* for Walters in 1939, given that he pitched 319 innings that year.

Using the formula for *WPR* and the given information, we have

$$WPR = \left(\frac{W}{W+L} - \frac{W_t}{W_t + L_t} \right)(IP) = \left(\frac{27}{27+11} - \frac{70}{70+46} \right)(319) = 34.16.$$

3. In 1971, the American League champion Baltimore Orioles won 101

games while losing 57. The Birds had four pitchers who won at least twenty games: Mike Cuellar, Pat Dobson, Dave McNally and Jim Palmer. Given the information below, compute the *WPR* for each pitcher.

Pitcher	W	L	IP	W_t	L_t
Cuellar	20	9	292⅓	81	48
Dobson	20	8	282⅓	81	49
McNally	21	5	224⅓	80	52
Palmer	20	9	282	81	48

Regarding Mike Cuellar's *WPR*, we employ the formula to obtain

$$WPR = \left(\frac{W}{W+L} - \frac{W_t}{W_t+L_t} \right)(IP) = \left(\frac{20}{20+9} - \frac{81}{81+48} \right)(292\tfrac{1}{3}) = 18.05;$$

for Pat Dobson's *WPR*, we have

$$WPR = \left(\frac{W}{W+L} - \frac{W_t}{W_t+L_t} \right)(IP) = \left(\frac{20}{20+8} - \frac{81}{81+49} \right)(282\tfrac{1}{3}) = 25.75;$$

Dave McNally's *WPR* is

$$WPR = \left(\frac{W}{W+L} - \frac{W_t}{W_t+L_t} \right)(IP) = \left(\frac{21}{21+5} - \frac{80}{80+52} \right)(224\tfrac{1}{3}) = 45.23;$$

lastly, Jim Palmer's *WPR* is computed to be

$$WPR = \left(\frac{W}{W+L} - \frac{W_t}{W_t+L_t} \right)(IP) = \left(\frac{20}{20+9} - \frac{81}{81+48} \right)(282) = 17.41.$$

These WPR numbers have a range of 42.23 – 17.41 = 24.82, even though three of the hurlers had 20 victories and the fourth had 21 wins. This is because McNally pitched the fewest number of innings, yet his number of losses were, relatively speaking, much less than those of his teammates.

4. In 1970, Hall of Famer Jim Palmer won 20 games while losing 10 as he pitched in 305 innings. His team, the World Champion Baltimore Orioles, won 108 games and lost 54 contests. Find Palmer's *WPR*.

The numbers which will be substituted into out *WPR* formula are as follows: $W=20$, $L=10$, $W_t=108-20=88$, $L_t=54-10=44$, $IP=305$. Therefore, Palmer's 1970 *WPR* is:

$$WPR = \left(\frac{20}{20+10} - \frac{88}{88+44} \right)(305) = 0\,(305) = 0.$$

5. Referring to the Problem 4, what would Palmer's 1970 *WPR* have been if he had pitched 400 innings?

Zero. This is due to the fact that his ratio of wins (*W*) to wins plus losses (*W*+*L*), is in the *same proportion* as the team's corresponding ratio, less Palmer's decisions. That is, *no matter how many or few innings* Palmer pitched that year, his *WPR* = 0, because

$$\frac{W}{W+L}=\frac{W_t}{W_t+L_t}.$$

6. In 1931 Philadelphia A's ace Lefty Grove had a *WPR* of 68.17. Find his number of innings pitched if his won-loss record was 31–4 and his team's won-loss record was 107–45.

We have the following statistics: $W=31$, $L=4$, $W_t=76=84$, $L_t=41$, $WPR=68.71$.

Solving for *IP* in the equation $WPR=\left(\dfrac{W}{W+L}-\dfrac{W_t}{W_t+L_t}\right)(IP)$, we have,

$IP=\dfrac{WPR}{\left(\dfrac{W}{W+L}-\dfrac{W_t}{W_t+L_t}\right)}$. Substituting our value we obtain,

$$IP=\frac{WPR}{\left(\dfrac{W}{W+L}-\dfrac{W_t}{W_t+L_t}\right)}=\frac{68.17}{\left(\dfrac{31}{31+4}-\dfrac{76}{76+41}\right)}=288.7$$

as the number of innings pitched by Grove that year.

7. Red Ruffing and Babe Ruth are both in the Hall of Fame. In 1916, Ruth had 35 pitching decisions, winning 23 and losing 12. He also set a league season record for shutouts by a lefthander with nine. His team, the World Champion Boston Red Sox, had a won-loss record of 91–63. Twenty years later, Ruffing posted a 20–12 pitching record for the World Champion New York Yankees, a team which won 102 games while losing 51 contests. Compare their *WPRs* given that Ruth hurled 323⅔ innings while Ruffing pitched in 271 frames.

The statistics are, for Ruth, $W=23$, $L=12$, $W_t=68$, $L_t=51$, $IP=323⅔$; and for Ruffing, $W=20$, $L=12$, $W_t=82$, $L_t=39$, $IP=271$.

Therefore, the *WPR* for Ruth becomes

$$WPR=\left(\frac{23}{23+12}-\frac{68}{68+51}\right)(323⅔)=27.75,$$

and Ruffing's *WPR* is

$$WPR=\left(\frac{20}{20+12}-\frac{82}{83+39}\right)(271)=-14.28.$$

Notice that even though Ruffing won 20 games, he was actually "below average" with respect to his team. That is, his team actually performed better without him. One should not infer from this, however, that Ruffing was not an asset for this team. In fact, over the four year span from 1936 through 1939, Ruffing won 82 games as the Yankees became the first team to win four consecutive World Series. In addition to his pitching, Ruffing was a very good hitter, finishing up with a career batting average of .269, a lifetime slugging percentage of .389 and had 36 home runs to his credit.

　8. Using the information in the Introduction section, compute Whitey Ford's 1961 *WPR* relative to the American League, given that there were 807 league games played that season.

　Since there were 807 games played that year, there clearly had to be both 807 wins and 807 losses. Therefore, the amount of games won by the league, minus Ford's total of 25, was 782, while the losses, subtracting Ford's 4 losses, was 803. Therefore, his *WPR* relative to the league was

$$WPR = \left(\frac{25}{25+4} - \frac{782}{782+803} \right)(283) = 104.34.$$

　9. In 1994 Major League Baseball suffered through a strike, thereby shortening the season. The Yankee's Jimmy Key had a *WPR* of 39.22, while pitching 168 innings and being involved in 21 decisions (wins and losses). Given the fact that the Yankees won 70 games while dropping 43 contests, how many games did Key win that year?

　We want to find *W*, which represents Key's win total, in the following equation:

$$WPR = 39.22 = \left(\frac{W}{W+L} - \frac{W_t}{W_t+L_t} \right)(IP).$$

　We know that *IP* = 168 and we also are given the fact that *W* + *L* = 21. So our equation can now be written as:

$$39.22 = \left(\frac{W}{21} - \frac{W_t}{W_t+L_t} \right)(168).$$

　Since the Yankees won 70 games that year, $W_t = 70 - W$, and because the Yankees were involved in 113 decisions, $W_t = L_t = 113 - 21 = 92$. Our equation now simplifies to

$$39.22 = \left(\frac{W}{21} - \frac{70-W}{92} \right)(168).$$

　Simplifying the right hand side by using 1932 as the least common denominator and then multiplying through by 168, we solve for *W* and determine that Key won 17 games for the Yankees in 1994.

　10. Referring again to the 1994 strike (see Problem 9), the Chicago White Sox were involved in 113 decisions. Pitcher Wilson Alvarez hurled 161⅔ innings while posting a 12–8 won-loss record, and attaining a *WPR* of 1.39. Determine the won-loss record of the White Sox for that year.

　With respect to our formula for the *WPR*, we have *IP* = 161⅔, *W* = 12, *L* = 8 and *WPR* = 1.39. We also know that $W_t + L_t = 113 - W - L = 113 - 20$

= 93, because $W + L$ is the total number of decisions accrued by Alvarez. So our formula now becomes

$$1.39 = \left(\frac{12}{12 + 8} - \frac{W_t}{93}\right)(161\frac{2}{3}).$$

Multiplying through by $161\frac{2}{3}$ on the right hand side of the equation and solving for W_t, we learn that $W_t = 55$. This means that the Twins won 55 games, not counting the wins credited to Alvarez. Therefore, Minnesota won $55 + 12 = 67$ games in 1994, and so lost $113 - 67 = 46$ games, giving them a won-loss record of 67–46 .

Practicing Sabermetrics

1. Three of the Yankees' twenty six World Championships were won in 1927, 1977 and 1998. Given the information below, find the *WPR* for each of the nine pitchers listed (3 from each team):

Pitcher	W	L	IP	W_t	L_t
Hoyt ('27)	22	7	256	110	44
Pennock ('27)	19	8	209⅔	110	44
Shocker ('27)	18	6	200	110	44
Figueroa ('77)	16	11	239⅓	100	62
Guidry ('77)	16	7	210⅔	100	62
Torrez ('77)	14	12	217	100	62
Cone ('98)	20	7	207⅔	114	48
Pettitte ('98)	16	11	216⅓	114	48
Wells ('98)	18	4	214	114⅓	48

[Answers: Hoyt (14.00), Pennock (–2.69), Shocker (8.46);
  Figueroa (–7.09), Guidry (19.24), Torrez (–20.37);
  Cone (9.23), Pettitte (–28.84), Wells (28.39).]

2. In 1931, Lefty Grove had a *WPR* of 68.17 (see Problem 6 in the Demonstrating Sabermetrics section). Compare Grove's mark to Hall of Famer Steve Carlton's 1972 *WPR*, when Carlton pitched 346⅓ innings and had a 27–10 won-loss record for his Phillies team which won 59 games while losing 97 contests.

[Answer: 159.58. This is an extremely high *WPR*.]

3. Using the information in the previous problem, find Carlton's 1972 *WPR* relative to the National League, given that there were 929 games played during the season.

[Answer: 81.17.]

4. In 2007, Tom Glavine of the New York Mets, won 13 games while losing eight. Find his *WPR*, given that he pitched in 200⅓ innings and his team had a won-loss record of 88–74.

[Answer: 17.45.]

5. Using the information from Problem 4, find the number of innings pitched by Mets hurler Oliver Perez in 2007 if he had a won-loss record of 15–10 and his *WPR* was 11.89.

[Answer: 177.]

6. Many teams have boasted of staffs which were bolstered by an excellent 1–2 pitching punch. Four such examples were the 1935 New York Giants which had Carl Hubbell and Hal Schumacher, the 1948 Boston Braves team with Johnny Sain and Warren Spahn, the 1964 Philadelphia Phillies with Jim Bunning and Chris Short, and 1965 Dodgers featuring Don Drysdale and Sandy Koufax. Given the information below, and using the *WPR*, sum up each of the duo's combinations to determine the highest total *WPR* of the four pairs of pitchers.

Pitcher	*W*	*L*	*IP*	W_t	L_t
Hubbell	23	12	302⅔	91	62
Schumacher	19	9	261⅓	91	62
Sain	24	15	314⅔	91	62
Spahn	15	12	257	91	62
Bunning	19	8	284⅓	92	70
Short	17	9	220⅔	92	70
Drysdale	23	12	308⅓	97	65
Koufax	26	8	335⅔	97	65

[Answers: Hubbell (24.48) + Schumacher (26.84) = 51.32;
Sain (8.70) + Spahn (–12.24) = –3.54;
Bunning (46.33) + Short (924.36) = 70.69;
Drysdale (22.96) + Koufax (70.50) = 93.46.]

7. Three of the greatest pitchers ever were Grover Cleveland Alexander, Walter Johnson and Christy Mathewson. Among this trio, they hurled eight seasons where they won thirty or more games (each performed these tasks in consecutive seasons). Given the information below, rank their seasons with respect to their *WPRs*.

Pitcher	W	L	IP	W_t	L_t
Mathewson (1903)	30	13	366⅓	84	55
Mathewson (1904)	33	12	367⅔	106	47
Mathewson (1905)	31	9	338⅔	105	48
Johnson (1912)	33	12	369	91	61
Johnson (1913)	36	7	346	90	64
Alexander (1915)	31	10	376⅓	90	62
Alexander (1916)	33	12	389	91	62
Alexander (1917)	30	13	388	87	65

[Answers: 1913 Johnson (121.35); 1915 Alexander (84.50); 1916 Alexander (76.36); 1912 Johnson (70.58); 1917 Alexander (67.80); 1903 Mathewson (49.51); 1905 Mathewson (40.69); 1904 Mathewson (21.11).]

8. Dizzy Dean of the 1934 St. Louis Cardinals had a won-loss record of 30–7 while his team won 95 games and lost 58 contests on the way to a seven game World Series victory over the Detroit Tigers. Dean pitched in 311⅔ innings that year. Find his *WPR*.

[Answer: 78.07.]

9. In 1968 the Detroit Tigers reversed the table on the St Louis Cardinals (see Problem 8), winning the World Series in seven games. The Tigers won 103 games, while losing 59 contests. Their pitching staff was spearheaded by right-hander Denny McLain, who had a won-loss record of 31–6. Given that McLain hurled 336 innings, find his *WPR*.

[Answer: 87.98.]

10. Consider the two 40-game winners below, both of whom are in the Hall of Fame. Find their *WPRs*.

Pitcher	W	L	Team	IP	W_t	L_t
Jack Chesbro (1904)	41	12	Yankees	454	92	59
Ed Walsh (1908)	40	15	White Sox	464	88	64

[Answers: Chesbro (114.94); Walsh (107.85).]

11. In 1981, Major League Baseball experienced a strike (much like 1994; see Problems 9 and 10 in the Demonstrating Sabermetrics section) which resulted in teams playing fewer than the usual 162 games. Oakland A's pitcher Steve McCatty accrued 21 decisions (wins and losses) while his team won 64 games and lost 45 contests. If McCatty pitched in 185⅔ innings and his *WPR* was 18.29, determine the number of games he won that year.

[Answer: 14.]

12. Referring to Problem 11, find the amount of games pitcher Mike Norris lost for the Oakland A's if he pitched in 172⅔ innings, had 21 decisions and had a *WPR* of –3.36.

[Answer: 9.]

13. Again referring to the 1981 strike, the Minnesota Twins were involved in 109 decisions. Twins pitcher Albert Williams won 6 games, while losing 10 contests; he pitched in 150 innings and had a *WPR* of –0.20. What was the won-loss record of the Twins for that year?

[Answer: The Twins won 41 games and lost 68 games.]

CHAPTER 13

Base-Out Percentage and Total Average

Introduction

A baseball writer from the *Washington Post*, Thomas Boswell, devised a simple but elegant statistic that attempted to measure offensive performance shortly after Barry Codell had developed a similar statistic. Each measures is essentially a ratio of bases gained to outs made, with some slight philosophical differences on how to count sacrifices. While some measurements tend to favor one type of hitter over another, these work to place all types of hitters on a more or less equal footing.

We note that Caught Stealing and Sacrifice Flies data has only been consistently available for both major leagues since 1954, Grounded Into Double Plays since 1939 and Sacrifice Hits since 1931. Prior to those years, they (and other numbers) were available for some seasons, but then not for subsequent seasons, and then available again, but sometimes not for both leagues.

Boswell's statistic is called Total Average, and, denoted by *TA*, has the formula

$$TA = \frac{(TB + BB + HBP + SB)}{(AB - H)}.$$

We will use this statistic for any evaluation of pre–1954 players' seasons.

Codell's measurement is called Base-Out-Percentage, is denoted by *BOP*, and has formula

$$BOP = \frac{(TB + BB + HBP + SB + SH + SF)}{(AB - H + SH + SF + CS + GIDP)}.$$

We will employ this formula for any seasons 1954 and after. Both statistical measures have a standard of about 0.900 for excellence in a season.

In 1932, "Old Double X," Jimmie Foxx, had one of the most remarkable seasons in baseball history. He won the American League's Most Valuable Player Award that year while playing for the then–Philadelphia Athletics, belting out 58 homers, driving in 169 runs, and batting 0.364. He missed out on a triple crown by 0.003 to Dale Alexander, who would not have had the required number of plate appearances by more modern rules.

Foxx's stats line looked like this:

AB	H	2B	3B	HR	BB	SB	CS	GIDP	HBP	SH	SF
585	213	33	9	58	116	3	7	–	0	–	–

Because of the unavailability of some of the statistics needed to use *BOP,* we will use *TA.*

We calculate his $TB = 213 + 33 + (2 \times 9) + (3 \times 58) = 438$, so his total average can be found as $TA = \dfrac{(TB + BB + HBP + SF)}{(AB - H)} = \dfrac{(438 + 116 + 0 + 3)}{(585 - 213)} = \dfrac{557}{372} = 1.50.$

As another example, we consider the 1962 National League. After beating the Dodgers in a three-game playoff to break a regular season tie for first place, the Giants came within a whisker of at least tying the Yankees in the ninth inning of Game 7 of the World Series that year. Maury Wills stole 104 bases in 1962, a record at the time, en route to winning the Most Valuable Player Award. However, a computation of his *BOP* would suggest that his value was not purely on the measurable offensive side. Wills' stats in 1962 are shown in the following table:

AB	H	2B	3B	HR	BB	SB	CS	GIDP	HBP	SH	SF
695	208	13	10	6	51	104	13	7	2	7	4

We calculate his $TB = 208 + 13 + (2 \times 10) + (3 \times 6) = 259$, and his

$$BOP = \frac{(TB + BB + HBP + SB + SH + SF)}{(AB - H + SH + SF + CS + GIDP)} = \frac{(259 + 51 + 2 + 104 + 7 + 4)}{(695 - 208 + 7 + 4 + 13 + 7)} = \frac{427}{518} = 0.824.$$

This means that Maury Wills gained around 0.82 bases for every out "spent." In fact, the best players of all time will have *BOP* numbers around 1.

As a league, the National League in 1962 had the following numbers:

AB	H	2B	3B	HR	BB	SB	CS	GIDP	HBP	SH	SF
55449	14453	2075	453	1449	5265	788	409	1251	373	656	410

Thus, the NL $14453 + 2075 + (2 \times 453) + (3 \times 1449) = 21781$ total bases, so the league

$$BOP = \frac{(21781 + 5265 + 373 + 788 + 656 + 410)}{(55449 - 14453 + 656 + 410 + 409 + 1251)} = \frac{29273}{43722} = 0.670.$$

As discussed in Chapter 4, we will calculate a relative statistic as the ratio of a player's measure relative to the league. Thus, Maury Wills' relative BOP
$= \frac{(\text{Wills'}\ BOP)}{(\text{League}\ BOP)} = \frac{0.824}{0.670} = 1.23$; or in other words, the MVP had a BOP that was 23 percent better than the league's percentage.

Willie Mays of the San Francisco Giants, who finished in second place in the MVP voting that year (seven points behind Wills), put up the following numbers:

AB	H	2B	3B	HR	BB	SB	CS	GIDP	HBP	SH	SF
621	189	36	5	49	78	18	2	19	4	0	3

We calculate his total bases to be $TB = 189 + 36 + (2 \times 5) + (3 \times 49) = 382$, and his

$$BOP = \frac{(TB + BB + HBP + SB + SH + SF)}{(AB - H + SH + SF + CS + GIDP)} =$$
$$\frac{(382 + 78 + 4 + 18 + 0 + 3)}{(621 - 189 + 0 + 3 + 2 + 19)} = \frac{485}{456} = 1.064.$$

His relative $BOP = \frac{(\text{Mays'}\ BOP)}{(\text{League}\ BOP)} = \frac{1.064}{0.670} = 1.59$, or a BOP that was 59 percent better than the league's. That's impressive.

Perhaps the ballparks had an effect on the numbers. Using PF (see Chapter 5), we can make an adjustment. Mays played his home games at Candlestick Park, while Wills played his at Dodger Stadium. Both teams played 165 official games because of the best-of-three playoffs at the end of the season. In the following table is the data needed to calculate a Park Factor (PF) for both stadiums. Since 1962 was the third year for Candlestick but the first year for Dodger Stadium, we will use the one-year statistic.

	Games (Home)	Games (Away)	R (Home)	RA (Home)	R (Away)	RA (Away)	PF
Giants	82	83	479	299	399	391	1
Dodgers	83	82	409	289	433	408	0.82

How did we determine the last column? For the Giants in 1962,

$$PF = \left(\frac{\left(\dfrac{R\,(Home) + RA\,(Home)}{Games\,(Home)} \right)}{\left(\dfrac{R\,(Road) + RA\,(Road)}{Games\,(Away)} \right)} \right) = \frac{\dfrac{479 + 299}{82}}{\dfrac{399 + 391}{83}} = 1.00,$$

which indicates that Candlestick Park was neutral, favoring neither offense nor defense; the league's park factor is also equal to 1, since it is the accumulation of all the numbers. Thus, Mays' *BOP* remains at 1.064, or *59* percent better than the league. For Wills and Dodger Stadium,

$$PF = \left(\frac{\left(\dfrac{R\,(Home) + RA\,(Home)}{Games\,(Home)} \right)}{\left(\dfrac{R\,(Road) + RA\,(Road)}{Games\,(Away)} \right)} \right) = \frac{\dfrac{409 + 299}{83}}{\dfrac{433 + 408}{82}} = 0.82,$$

= indicating a ballpark that suppressed offense by 18 percent.

We can now determine a Park Adjusted *BOP* for Wills in 1962, calculated as follows: *Adj BOP* = *BOP* + [(1 – *PF*) *BOP*] × 0.5 = 0.820 + [(1 – 0.82) 0.820] × 0.5 = 0.898.

Wills' relative park adjusted $BOP = \dfrac{(Mays'\ Adj\ BOP)}{(League\ BOP)} = \dfrac{0.898}{0.670} = 1.34,$

or Wills was 34 percent better than the league average.

Demonstrating Sabermetrics

1. Hall of Famer Al "Bucketfoot" Simmons played 20 major league seasons, mostly for the Philadelphia Athletics of the American League. His finest season was probably 1930, a year in which many players had great offensive numbers. Calculate his *TA*, given his statistics in the following table.

AB	*H*	*2B*	*3B*	*HR*	*BB*	*SB*	*HBP*
585	211	41	16	36	39	9	1

First, we find Simmons' total bases: *TB* = 211 + 41 + (2 × 16) + (3 × 36)

$= 392.\ TA = \dfrac{(TB + BB + HBP + SB)}{(AB - H)} = \dfrac{(392 + 39 + 1 + 9)}{(585 - 211)} = \dfrac{440}{343} = 1.28.$

2. Using the table below, compute the American League's *TA* for 1930, and use it to determine Simmons' relative *TA* for the season. Interpret the meaning of this result.

AB	H	2B	3B	HR	BB	SB	HBP
42882	12338	2375	655	673	3975	598	203

$TB = 12338 + 2375 + (2 \times 655) + (3 \times 673) = 18042$, *so*

$$TA = \frac{(TB + BB + HBP + SB)}{(AB - H)} = \frac{(18042 + 3975 + 203 + 598)}{(42882 - 12338)} = \frac{22818}{30544} = 0.747.$$

Relative $TA = \dfrac{(\text{Simmons } TA)}{(\text{League } TA)} = \dfrac{1.28}{0.747} = 1.71$, so Simmons was 71 percent better than the league in 1930.

3. Hall of Famer Tris Speaker, by no means a home run hitter, put up impressive career numbers. Using the chart below, calculate the career TA for the "Grey Eagle."

AB	H	2B	3B	HR	BB	SB	HBP
10195	3514	792	222	117	1381	432	103

First, Speaker's total bases: $TB = 3514 + 792 + (2 \times 222) + (3 \times 117) = 5101$.

$$TA = \frac{(TB + BB + HBP + SB)}{(AB - H)} = \frac{(5101 + 1381 + 103 + 432)}{(10195 - 3514)} = \frac{7017}{6681} = 1.05.$$

4. Albert Pujols has become one of the most feared hitters in all of baseball. In 2005, he had an MVP season for the World Champion St. Louis Cardinals. Calculate his BOP, given his numbers in the following table.

AB	H	2B	3B	HR	BB	SB	CS	GIDP	HBP	SH	SF
591	195	38	2	41	97	16	2	19	9	9	3

$TB = 195 + 38 + (2 \times 2) + (3 \times 41) = 360$, and his $BOP =$

$$\frac{(TB + BB + HBP + SB + SH + SF)}{(AB - H + SH + SF + CS + GIDP)} = \frac{(360 + 97 + 9 + 16 + 9 + 3)}{(591 - 195 + 9 + 3 + 2 + 19)} = \frac{485}{420} = 1.16.$$

5. The NL in 2005 had the statistics shown in the table below. Calculate the league BOP, and then find and interpret Pujols' relative BOP.

AB	H	2B	3B	HR	BB	SB	CS	GIDP	HBP	SH	SF
88120	23058	36488	8396	1349	560	2052	980	1151	669	88120	23058

The league $BOP = \dfrac{(TB + BB + HBP + SB + SH + SF)}{(AB - H + SH + SF + CS + GIDP)}$

$$= \frac{(36488 + 8396 + 980 + 1349 + 1151 + 669)}{(88120 - 23058 + 1151 + 669 + 560 + 2052)} = \frac{49033}{69494} = 0.706.$$

Relative $BOP = \dfrac{(\text{Pujols'} \; BOP)}{(\text{League} \; BOP)} = \dfrac{1.155}{0.706} = 1.63,$ so Pujols was 63 percent better than the National League in 2005.

6. Hall of Famer Frank Robinson finished fourth in the MVP voting in 1962, putting up the following statistics for the Cincinnati Reds:

AB	H	2B	3B	HR	BB	SB	CS	GIDP	HBP	SH	SF
609	208	380	76	18	9	13	11	0	5	609	208

Find his *BOP*.

$$BOP = \frac{(TB + BB + HBP + SB + SH + SF)}{(AB - H + SH + SF + CS + GIDP)} = \frac{(380 + 76 + 11 + 18 + 0 + 5)}{(609 - 208 + 0 + 5 + 9 + 13)}$$

$$= \frac{490}{428} = 1.145.$$

7. Using the 1962 NL *BOP* of 0.670, calculate and interpret Frank Robinson's relative *BOP.*

Relative $BOP = \dfrac{(\text{Robinson's} \; BOP)}{(\text{League} \; BOP)} = \dfrac{1.145}{0.670} = 1.71,$ or Robinson was 71 percent better than the league.

8. Tommy Davis finished third in the MVP voting in 1962, and his statistics are in the following table. We have determined total bases in the table.

AB	H	TB	BB	SB	CS	GIDP	HBP	SH	SF
665	230	356	33	18	6	17	2	3	8

Find his *BOP*.

$$BOP = \frac{(TB + BB + HBP + SB + SH + SF)}{(AB - H + SH + SF + CS + GIDP)} = \frac{(356 + 33 + 2 + 18 + 3 + 8)}{(665 - 230 + 3 + 8 + 6 + 17)}$$

$$= \frac{420}{469} = 0.896.$$

9. Using the answer to Problem 8, calculate and interpret Tommy Davis' relative *BOP.*

Relative $BOP = \dfrac{(\text{Robinson's} \; BOP)}{(\text{League} \; BOP)} = \dfrac{0.896}{0.670} = 1.34,$ or Davis was 34 percent better than the league.

10. Using the 1962 Park Factor for Dodger Stadium (0.82), find Tommy Davis' adjusted *BOP* and his Park Adjusted Relative *BOP.*

The Park Adjusted *BOP* for Davis in 1962 is found to be
$PA(BOP_{1962}) = BOP + [(1 - PF) \; BOP] \times 0.5 = 0.896 + [(1 - 0.82) \; 0.896] \times 0.5 = 0.977.$

So, Davis' Park Adjusted Relative $BOP = \dfrac{\text{(Davis' Adj } BOP)}{\text{(League } BOP)} = \dfrac{0.977}{0.670} = 1.46$,

or 46 percent better than the league average.

11. Jim Rice during his Hall of Fame career had the numbers in the following table:

AB	H	TB	BB	SB	CS	GIDP	HBP	SH	SF
8225	2452	4129	670	58	34	315	64	5	94

Find his *BOP*.

$$BOP = \frac{(TB + BB + HBP + SB + SH + SF)}{(AB - H + SH + SF + CS + GIDP)}$$

$$= \frac{(4129 + 670 + 64 + 58 + 5 + 94)}{(8225 - 2452 + 5 + 94 + 34 + 315)} = \frac{5020}{6221} = 0.807.$$

12. When Houston Astros player Craig Biggio topped both 50 stolen bases and 50 doubles in 1998, he was the first player to do so since Tris Speaker in 1912. Find the *TA* for both players, using the data below.

	AB	H	2B	3B	HR	BB	SB	HBP
Speaker 1912	580	222	53	12	10	82	52	6
Biggio 1998	646	210	51	2	20	64	50	23

Speaker had 339 TB, and $TA = \dfrac{(TB + BB + HBP + SB)}{(AB - H)} =$

$\dfrac{(339 + 82 + 6 + 52)}{(580 - 222)} = \dfrac{479}{358} = 1.34.$

Biggio had 325 TB, and $TA = \dfrac{(TB + BB + HBP + SB)}{(AB - H)} = \dfrac{(325 + 64 + 23 + 50)}{(646 - 210)}$

$= \dfrac{462}{436} = 1.06.$

Practicing Sabermetrics

The 1960 AL MVP race saw two Yankees teammates, Roger Maris and Mickey Mantle, finish 1–2 (respectively), separated only by three points in the final vote tally. In Problems 1–10, we will analyze their respective *BOP* measures, relative *BOP*, and also adjust these measures with park factors. Here are their data:

	AB	H	TB	BB	SB	CS	GIDP	HBP	SH	SF
Maris	499	141	290	70	2	2	6	2	1	5
Mantle	527	145	294	111	14	3	11	1	5	6

1. Calculate Maris' *BOP.*

[Answer: 0.997.]

2. Calculate Mantle's *BOP.*

[Answer: 1.059.]

3. Calculate the *BOP* for the American league in 1960, given the table below.

AB	H	TB	BB	SB	CS	GIDP	HBP	SH	SF
41838	10689	16215	4447	422	234	6	2	1	5

[Answer: 0.668.]

4. Find and interpret Maris' *relative BOP.*

[Answer: 1.493, or 49 percent better than the league's.]

5. Find and interpret Mantle's *relative BOP.*

[Answer: 1.585, or almost 59 percent better than the league's.]

6. Find and interpret the *PF* for Yankee Stadium in 1960, given the table below. Did it favor hitters or pitchers?

	Games (Home)	Games (Away)	R (Home)	RA (Home)	R (Away)	RA (Away)
Yankee Stadium	77	77	350	273	396	354

[Answer: *PF* = 0.831, which indicates that pitchers were favored.]

7. Determine Maris' park-adjusted *BOP.*

[Answer: 1.081.]

8. Determine Mantle's park-adjusted *BOP.*

[Answer: 1.148.]

9. Determine Maris' park-adjusted relative *BOP.*

[Answer: 1.619.]

10. Determine Mantle's park-adjusted relative *BOP.*

[Answer: 1.719.]

11. Given the data in Problems 9 and 10, how well did the writers do in selecting the AL MVP for 1960?

[Answer: Offensively, Mantle seemed to have a better season than Maris.]

12. Find Hank Aaron's *BOP* for 1962.

[Answer: 1.065.]

13. Using the data in the Introduction, find and interpret Aaron's relative *BOP* for 1962.

[Answer: 1.590, or 59 percent better than the league.]

CHAPTER 14

OPS, *POP* and the *SLOB*

Introduction

That sabermetrics has an influence on the analysis of baseball has no greater proof than the prevalent application of the statistic *OPS* , or "On base Plus Slugging," i.e., On Base Average (*OBA*) plus Slugging Average (*SLG*). As discussed in their marvelous book *The Hidden Game of Baseball,* John Thorn and Pete Palmer laud these measures as compensating for the shortcomings of batting average.

By way of review, to calculate On Base Average, we will use the formula

$$OBA = \frac{H + BB + HBP}{AB + BB + HBP}.$$

The official formula *OBA* used by Major League Baseball only can be used for seasons 1954 and later. To differentiate it from *OBA*, we will call it the On Base Percentage (*OBP*). Its formula is

$$OBP = \frac{H + BB + HBP}{AB + BB + HBP + SF}.$$

This particular form of the statistic is unusual in that a player could, hypothetically, have a lower *OBP* than batting average. For example, if a player has 300 *AB*, 100 *H,* 0 *BB,* 0 *HBP*, and 5 *SF*, then his batting average would be $\frac{H}{AB} = \frac{100}{300} = 0.333$ and his $OBP = \frac{H + BB + HBP}{AB + BB + HBP + SF} = \frac{100 + 0 + 0}{300 + 0 + 0 + 5} = 0.328$. The player's *OBA* would be the same as the batting average, i.e. $OBA = \frac{H + BB + HBP}{AB + BB + HBP} = \frac{100 + 0 + 0}{AB + 0 + 0} = 0.333$.

We will use the *OBA* formula, noting that it can be applied for all seasons, facilitating comparison between players across eras, and having the added benefit that we can avoid the anomaly of a higher bating average than on base average.

As mentioned in Chapter 13, Jimmie Foxx had a near–Triple Crown season in 1932. His impressive line appears in the following table.

AB	H	2B	3B	HR	BB	HBP
585	213	33	9	58	116	0

Foxx's $OBA = \dfrac{H + BB + HBP}{AB + BB + HBP} = \dfrac{213 + 116 + 0}{585 + 116 + 0} = 0.469.$

Recall that slugging average is calculated by dividing the total bases gained on safe hits by the total number of at bats, i.e., $SLG = \dfrac{TB}{AB}$.

In Chapter 13, we calculated Foxx's $TB = 213 + 33 + (2 \times 9) + (3 \times 58) = 438$. With 585 AB, this translates to a $SLG = \dfrac{TB}{AB} = \dfrac{438}{585} = 0.749.$

An OPS close to 1.000 signifies an excellent season. Foxx in 1932 had an $OPS = OBA + SLG = 0.469 + 0.749 = 1.218$. This definitely qualifies as excellent.

Since OBA and SLG have different denominators, some mathematical purists blanch at adding the two quantities together. For such people, the next best way to combine the two statistics is the $SLOB$, or "Slugging times On Base average." For Jimmie Foxx, his 1932 $SLOB = SLG \times OBA = 0.749 \times 0.469 = 0.351$.

As a point of reference, a 1.000 OPS can be achieved with $SLG = 0.600$ and $OBA = 0.400$ (among other possibilities). This translates to a $SLOB = 0.600 \times 0.400 = 0.240$.

Elements of relativity and park adjustment can also be applied to these numbers.

The American League hitters in 1932 put up the numbers in the following table:

AB	H	2B	3B	HR	BB	HBP
43430	12017	2287	570	707	4405	719

We calculate $TB = 12017 + 2287 + (2 \times 570) + (3 \times 707) = 17565$. With 43430 AB, this translates to a league $SLG = \dfrac{TB}{AB} = \dfrac{17565}{43430} = 0.404$. That is a high number for a league, signifying 40 percent of a base per at bat. Further,

$$\text{League } OBA = \frac{H + BB + HBP}{AB + BB + HBP} = \frac{12017 + 4405 + 719}{43430 + 4405 + 719} = 0.353.$$

Thus, the American League in 1932 had an $OPS = OBA + SLG = 0.353 + 0.404 = 0.757$, and a $SLOB = SLG \times OBA = 0.404 \times 0.353 = 0.143$. Therefore, 1932 was a year of heightened offense in the AL.

Back to Jimmie Foxx. Foxx had a relative $OPS = \dfrac{\text{Foxx} - OPS}{\text{AL} - OPS} = \dfrac{1.218}{0.757}$

$= 1.608$, or a figure almost 61 percent better than the league's. His relative *SLOB* can be found as

$$SLOB = \frac{\text{Foxx} - SLOB}{\text{AL} - SLOB} = \frac{0.351}{0.143} = 2.455, \text{ or } 145 \text{ percent better than the league's}$$

SLOB.

The Philadelphia Athletics played their home games in Shibe Park. In the table below are Shibe Park's numbers for 1932.

Games (Home)	Games (Away)	R (Home)	RA (Home)	R (Away)	RA (Away)
77	77	572	406	409	346

We use this to determine the park factor (see Chapter 5 for more on Park Factors). Thus,

$$PF = \left(\frac{\left(\dfrac{R(\text{Home}) + RA(\text{Home})}{\text{Games (Home)}} \right)}{\left(\dfrac{R(\text{Road}) + RA(\text{Road})}{\text{Games (Away)}} \right)} \right) = \frac{\dfrac{572 + 406}{77}}{\dfrac{409 + 346}{77}} = 1.29,$$

indicating a very large swing towards a hitter's park.

Recalculating Foxx's relative *SLOB* and relative *OPS* with this adjustment to the park, $Adj\ SLOB = SLOB + [(1 - PF)\ SLOB] \times 0.5 = 0.351 + [(1 - 1.29)\ 0.351] \times 0.5 = 0.300$, adjusting his relative *SLOB* to be

$\dfrac{\text{Foxx} - Adj\ SLOB}{\text{AL} - SLOB} = \dfrac{0.300}{0.143} = 2.098$, still more than 100 percent better than

the league. Similarly, his $Adj\ OPS = OPS + [(1 - PF)\ OPS] \times 0.5 = 01.218 + [(1 - 1.29)\ 1.218] \times 0.5 = 1.041$, adjusting his relative *OPS* to be

$\dfrac{\text{Foxx} - Adj\ OPS}{\text{AL} - OPS} = \dfrac{1.041}{0.757} = 1.375$, or around 38 percent better than the

league's *OPS*.

Thorn and Palmer adopt an adjustment for *OPS* that makes a value of 100 the league's average for the statistic. They call it *Adjusted OPS* and it is calculated as follows:

$$\text{Adjusted OPS} = \frac{\left(\dfrac{\text{Player } OBA}{\text{League } OBA} + \dfrac{\text{Player } SLG}{\text{League } SLG}\right) - 1}{PF}$$. They further adjust the

statistic by removing the pitchers' batting statistics. We will leave them in, and determine for Jimmie Foxx in 1932,

$$\text{Adjusted OPS} = \frac{\left(\dfrac{\text{Player } OBA}{\text{League } OBA} + \dfrac{\text{Player } SLG}{\text{League } SLG}\right) - 1}{PF} =$$

$$\frac{\left(\dfrac{0.469}{0.353} + \dfrac{0.749}{0.404}\right) - 1}{1.295} = 1.68.$$

Statistics such as the *OPS* and *SLOB* shed light on players' true contributions to the team, especially since they are more telling than batting average. The creator or creators of the *POP* Award (http://www.popaward.com/htdocs/index.htm) have come up with an extension of the *OPS* formula to include batting average, calling it *POP*, which sums *OPS* and *BA*, i.e., *POP* = *OBA* + *SLG* + *BA*. The one proviso for this statistic is that it is only used for players with a minimum batting average of .300, an on-base percentage of .400, and a slugging percentage of .500, which yields a minimum *POP* = *BA* + *OB* + *SLG* = 0.300 + 0 .400 + 0.500 = 1.200.

Jimmie Foxx in 1932 met these minimums, so we can compute his *POP*. We calculate his $BA = \dfrac{H}{AB} = \dfrac{213}{585} = 0.364$, and *POP* = *BA* + *OB* + *SLG* = 0.364 + 0.469 + 0.749 = *OPS* + *BA* = 1.218 + 0.364 = 1.582.

Ken Griffey, Jr., became the sixth member of the 600 Home Run Club in 2008. His career numbers through the 2008 season are in the following table:

AB	H	2B	3B	HR	BB	HBP
9316	2680	503	38	611	1240	80

Griffey's $OBA = \dfrac{H + BB + HBP}{AB + BB + HBP} = \dfrac{2680 + 1240 + 80}{9316 + 1240 + 80} = 0.376$. Next, we determine that his $SLG = \dfrac{TB}{AB} = \dfrac{5092}{9316} = 0.547$. Thus, his *OPS* = *OBA* + *SLG*

= 0.376 + 0.547 = 0.923, while his *SLOB* = *SLG* × *OBA* = 0.547 × 0.376 = 0.206. Since Griffey's *BA* and *OBA* are not at the levels of 0.300 and .400 (respectively), we do not calculate his *POP*.

Speaking of his "Pop," Ken Griffey, Sr., put up the following career numbers:

AB	H	2B	3B	HR	BB	HBP
7229	2143	364	77	152	719	14

which lead to his $SLG = \dfrac{TB}{AB} = \dfrac{3117}{7229} = 0.431$, his $OBA = \dfrac{H + BB + HBP}{AB + BB + HBP} =$ $\dfrac{2143 + 719 + 14}{7229 + 719 + 14} = 0.361$, his $OPS = OBA + SLG = 0.361 + 0.431 = 0.792$, while his $SLOB = SLG \times OBA = 0.361 \times 0.431 = 0.156$.

Demonstrating Sabermetrics

1. Besides the Griffeys, the small Pennsylvania town of Donora produced another All-Star outfielder, Cardinals Hall of Famer Stan "The Man" Musial. Using his career numbers, calculate his *OBA* and *SLG*.

AB	H	2B	3B	HR	BB	HBP
10972	3630	725	177	475	1599	53

First, we find Musial's total bases: $TB = 3630 + 725 + (2 \times 177) + (3 \times 475) = 6134$. Musial's $SLG = \dfrac{TB}{AB} = \dfrac{6134}{10972} = 0.559$, while his $OBA = \dfrac{H + BB + HBP}{AB + BB + HBP} = \dfrac{3630 + 1599 + 53}{10972 + 1599 + 53} = 0.418$.

2. Find Musial's career *OPS* and *SLOB*.

Using our work from Problem 1, $OPS = OBA + SLG = 0.418 + 0.559 = 0.977$, and his $SLOB = SLG \times OBA = 0.559 \times 0.418 = 0.234$.

3. Calculate Musial's career batting average. Do his career numbers qualify for a *POP* calculation? If so, find his career *POP.*

Musial's $BA = \dfrac{3630}{10972} = 0.331$, so his batting average is greater than 0.300, his on-base percentage is greater than 0.400, and slugging percentage is greater than 0.500. $POP = BA + OBA + SLG = 0.331 + 0.418 + 0.559 = 1.308$, which is astounding.

4. Barry Bonds' 2001 season was one of the better ones in history. Calculate his *OBA* and *SLG*.

AB	H	2B	3B	HR	BB	HBP	TB
476	156	32	2	73	177	9	411

Bonds had a $SLG = \dfrac{TB}{AB} = \dfrac{411}{476} = 0.863$, the greatest single season SLG of all time, while his $OBA = \dfrac{H + BB + HBP}{AB + BB + HBP} = \dfrac{156 + 177 + 9}{476 + 177 + 9} = 0.517$.

5. Find Bonds' *OPS* and *SLOB* for 2001.

Using our work from Problem 4, his *OPS* = *OBA* + *SLG* = 0.517 + 0.863 = 1.380, and a *SLOB* = *SLG* × *OBA* = 0.517 × 0.863 = 0.446.

6. Calculate Bonds' 2001 batting average. Do his numbers qualify for a *POP* calculation? If so, find his *POP*.

Barry's $BA = \dfrac{156}{477} = 0.328$, so his batting average is greater than 0.300, his on-base percentage is greater than 0.400, and slugging percentage is greater than 0.500. *POP* = *BA* + *OBA* + *SLG* = 0.328 + 0 .517 + 0.863 = 1.708, which is amazing.

7. Calculate the *OBA* for the National League in 2001, given the following statistics:

AB	H	BB	HBP	SLG
88100	23027	8567	1074	0.425

$OBA = \dfrac{H + BB + HBP}{AB + BB + HBP} = \dfrac{23027 + 8567 + 1074}{88100 + 8567 + 1074} = 0.334$.

8. Find Barry Bonds' relative *SLOB* for 2001.

From Problem 5, Bonds' *SLOB* = 0.446. From Problem 7, the National League in 2001 had a *SLOB* = *SLG* × *OBA* = 0.425 × 0.334 = 0.142. Therefore, Bonds' relative $SLOB = \dfrac{\text{Bonds} - SLOB}{\text{NL} - SLOB} = \dfrac{0.446}{0.142} = 3.141$.

9. Find Barry Bonds' relative *OPS* for 2001.

From Problem 5, Bonds' *OPS* = *1.380*. From Problem 7, the National League in 2001 had an *OPS* = *OBA* + *SLG* = 0.334 + 0.425 = 0.759. So, Bonds' relative $OPS = \dfrac{\text{Bonds} - OPS}{\text{NL} - OPS} = \dfrac{0.1.380}{0.759} = 1.818$.

10. In 1967, Carl Yastrzemski of the Boston Red Sox was the last major leaguer to achieve a Triple Crown (i.e., leading his league in batting average, home runs and runs batted in). Using his data in the chart, calculate his relative *OBA* and relative *SLG*.

	AB	H	BB	HBP	SLG	OBA
Yastrzemski	579	189	91	4	0.621	0.418
AL	54179	12766	4993	751	0.351	0.303

Yaz's relative $OBA = \dfrac{0.418}{0.303} = 1.49$. His relative $SLG = \dfrac{0.621}{0.351} = 1.77$.

11. Using the data from Problem 10, find Carl Yastrzemski's relative *OPS* for 1967.

Yaz's $OPS = OBA + SLG = 0.621 + .418 = 1.039$. The League $OPS = OBA + SLG = 0.351 + 0.303 = 0.654$. Thus, Yaz's' relative $OPS = \dfrac{1.039}{0.654} = 1.59$.

12. Carl Yastrzemski's league-leading batting average in 1967 was .326. Calculate his *POP.*

Yastrzemski's $POP = BA + OBA + SLG = 0.326 + 0.621 + .418 = 1.365$.

13. Find the *PF* for the Red Sox, 1967.

Games (Home)	Games (Away)	R (Home)	RA (Home)	R (Away)	RA (Away)
81	81	408	355	314	259

$$PF = \left(\frac{\left(\dfrac{R\,(\text{Home}) + RA\,(\text{Home})}{\text{Games}\,(\text{Home})} \right)}{\left(\dfrac{R\,(\text{Road}) + RA\,(\text{Road})}{\text{Games}\,(\text{Away})} \right)} \right) = \frac{\dfrac{408 + 355}{81}}{\dfrac{314 + 259}{81}} = 1.33 \,.$$

14. Using the answers to Problems 10 and 13 above, find Carl Yastrzemski's 1967 *Adjusted OPS.*

$$Adjusted\ OPS = \frac{\left(\dfrac{\text{Player } OBA}{\text{League } OBA} + \dfrac{\text{Player } SLG}{\text{League } SLG} \right) - 1}{PF} = \frac{(1.49 + 1.77) - 1}{1.33} = 1.617,$$

or 162.

Practicing Sabermetrics

The 1960 American League Most Valuable Player race saw two Yankees teammates, Roger Maris and Mickey Mantle, finish 1–2 (respectively), separated only by three points. In Problems 1 through 7, we will analyze their respective *OPS* numbers, relative *OPS,* and adjust them for park.

Here are their data:

	AB	H	TB	BB	SB	CS	GDP	HBP	SH	SF
Maris	499	141	290	70	2	2	6	2	1	5
Mantle	527	145	294	111	14	3	11	1	5	6

1. Calculate Maris' *BA, SLG,* and *OBA.* Does he qualify for *POP* consideration?

[Answers: *BA* = 0.283; *SLG* = 0.581; *OBA* = 0.374; he does not qualify for *POP*, as his *OBA* and *BA* are below the minimum values necessary.]

2. Calculate Mantle's *BA, SLG,* and *OBA.* Does he qualify for *POP* consideration?

[Answers: *BA* = 0.275; *SLG* = 0.558; *OBA* = 0.402; he does not qualify for *POP*, as his *BA* is below the minimum value necessary.]

3. Calculate the *OPS* for Maris and Mantle, 1960.

[Answers: Maris' *OPS* = 0.955; Mantle's *OPS* = 0.960.]

4. Calculate the *SLOB* for Maris and Mantle, 1960.

[Answers: Maris' *SLOB* = 0.217; Mantle's *SLOB* = 0.224.]

5. Find the *OBA* and *SLG* for the American league in 1960, given the information below.

AB	H	TB	BB	SB	CS	GDP	HBP	SH	SF
41838	10689	16215	4447	422	234	6	2	1	5

[Answers: *OBA* = 0.331; *SLG* = 0.388.]

6. Find Maris' and Mantle's relative *OBA* and relative *SLG* for 1960.

[Answers: Maris' relative *OBA* = 1.130, Maris' relative *SLG* = 1.500;
        Mantle's relative *OBA* = 1.215, Mantle's relative *SLG* = 1.438.]

7. Find Maris' and Mantle's *Adjusted OPS.* Recall that the Park Factor (*PF*) for Yankee Stadium in 1960 was calculated in Chapter 13 to be 0.83.

[Answers: Maris *Adjusted OPS* = 1.963, or 196;
        Mantle *Adjusted OPS* = 1.991, or 199.]

8. Willie Mays in 1962 put up the following numbers. Find his *OBA* and *SLG.*

AB	H	2B	3B	HR	BB	HBP	TB
621	189	36	5	49	78	4	382

[Answers: *OBA* = 0.385; *SLG* = 0.615.]

9. Calculate Mays' *OPS* and *SLOB* for 1962.

[Answers: *OPS* = 1.000; *SLOB* = 0.237.]

10. The National League numbers for 1962 are given below. Find the NL's *OBA* and *SLG*.

AB	H	2B	3B	HR	BB	HBP	TB
55449	14453	2075	453	1449	5265	373	21781

[Answers: *OBA* = 0.329; *SLG* = 0.393.]

11. Candlestick Park was calculated in Chapter 13 to be neutral, i.e., having a *PF* = 1.00. Using the answers from Problems 8 and 10, find Mays' *Adjusted OPS*.

[Answer: *Adjusted OPS* = 1.735, or 174.]

12. Calculate Babe Ruth's *BA, OBA,* and *SLG* for 1920, given his stats below.

AB	H	2B	3B	HR	BB	HBP	TB
457	172	36	9	54	150	3	388

[Answers: *BA* = 0.376; *OBA* = 0.533; *SLG* = 0.839.]

13. Calculate the American League's *BA, OBA,* and *SLG* for 1920.

AB	H	2B	3B	HR	BB	HBP	TB
41986	11902	2009	620	369	3809	1639	16258

[Answers: *BA* = 0.283; *OBA* = 0.366; *SLG* = 0.387.]

14. Find Babe Ruth's *POP* for 1920. Then calculate his relative *POP* = relative *BA* + relative *OBA* + relative *SLG*.

[Answers: *POP* = 1.748; relative *POP* = 4.95.]

CHAPTER 15

Total Power Quotient

Introduction

The Total Power Quotient (*TPQ*) is an instrument that is both cumulative (the "total" part) and relative (the "quotient" part). It can be used for an individual player, a team or a league. It is computed by first summing up three traditional *power* measures: home runs (*HR*), total bases (*TB*) and runs batted in (*RBI*). Once this total is computed, it is divided by the number of at-bats (*AB*). That is,

$$TPQ = \frac{HR + TB + RBI}{AB}.$$

As an example, in 1920, Hall of Famer Babe Ruth slugged 54 home runs, accrued 388 total bases, drove in 137 runs, while batting 457 times. So his 1920 *TPQ* is given by

$$TPQ = \frac{HR + TB + RBI}{AB} = \frac{54 + 388 + 137}{457} = 1.2670.$$

We will always compute the *TPQ* to four decimal places. In general, a *seasonal TPQ* score of 1.0000 of higher indicates a superior performance. Similarly, a *career TPQ* of 0.7500 or higher reflects excellent lifetime power numbers.

One can use a *relativity* approach with respect to the total power quotient. We symbolize this by *RTPQ* and compute it by dividing the individual player's total power quotient, TPQ_i, by an appropriate total power quotient term, TPQ_n. This yields a normalization number (see Chapter 4 on Relativity and Normalization). Symbolically,

$$RTPQ = \frac{TPQ_i}{TPQ_n}.$$

For example, in 1932 firstbaseman Jimmie Foxx had the following totals: 58 *HR*, 438 *TB* and 169 *RBI* in 585 *AB*. This gave him a TPQ_i of 1.1368.

That season his team, the Philadelphia Athletics, hit 172 *HR*, accumulated 2530 *TB* and had 923 *RBI*, all in 5537 *AB*. This led to a team TPQ_n of 0.6547. Therefore, Foxx's 1932 *RTPQ*, relative to his team, was

$$RTPQ = \frac{TPQ_i}{TPQ_n} = \frac{1.1368}{0.6547} = 1.7363.$$

As is the case for the *TPQ*, the *RTPQ* will also be computed to four decimal places. A relative *TPQ* value greater than 1 indicates that the player's *TPQ* was "better than the average," while a *RTPQ* less than 1 means that the player performed "below average." Clearly, if his *RTPQ* = 1, the player's performance was exactly the same as the normalizing *TPQ*. When the context of the situation is clear, the subscripts *i* and *n* may be dropped.

The Jimmie Foxx example suggests that we may use *TPQ* with respect to teams, leagues and eras of baseball. We can also use this approach with regard to *composite TPQs* (see Problem 6 and Problem 7 in the Demonstrating Sabermetrics section). Finally, it should be pointed out that *TPQ* scores can be both *scaled* and *weighted*. For example, suppose we separate each term in the numerator and rewrite the formula for *TPQ* as follows:

$$TPQ = \frac{HR + TB + RBI}{AB} = \frac{HR}{AB} + \frac{TB}{AB} + \frac{RBI}{AB}.$$

Next, let us "scale down" each term on the right hand side by multiplying by a factor of one-third. We denote this scaling by TPQ_s, which gives us

$$TPQ_s = \left(\frac{1}{3}\right)\frac{HR}{AB} + \left(\frac{1}{3}\right)\frac{TB}{AB} + \left(\frac{1}{3}\right)\frac{RBI}{AB}.$$

This, in itself, does not change the rankings of the *TPQ*. If Player A has a *TPQ* = 0.9000 and Player B has a *TPQ* = 0.6000, their scaled *TPQ* marks (in this particular scaling of ⅓ would become 0.3000 and 0.2000, respectively, with Player A still ranked ahead of Player B. Scaling is generally used to simplify an analysis by putting the numbers into a more convenient form.

Suppose, however, that we wish to change scaling by altering the coefficients of three factors. Often we may need to assign a different weight to each coefficient. For example, let us tweak the above formula for TPQ_s as follows:

$$TPQ_{sw} = \left(\frac{1}{6}\right)\frac{HR}{AB} + \left(\frac{1}{3}\right)\frac{TB}{AB} + \left(\frac{1}{2}\right)\frac{RBI}{AB}.$$

Since we have given different weights to this scaled formula, we will now denote it as TPQ_{sw}. This approach allows us to weigh the *RBI* statistic heavier that the *HR* total. The choice of the values of the weights is clearly up to the individual. By convention, the *sum* of the weights (coefficients) is usually 1. That is,

$$\frac{1}{6} + \frac{1}{3} + \frac{1}{2} = 1.$$

As in the case of the *RTPQ*, the subscripts *s* and *w* may be omitted when the context of the situation is clear.

Demonstrating Sabermetrics

1. In the 1934 All Star Game at the Polo Grounds, Giants southpaw Carl Hubbell electrified the crowd by striking out, in succession, five American League sluggers: Babe Ruth, Lou Gehrig, Jimmie Foxx, Al Simmons and Joe Cronin. Given the information below, find the career *TPQs* for these five American League stars.

Player	HR	TB	RBI	AB
Ruth	714	5793	2217	8398
Gehrig	493	5060	1995	8001
Foxx	534	4956	1922	8134
Simmons	307	4685	1827	8759
Cronin	170	3546	1424	7579

The *TPQs* are as follows:

for Ruth, $TPQ = \dfrac{HR + TB + RBI}{AB} = \dfrac{714 + 5793 + 2217}{8198} = 1.0388;$

for Gehrig, $TPQ = \dfrac{HR + TB + RBI}{AB} = \dfrac{493 + 5060 + 1995}{8001} = 0.9434;$

for Foxx, $TPQ = \dfrac{HR + TB + RBI}{AB} = \dfrac{534 + 4956 + 1922}{8134} = 0.9112;$

for Simmons, $TPQ = \dfrac{HR + TB + RBI}{AB} = \dfrac{307 + 4685 + 1827}{8759} = 0.7785;$

and for Cronin, $TPQ = \dfrac{HR + TB + RBI}{AB} = \dfrac{170 + 3546 + 1424}{7579} = 0.6782.$

Ruth's lifetime *TPQ* is the highest ever recorded.

2. In 1998 Chicago Cubs outfielder Sammy Sosa and St. Louis Cardinals first baseman Mark McGwire were involved in a season-long home run battle. Sosa hit 66 home runs, accrued 416 total bases and drove in 158 runs while batting 643 times. McGwire slugged 70 round trippers, had 383 total bases, drove in 147 runs and batted 509 times. Compare their 1998 *TPQs*.

For Sammy Sosa, $TPQ = \dfrac{HR + TB + RBI}{AB} = \dfrac{66 + 416 + 158}{643} = 0.9953.$

For Mark McGwire, $TPQ = \dfrac{HR + TB + RBI}{AB} = \dfrac{70 + 383 + 147}{509} = 1.1788.$

Though Sosa had but four fewer *HRs*, he topped McGwire in both *RBIs* and *TBs*. The reason McGwire had a super *TPQ* was because Sosa had 134 more *ABs*.

3. In 2001, Barry Bonds of the San Francisco Giants had a great year, when he hit 73 *HR*, had 411 *TB*, drove in 137 runs and batted 476 times. Find his *TPQ*.

For the 2001 season, Bonds' $TPQ = \dfrac{HR + TB + RBI}{AB} = \dfrac{73 + 411 + 137}{476} = 1.3046.$

Bonds' 2001 *TPQ* is the highest seasonal mark ever recorded.

4. Relative to their teams and using the information in the two previous problems, find the 1998 *RTPQ* for both Sammy Sosa and Mark McGwire and the 2001 *RTPQ* for Barry Bonds given the following information:

Team	HR	TB	RBI	AB
1998 Cardinals	223	2467	781	5593
1998 Cubs	212	2446	788	5649
2001 Giants	235	2582	775	5612

The 1998 Cards had a team $TPQ = \dfrac{HR + TB + RBI}{AB} = \dfrac{223 + 2467 + 781}{5593} = 0.6206,$

while the 1998 Cubs $TPQ = \dfrac{HR + TB + RBI}{AB} = \dfrac{212 + 2446 + 788}{5649} = 0.6100,$

and the 2001 Giants had a $TPQ = \dfrac{HR + TB + RBI}{AB} = \dfrac{235 + 2582 + 775}{5612} = 0.6401.$

Therefore, McGwire's *RTPQ* is given by $RTPQ = \dfrac{TPQ_i}{TPQ_n} = \dfrac{1.1788}{.6206} = 1.8995,$

Sosa's *RTPQ* is given by $RTPQ = \dfrac{TPQ_i}{TPQ_n} = \dfrac{0.9953}{.6100} = 1.6316,$

and Bonds' *RTPQ* is given by $RTPQ = \dfrac{TPQ_i}{TPQ_n} = \dfrac{1.3046}{.6401} = 2.0381.$

5. Future Hall of Famer Mike Piazza had a lifetime *TPQ* of 0.8002 during a career in which he hit 427 home runs and drove in 1335 runs. Find the number of total bases which he accumulated in his career, given the fact that he had 6911 at-bats.

Using the formula for *TPQ*, and substituting in our values we have the equation, $TPQ = 0.8002 = \dfrac{HR + TB + RBI}{AB} = \dfrac{427 + TB + 1335}{6911}.$

Multiplying through by 6911 and solving for *TB*, we find that Piazza had 3768 total bases in his career.

6. Two of the greatest teams in the history of the Yankees were their

World Championship clubs of 1927 and 1961. Both teams featured teammates vying for the seasonal home run record: Babe Ruth and Lou Gehrig in 1927 and Roger Maris and Mickey Mantle in 1961. Given the information below, calculate the combined *TPQs* of the Ruth–Gehrig and Maris–Mantle duos.

Player	HR	TB	RBI	AB
1927 Ruth	60	417	164	540
1927 Gehrig	47	447	175	584
1961 Maris	54	353	128	514
1961 Mantle	61	366	142	590

The composite totals for the Ruth–Gehrig combination are: 107 home runs, 864 total bases, 339 runs batted in and 1124 at-bats. The same totals for the Maris–Mantle one-two punch are 115 *HR*, 719 *TB*, 270 *RBI* and 1104 *AB*, respectively. So the Ruth–Gehrig

$$TPQ = \frac{HR + TB + RBI}{AB} = \frac{107 + 864 + 339}{1124} = 1.1655,$$ while the same formula yields

a *TPQ* of 1.000 for the Maris–Mantle tandem.

7. Using the information below, and referring to Problem 6, find the seasonal *RTPQ* of each duo, relative to their teams.

Team	HR	TB	RBI	AB
1927 Yankees	158	2415	908	5347
1961 Yankees	240	2457	782	5559

By definition, the *TPQ* for the 1927 Murderer's Row club is given by

$$TPQ = \frac{HR + TB + RBI}{AB} = \frac{158 + 2415 + 908}{5347} = 0.6510;$$ the same formula gives a

team *TPQ* value of 0.6258 for the 1961 Bronx Bombers. So, the *RTQP* for

the Ruth–Gehrig duo is given by $RTPQ = \dfrac{TPQ_i}{TPQ_n} = \dfrac{1.1655}{.6510} = 1.7902,$

while the same metric yields a *RTPQ* of 1.5979 for the Maris–Mantle combination.

8. In 1941, outfielders Joe DiMaggio and Ted Williams had terrific seasons: DiMaggio hit in 56 consecutive games, while Williams batted .406 for the season. Given the information below, find both their seasonal *TPQs* and a *scaled* and *weighted TPQ* which is defined as follows:

$$TPQ_{sw} = \left(\frac{1}{4}\right)\frac{HR}{AB} + \left(\frac{3}{8}\right)\frac{TB}{AB} + \left(\frac{3}{8}\right)\frac{RBI}{AB}.$$

Player	HR	TB	RBI	AB
1941 DiMaggio	30	348	125	541
1941 Williams	37	335	120	456

Starting with $TPQ = \dfrac{HR + TB + RBI}{AB}$ we find that DiMaggio had a TPQ = 0.9298 and that Williams had a TPQ = 1.0790. Regarding the scaled and weighted TPQ_{sw}, for the "Yankee Clipper," we have:

$$TPQ_{sw} = \left(\frac{1}{4}\right)\frac{HR}{AB} + \left(\frac{3}{8}\right)\frac{TB}{AB} + \left(\frac{3}{8}\right)\frac{RBI}{AB} = \left(\frac{1}{4}\right)\frac{30}{541} + \left(\frac{3}{8}\right)\frac{348}{541} + \left(\frac{3}{8}\right)\frac{125}{541} = 0.3417.$$

In the case of the "Splendid Splinter," we have:

$$TPQ_{sw} = \left(\frac{1}{4}\right)\frac{HR}{AB} + \left(\frac{3}{8}\right)\frac{TB}{AB} + \left(\frac{3}{8}\right)\frac{RBI}{AB} = \left(\frac{1}{4}\right)\frac{37}{456} + \left(\frac{3}{8}\right)\frac{335}{456} + \left(\frac{3}{8}\right)\frac{120}{456} = 0.3944.$$

Practicing Sabermetrics

1. Find the lifetime TPQ of Barry Bonds, through the 2007 season, given that he accumulated the following career statistics: 762 homeruns, 5796 total bases, 1996 runs batted in and 9847 at-bats.

[Answer: 0.8686.]

2. In the Demonstrating Sabermetrics section of this chapter, we showed that Babe Ruth had a TPQ of 1.2670 in 1920. This was Ruth's first year with the Yankees. Find his $RTPQ$ relative to his team, given that the Yankees blasted 115 home runs, accrued 2205 total bases, drove in 745 runs and had 5176 at-bats.

[Answer: 2.1396.]

3. Find Babe Ruth's $RTPQ$ relative to his team for the 1921 season, given the following data:

	HR	TB	RBI	AB
1921 Ruth	59	457	171	540
1921 Yankees	134	2436	863	5249

[Answer: 1.9452.]

4. The career statistics for four power hitting first basemen who played most of their careers in the National League are listed below. Rank them according to their $TPQs$.

Player	HR	TB	RBI	AB
Orlando Cepeda	379	3959	1365	7927
Gil Hodges	370	3422	1274	7030
Ted Kluszewski	279	2951	1028	5929
Tony Perez	379	4532	1652	9778

[Answers: Hodges (0.7206), Cepeda (0.7194),
　　　　Kluszewski (0.7182), Perez (0.6712).]

5. First basemen and Hall of Famers George Sisler and Bill Terry were both great hitters. Sisler hit .407 in 1920 and again batted .420 two years later. Terry had a batting average of .401 in 1930. Compare the *TPQs* for their seasons when they hit over .400 and calculate their lifetime *TPQs*, given the data below.

Player	HR	TB	RBI	AB
Sisler (1920)	19	399	122	631
Sisler (1922)	8	348	105	586
Sisler (Career)	102	3871	1175	8267
Terry (1930)	23	392	129	633
Terry (Career)	154	3252	1078	6428

[Answers: 1920 Sisler (0.8558), 1922 Sisler (0.7867), Career Sisler
　　　　(0.6227); 1930 Terry (0.8594); Career Terry (0.6976).]

6. The following table gives the lifetime statistics for five Hall of Fame catchers. Find the unknown quantities, denoted as v, w, x, y, and z.

Player	HR	TB	RBI	AB	TPQ
Johnny Bench	389	v	1376	7658	0.7063
Yogi Berra	358	3643	w	7555	0.7189
Roy Campanella	x	2101	856	4205	0.7608
Mickey Cochrane	119	2470	832	y	0.6618
Bill Dickey	202	2470	1209	6300	z

[Answers: v = 3644, w = 1430, x = 242, y = 5169, z = 0.6160.]

7. Consider the career World Series totals for the following outfielders:

Player	HR	TB	RBI	AB
Joe DiMaggio	8	84	19	199
Duke Snider	11	79	26	133
Mickey Mantle	18	123	40	230

Find their *TPQ*s and their scaled and weighted Total Power Quotients (TPQ_{sw}) using the following scheme for the latter:

$$TPQ_{sw} = \left(\frac{1}{2}\right)\frac{HR}{AB} + \left(\frac{1}{6}\right)\frac{TB}{AB} + \left(\frac{1}{3}\right)\frac{RBI}{AB}.$$

[Answers: *TPQ*: DiMaggio (0.5578), Snider (0.8722), Mantle (0.7870); TPQ_{sw}: DiMaggio (0.1222), Snider (0.2055); Mantle (0.1862).]

8. St. Louis Cardinals Stan Musial was one of the greatest and most beloved players of all time. His career statistics are as follows:

HR	TB	RBI	AB
475	6134	1951	10972

His lifetime *TPQ* is 0.7802. Suppose we use Musial's numbers with regard to a scaled and weighted *TPQ* with a formula given by

$$TPQ_{sw} = \frac{aHR + bTB + cRBI}{AB},$$ where *a, b* and *c* are to be determined (these numbers are sometimes called *parameters*). If we further suppose that the sum *a* + *b* + *c* does not necessarily equal 1, find the value of *a*, for the given values of *b* = 1.5 and *c* = 3.7; that is, $TPQ_{sw} = \frac{a\,HR + 1.5\,TB + 3.7\,RBI}{AB}.$

Using this definition, if Musial had a lifetime TPQ_{sw} = 1.6000, find the value of the parameter *a*, rounded off to one decimal place.

[Answer: *a* = 2.4.]

9. Hank Greenberg was a slugging first baseman and outfielder who starred in the 1930s and the 1940s. He had two terrific seasons in 1937 and 1938 when he posted the following numbers:

Year	HR	TB	RBI	AB
1937	40	397	183	594
1938	58	380	146	556

[Answers: 1937 Greenberg (1.0438); 1938 Greenberg (1.0504).]

10. Suppose we have developed a situational TPQ_{sw} which is defined as

$$TPQ_{sw} = \frac{x\,HR + y\,TB + 3.5\,RBI}{AB},$$ where the parameters *x* and *y* are to be determined. Using the information in Problem 9, assume that Greenberg's

1937 TPQ_{sw} = 3.9500 and his 1938 TPQ_{sw} = 4.2000. To one decimal place, determine the values of x and y.

The solution of this problem requires simultaneously solving two equations in two unknowns.

[Answers: x = 9.7, y = 3.3.]

CHAPTER 16

Isolated Power, Power Factor and Power Average

Introduction

In this chapter we consider three simple measures of *power*. The first is called *Isolated Power* (*ISO*) and is defined as the difference between slugging percentage (*SLG*) and batting average (*BA*). We recall that the former is the ratio of the number of total bases (*TB*) divided by the number of at-bats (*AB*), while the latter is the number of hits (*H*) divided by the number of at-bats. That is,

$$ISO = SLG - BA = \frac{TB}{AB} - \frac{H}{AB} = \frac{TB - H}{AB}.$$

For example, Hall of Famer Willie Mays had a lifetime *BA* = .302 and a career *SLG* = .557. Therefore, his lifetime *ISO* = .557 × .302 = 0.255

Because of the way it is defined, isolated power can be thought of as a measure of power "beyond first base." If a player does not get many extra base hits (doubles, triples, and home runs), then his *ISO* will not be much greater than 0.000. The minimum value which the *ISO* can attain is .000 (no extra base hits), while the maximum value is 3.000 (a home run in every at-bat).

The next metric we wish to define is known as the *Power Factor* (*PwrF*), as is defined as the ratio of slugging percentage to batting average. That is,

$$PwrF = \frac{SLG}{BA} = \frac{\left(\dfrac{TB}{AB}\right)}{\left(\dfrac{H}{AB}\right)} = \frac{TB}{H}.$$ So, the career *PwrF* of Willie Mays is

$$PF = \frac{SLG}{BA} = \frac{.557}{.302} = 1.844.$$

The power factor is a measure of total bases per hit. If a player does not get many extra base hits, his *PwrF* will not be much greater than 1.000. The minimum value which the *PwrF* can reach is 1.000 (no extra base hits), while highest value it can attain is 4.000 (a home run in every at-bat). A career *PwrF* > 1.750 is an indication that the batter compiled some very good "power" numbers while playing. The players with lifetime marks of *PwrF* > 2.000 are few and far between.

Our last measure is known as the Power Average (*PwrA*). The number is defined as the sum of hits plus home runs (*HR*), all divided by *AB*. Namely,

$$PwrA = \frac{H + HR}{AB}.$$

To continue our example, in his career Willie Mays slugged 660 *HR*, while obtaining 3283 *H* in 10,881 *AB*. So his lifetime power average number is $PwrA = \dfrac{H + HR}{AB} = \dfrac{3283 + 660}{10,881} = 0.362$. The power average statistic gives "equal weight" to both hits and home runs and can be used in analyses of home run hitters who also hit for a high average. We can modify this measure by changing the weights, making it somewhat like the *SLG* metric. See Problem 14 in the Demonstrating Sabermetrics section for an example.

With respect to the three instruments of *SLG*, *PwrA* and *ISO*, we will take our calculations out to three decimal places.

Demonstrating Sabermetrics

1. Through the end of the 2008 season, only three hitters in the history of Major League Baseball have hit at least 700 home runs: Hank Aaron, Barry Bonds and Babe Ruth. Given the information below, find their career numbers for isolated power, power factor and power average.

Player	AB	H	HR	TB	BA	SLG
Aaron	12364	3771	755	6856	.305	.555
Bonds	9847	2935	762	5976	.298	.607
Ruth	8398	2873	714	5793	.342	.690

Aaron's *ISO* = *SLG* – *BA* = .555 – .305 = 0.250, his

$PwrF = \dfrac{SLG}{BA} = \dfrac{.555}{.305} = 1.819$, and his $PwrA = \dfrac{H + HR}{AB} = \dfrac{3771 + 755}{12,346} = 0.366$.

Bonds' numbers are *ISO* = *SLG* – *BA* = .607 – .298 = 0.309,

$PwrF = \dfrac{SLG}{BA} = \dfrac{.607}{.298} = 2.036$, and $PwrA = \dfrac{H + HR}{AB} = \dfrac{2935 + 762}{9847} = 0.375$.

In Ruth's case, we find that his $ISO = SLG - BA = .690 - .342 = 0.348$, his $PwrF = \dfrac{SLG}{BA} = \dfrac{.690}{.342} = 2.017$, and his $PwrA = \dfrac{H + HR}{AB} = \dfrac{2873 + 714}{8398} = 0.427$.

To summarize our results,

Player	ISO	PwrF	PwrA
Aaron	0.250	1.819	0.366
Bonds	0.309	2.036	0.375
Ruth	0.348	2.017	0.427

Ruth's *SLG*, *PwrA* and *ISO* are the highest career values in history.

2. Mark McGwire was the first player to hit 70 home runs in a season. He also has the best career home run percentage (home runs per at-bat) in history. Determine his career *ISO*, *PwrF* and *PwrA*, based on the following data: $AB = 6187$, $H = 1626$, $HR = 583$, $TB = 3639$, $BA = .263$ and $SLG = .588$.

Using the formula, "Big Mac's" $ISO = SLG - BA = .588 - .263 = 0.325$, while his $PwrF = \dfrac{SLG}{BA} = \dfrac{.588}{.263} = 2.238$, and his

$PwrA = \dfrac{H + HR}{AB} = \dfrac{1626 + 583}{6187} = 0.357$. McGwire's *PwrF* is the highest in history.

3. For much of his career, journeyman Dave Kingman had power statistics similar to those of Mark McGwire (see Problem 2). Given the information below, compare Kingman's *ISO*, *PwrF* and *PwrA* to those of McGwire.

AB	H	HR	TB	BA	SLG
6677	1575	442	3191	.236	.478

Using the same approach, Kingman's $ISO = SLG - BA = .478 - .236 = 0.242$. His $PwrF = \dfrac{SLG}{BA} = \dfrac{.478}{.236} = 2.025$, and his

$PwrA = \dfrac{H + HR}{AB} = \dfrac{1575 + 442}{6677} = 0.302$. While Kingman's *PwrF* is impressive, his two other statistics are well below those of McGwire.

4. Ted Williams had a career $BA = .344$. If his lifetime $ISO = 0.290$, find his *SLG*.

Solving for *SLG* in the following equations, $ISO = SLG - BA$ and $0.290 = SLG - .344$, we find that William's $SLG = .634$.

5. Through the end of the 2007 season, outfielder Sammy Sosa had a

career $PwrF = 1.955$. Given that Sosa had 2408 H, find his lifetime number of TB.

Since the $PwrF$ can be computed as follows, $PwrF = \dfrac{TB}{H}$, we can substitute our given values to obtain the equation $1.995 = \dfrac{TB}{2408}$. Solving for the unknown, we find that $TB = 4707$.

6. Yankee first baseman Lou Gehrig had many great seasons. Two of his finest occurred in 1927 and 1934. Given the data below, contrast his seasonal ISO, $PwrF$ and $PwrA$ numbers. Based on these numbers, which was the "better" year for the "Iron Horse"?

Year	AB	H	HR	TB	BA	SLG
1927	584	218	47	447	.373	.765
1934	579	210	49	409	.363	.706

For 1927, Gehrig's stats are $ISO = SLG - BA = .765 - .373 = 0.392$, with

$PwrF = \dfrac{SLG}{BA} = \dfrac{.765}{.373} = 2.051$, and $PwrA = \dfrac{H + HR}{AB} = \dfrac{218 + 47}{584} = 0.454$, while for

1934, his statistics are $ISO = SLG - BA = .706 - .363 = 0.447$,

$PwrF = \dfrac{SLG}{BA} = \dfrac{.706}{.363} = 1.945$, and his $PwrA = \dfrac{H + HR}{AB} = \dfrac{210 + 49}{579} = 0.447$.

Based on these three metrics, it would seem that Gehrig had a better year in 1927. In 1927, Gehrig drove in 175 runs. What is amazing about this feat is that he followed Babe Ruth in the Yankee lineup. Since Ruth hit 60 home runs that season, Gehrig came to the plate with the bases empty at least sixty times that year.

7. Hall of Famer Rogers Hornsby has been called by many baseball experts the "greatest right-handed batter" who ever played the game. Find his career hit total, given that he batted 8173 times, hit 301 home runs and had a power average figure of .395.

Using the formula for $PwrA$, we have $PwrA = \dfrac{H + HR}{AB}$, or,

$0.395 = \dfrac{H + 301}{8173}$. Cross-multiplying and solving for H yields a hit total of 2927. Hornsby's actual hit total was 2930. The discrepancy is caused by round-off from his batting average, which affects the $PwrA$.

8. Using the information from Problem 7, find Hornsby's lifetime batting average.

Since $BA = \dfrac{H}{AB}$, we obtain $BA = \dfrac{2930}{8137} = .358$.

9. Using the information from Problems 7 and 8, calculate Hornsby's lifetime *SLG* and *PwrF*, given that his career *ISO* = 0.219.

Using the formula for *ISO*, we have *ISO* = *SLG* − *BA*, or, 0.219 = *SLG* − .358, which gives *SLG* = .577. Regarding the *PwrF* metric, since

$PwrF = \dfrac{SLG}{BA}$, we find that Hornsby's lifetime mark is $PwrF = \dfrac{.577}{.358} = 1.612$.

10. In 1934, Hall of Famer Joe Medwick had an *ISO* = 0.210 and a *PwrF* = 1.658 for the World Champion St. Louis Cardinals. Find his seasonal *SLG* and *BA* marks.

We have two equations in two unknowns, since we know *ISO* = 0.210 = *SLG* − *BA* and $PwrF = 1.658 = \dfrac{SLG}{.BA}$. Multiplying both sides by BA yields 1.658 *BA* = *SLG*. We then substitute this expression into the first equation to get the transformed equality 0.210 = 1.658 *BA* − *BA* = 0.658 *BA*. Solving this equation for *BA*, gives us $BA = \dfrac{.210}{0.658} = .319$. We can now determine the *SLG* using the *ISO* equation, *ISO* = 0.210 = *SLG* − *BA*, or, 0.210 = *SLG* − .319, which finally yields *SLG* = .529.

11. In 2001, Chipper Jones of the Atlanta Braves slugged 38 home runs and had a *PwrA* = 0.397 in 572 at-bats. Calculate his batting average for that year.

We must determine the number of hits (*H*) amassed by Jones. Using the *PwrA* formula we have $PwrA = \dfrac{H + HR}{AB} = \dfrac{H + 38}{572} = 0.397$. This yields a hit total of *H* = 189. Dividing this number by *AB* = 572 gives *BA* = .330.

12. Using the information from Problem 11, find Jones' *SLG*, if his 2001 *PwrF* = 1.833.

Since $PwrF = \dfrac{SLG}{BA} = \dfrac{SLG}{.330} = 1.833$, *SLG* = .605.

13. Based on Problems 11 and 12, find Jones' *ISO* for 2001.

Since *ISO* = *SLG* − *BA*, we have ISO = .605 − .330 = 0.275.

14. Pittsburgh Pirates legend Willie Stargell had a career *PwrA* = 0.341; in 7927 *AB*, he amassed 2232 *H*, which included 475 *HR*. Using the three modifications of *PwrA* below, find Stargell's power average totals. Also, which of the three is the closest to his true *PwrA*?

$$PwrA_1 = \dfrac{2H + HR}{2AB} \qquad PwrA_1 = \dfrac{H + 2HR}{3AB} \qquad PwrA_1 = \dfrac{3H + 4HR}{5AB}$$

For the first modified metric, $PwrA_1 = \dfrac{2H + HR}{2AB} = \dfrac{2(2232) + 475}{2(7927)} = 0.312.$

For the second modified metric, $PwrA_2 = \dfrac{H + 2HR}{3AB} = \dfrac{2232 + 2(475)}{3(7927)} = 0.134,$

and for the last measure, $PwrA_3 = \dfrac{3H + 4HR}{5AB} = \dfrac{3(2232) + 4(475)}{5(7927)} = 0.217.$

The $PwrA_1$ value of 0.312 is the closest to Stargell's true $PwrA$ mark of 0.341. See Problem 12 in the Practicing Sabermetrics section for another example. The coefficients of the H, HR and AB terms are sometimes called parameters. These parameters are varied as we "tweak" the $PwrA$ model. This process can sometimes give us new information which was not revealed by the original instrument.

Practicing Sabermetrics

1. Hall of Fame sluggers Jimmie Foxx and Mickey Mantle had approximately the same number of home runs in a similar number of at-bats. Compare their career *ISO*, *PwrF* and *PwrA* measures, given the following information:

Player	AB	H	HR	TB	BA	SLG
Foxx	8134	2646	534	4956	.325	.609
Mantle	8102	2415	536	4511	.298	.557

[Answers: Foxx: *ISO* = 0.284, *PwrF F* = 1.874, *PwrA* = 0.391;
Mantle: *ISO* = 0.259, *PwrF* = 1.869, *PwrA* = 0.364.]

2. Two of baseball's current stars are Albert Pujols and Alex Rodriguez. Through the end of the 2007 season, each had compiled the following statistics:

Player	AB	H	HR	TB	BA	SLG
Pujols	4054	1346	282	2514	.332	.620
Rodriguez	7350	2250	518	4315	.306	.587

Determine their career *ISO*, *PwrF* and *PwrA* statistics.

[Answers: Pujols: *ISO* = 0.288, *PwrF* = 1.868, *PwrA* = 0.402;
Rodriguez: *ISO* = 0.281, *PwrF* = 1.918, *PwrA* = 0.377.]

3. In 1941, Joe DiMaggio of the Yankees hit safely in 56 consecutive

games, while Ted Williams of the Red Sox hit .406 for the season. Given the information below, find their seasonal *ISO*, *PwrF* and *PwrA* totals

Player	AB	H	HR	TB	BA	SLG
DiMaggio	541	193	30	348	.357	.643
Williams	456	185	37	335	.406	.735

[Answers: DiMaggio: *ISO* = 0.286, *PwrF* = 1.801, *PwrA* = 0.412;
     Williams: *ISO* = 0.329, *PwrF* = 1.810, *PwrA* = 0.487.]

4. Detroit Tiger Hall of Fame outfielder Harry Heilmann won four American League batting titles in the 1920s. Given the data below, determine his best year using the metrics of *ISO*, *PwrF* and *PwrA*.

Year	AB	H	HR	TB	BA	SLG
1921	602	237	19	365	.394	.606
1923	524	211	18	331	.403	.632
1925	573	225	13	326	.393	.569
1927	505	201	14	311	.398	.616

[Answers: 1921: *ISO* = 0.212, *PwrF* = 1.538, *PwrA* = 0.425;
     1923: *ISO* = 0.229, *PwrF* = 1.568, *PwrA* = 0.437;
     1925: *ISO* = 0.176, *PwrF* = 1.448, *PwrA* = 0.415;
     1927: *ISO* = 0.218, *PwrF* = 1.548, *PwrA* = 0.426.
Based on these three statistics, it would seem that Heilmann's 1923 season was the best of the four under consideration.]

5. The first two decades of the 1900s are sometimes referred to as the "Dead Ball Era." Two of the brightest stars during this time period were Ty Cobb and Honus Wagner, both charter members of the Hall of Fame. Find their career totals for *ISO*, *PwrF* and *PwrA*, using the information below.

Player	AB	H	HR	TB	BA	SLG
Cobb	11434	4189	117	5854	.366	.512
Wagner	10430	3415	101	4862	.327	.466

[Answers: Cobb: *ISO* = 0.146, *PwrF* = 1.399, *PwrA* = 0.377;
     Wagner: *ISO* = 0.139, *PwrF* = 1.425, *PwrA* = 0.337.
     Cobb's career *BA* of .366 is the highest ever recorded.]

6. All time hit leader Pete Rose and Ty Cobb (see the previous problem) are the only players in history to reach the 4000 hit plateau. Find Rose's

ISO, *PwrF* and *PwrA*, given the following data: *AB* = 14053, *H* = 4256, *HR* = 160, *TB* = 5752, *BA* = .303, *SLG* = .409.

[Answer: *ISO* = 0.106, *PwrF* = 1.350, *PwrA* = 0.314.]

    7. The famed $100,000 Infield of Connie Mack's Philadelphia A's was comprised of first baseman Stuffy McInnis, second baseman Eddie Collins, shortstop Jack Barry and third baseman Home Run Baker. Given their lifetime statistics below, solve for the unknowns *w*, *x*, *y*, and *z*.

Player	AB	H	HR	PwrA
McInnis	*w*	2405	20	0.310
Collins	9949	*x*	47	0.338
Barry	4146	1009	*y*	0.246
Baker	5984	1838	96	*z*

[Answers: *w* = 7822; *x* = 3315; *y* = 10; *z* = .323.]

    8. In 1980, third baseman and Hall of Famer Mike Schmidt a *PwrF* = 2.182 and an *ISO* = 0.338 for the World Champion Philadelphia Phillies. Find his seasonal *BA* and *SLG* marks.

[Answers: *BA* = .286; *SLG* = .624.]

    9. In 2007 Jimmy Rollins of the Phillies had a *PwrA* = 0.338 in 716 at-bats. Find his batting average for that year, given that he hit 30 home runs.

[Answer: *BA* = .296.]

    10. In 1924 Hall of Famer Rogers Hornsby batted .424 for the season. Given that he hit 25 home runs and had a slugging percentage of .696, find his seasonal totals for: a) hits; b) power average; c) power factor; and d) isolated power.

[Answers: a) *H* = 227; b) *PwrA* = 0.466; c) *PwrF* = 1.642; d) *ISO* = 0.272.]

    11. Five members of the 500 Home Run Club are Ernie Banks, Reggie Jackson, Eddie Mathews, Mel Ott and Frank Robinson. On the basis of the measures of *ISO*, *PwrF* and *PwrA*, determine which Hall of Famer in this group had the best power numbers, given the data below.

Player	AB	H	HR	TB	BA	SLG
Banks	9421	2583	512	4706	.274	.500
Jackson	9864	2584	563	4834	.262	.490
Mathews	8537	2315	512	4349	.271	.509
Ott	9456	2876	511	5041	.304	.533
Robinson	10006	2943	586	5373	.294	.537

[Answers: Banks: *ISO* = 0.226, *PwrF* = 1.825, *PwrA* = 0.329;
            Jackson: *ISO* = 0.228, *PwrF* = 1.870, *PwrA* = 0.319;
            Mathews: *ISO* = 0.238, *PwrF* = 1.878, *PwrA* = 0.331;
            Ott: *ISO* = 0.229, *PwrF* = 1.753, *PwrA* = 0.358.
            Robinson: *ISO* = 0.243, *PwrF* = 1.839, *PwrA* = 0.353.
Based on these three statistics, it would seem that Frank Robinson had the best power numbers.]

12. Harmon Killebrew was a powerful slugger and is a member of the Hall of Fame. His lifetime marks of 573 *HR* and 2086 *H* in 8147 *AB* gave him a career *PwrA* = .326 Using the three modifications of the *PA* metric discussed in Problem 14 of the Demonstrating Sabermetrics section, calculate $PwrA_1$, $PwrA_2$ and $PwrA_3$.

[Answers: $PwrA_1$ = 0.291; $PwrA_2$ = 0.132; $PwrA_3$ = 0.210.]

CHAPTER 17

Power-Speed Number

Introduction

When he introduced the statistic in the 1982 *The Bill James Baseball Abstract*, Bill James called the Power-Speed Number (*PSN*) a "freak show stat," one in which we learn nothing other than where names go on a list. However, it is an interesting way to rate a combination of accomplishments, where one must be equally adept at two disparate baseball skills, stealing bases and hitting home runs. The formula for *PSN* is very simple;

$$PSN = \frac{2 \times (HR \times SB)}{HR + SB}.$$

As stated above, one must be adept at both skills to score high in this statistic.

For example, in 1961, Tigers' Hall of Fame right fielder, Al Kaline, had 19 *HR* and 14 *SB*, for a $PSN = \dfrac{2 \times (HR \times SB)}{HR + SB} = \dfrac{2 \times (19 \times 14)}{19 + 14} = \dfrac{532}{33} = 16.12$.

However, Roger Maris, who hit 61 *HR* that same season, had a *PSN* of 0, because he had 0 *SB*, i.e., $PSN = \dfrac{2 \times (HR \times SB)}{HR + SB} = \dfrac{2 \times (61 \times 0)}{61 + 0} = \dfrac{0}{61} = 0$.

Similarly, in 1897, all-time great "Wee Willie" Keeler, had 239 hits for the legendary Baltimore Orioles of the National League, stealing 64 bases but hitting no home runs. Therefore, his $PSN = \dfrac{2 \times (HR \times SB)}{HR + SB} = \dfrac{2 \times (0 \times 64)}{0 + 64} = \dfrac{0}{64} = 0$. We will carry calculations to two decimal places, unless the *PSN* equals zero.

When the player has an equal number of homers and steals, the *PSN* is exactly that common value. For example, say a player has *N HR* and *N SB*.

His $PSN = \dfrac{2 \times (HR \times SB)}{HR + SB} = \dfrac{2 \times (N \times N)}{N + N} = \dfrac{2 \times N \times N}{2 \times N} = N$. Thus, Colorado

Rockies' Dante Bichette, with his 1996 marks of 31 *HR* and 31 *SB*, had a *PSN* of 31.

The informal measure of the ability of a player in both of these areas has become the "30–30" season, in which a player hits at least 30 *HR* and has at least 30 *SB*. The first such season was posted by Ken Williams of the American League St. Louis Browns in 1922, when he hit a league leading 39 home runs while stealing 37 bases. His $PSN = \dfrac{2 \times (HR \times SB)}{HR + SB} =$

$\dfrac{2 \times (39 \times 37)}{39 + 37} = \dfrac{2886}{76} = 37.97.$

The next "30–30" season did not occur until 1956 and 1957, when New York Giants great Willie Mays accomplished the feat in back-to-back seasons. He hit 35 home runs and stole 38 bases in 1957, for a $PSN = \dfrac{2 \times (HR \times SB)}{HR + SB}$

$= \dfrac{2 \times (35 \times 38)}{35 + 38} = \dfrac{2660}{73} = 36.44.$

However, in 1988, Jose Canseco became the first player to record a "40–40" season, or at least 40 *HR* and 40 *SB* in the same season. Canseco's numbers, 42 *HR* and 40 *SB* translate to $PSN = \dfrac{2 \times (HR \times SB)}{HR + SB} =$

$\dfrac{2 \times (42 \times 40)}{42 + 40} = \dfrac{3360}{82} = 40.98.$ As of this writing, there have been three other such notable seasons. No one has yet to have a "50–50" season.

In 1990, playing for Oakland, Rickey Henderson had a *PSN* that translated to a "30–30" season, even though he did not actually do so. His numbers of 28 homers and 65 successful swipes give a

$$PSN = \dfrac{2 \times (HR \times SB)}{HR + SB} = \dfrac{2 \times (28 \times 65)}{28 + 65} = \dfrac{3640}{93} = 39.14.$$

We will call this a "virtual 30–30" season.

There were two "legitimate 30–30 seasons" in the 1960s, five in the '70s, seven in the '80s, and twenty in the '90s, including four each in 1996 and 1997. Does that mean that players have become more talented than in the past? Let's investigate.

In 1908, Honus Wagner, the Pirates' Hall of Fame Shortstop, had 10 home runs and 53 stolen bases. His actual

$$PSN = \dfrac{2 \times (HR \times SB)}{HR + SB} = \dfrac{2 \times (10 \times 53)}{10 + 53} = \dfrac{1060}{63} = 16.83.$$

This seems unimpressive compared to other players we have discussed, but the National League in 1908 was an eight team league, with a total of 151 home runs and 1372 stolen bases. By comparison, the National League in 1997 had

2163 home runs and 1817 stolen bases, with seven of the fourteen teams exceeding the 151 homers of the entire league in 1908. Clearly, Wagner toiled in an environment where home runs were far rarer than in 1997. He hit roughly 6.6 percent of the NL's home runs in 1908. For a player in 1997 to do so, he would have had to hit around 143 home runs.

When the number of "30–30" seasons started to tick upward in the late 1980s and early 1990s, the *USA Baseball Weekly* developed a "Degree of Difficulty" for the "30–30" seasons. Let's use 1908 as the example. Since there were 151 *HR* and 8 teams, this translates to 18.875 *HR* per team. Each team has 9 batting slots, but since many pitchers are notoriously bad hitters, *USA Baseball Weekly* used 8.5 as the number of batting order slots per team. (In a league that uses a designated hitter, we would use 9 instead of 8.5). So, if we divide 18.875 by 8.5, we obtain 2.22, meaning an average slot in the batting order might be "expected" to produce 2.22 home runs in a season. Now, we are well aware of the fact that there are different baseball expectations for different batting order slots. We are talking about a naïve "mathematical expectation."

By a similar calculation, the expected number of stolen bases for a batting order slot in the National League in 1908 is $\dfrac{\left(\dfrac{1372}{8}\right)}{8.5} = 20.17$, or 20.17 *SB* per batting order slot.

Now we compute the "Degree of Difficulty" (*DOD*) for Wagner's season. If we divide his *HR* total by the expected total, we obtain $DOD - HR = \dfrac{\text{Player } HR}{\text{Expected } HR} = \dfrac{10}{2.22} = 4.5$, meaning Wagner had 4.5 times the average home runs for that season. His $DOD - SB = \dfrac{\text{Player } SB}{\text{Expected } SB} = \dfrac{53}{20.17} = 2.6$, or 2.6 times the average stolen bases for the season. We compute Wagner's total *DOD* for 1908 as $DOD = DOD - HR + DOD - SB = 4.5 + 2.6 = 7.1$.

The 14-team National League in 1996 had an Expected $HR = \dfrac{\left(\dfrac{2163}{14}\right)}{8.5} = 18.17$, and an Expected $SB = \dfrac{\left(\dfrac{1817}{14}\right)}{8.5} = 15.26$. Jeff Bagwell in 1996 slugged 43 home runs and stole 31 bases. His $PSN = \dfrac{2 \times (HR \times SB)}{HR + SB} = \dfrac{2 \times (43 \times 31)}{43 + 31} = \dfrac{2666}{74} = 36.03$, while his $DOD = DOD - HR + DOD - SB =$

$$\frac{\text{Player } HR}{\text{Expected } HR} + \frac{\text{Player } SB}{\text{Expected } SB} = \frac{43}{18.17} + \frac{31}{15.26} = 2.4 + 2.0 = 4.4.$$ Thus, by this measure, Wagner's season was a more difficult and impressive achievement than Bagwell's, when viewed in the context of the respective leagues in which they played.

Suppose the 1908 Wagner had played in 1996? If we apply his $DOD - HR$ and $DOD - SB$ numbers, we can see what he might have done in 1996. If we multiply his $DOD - HR$ by the Expected HR for 1996, we obtain 18.17 × 4.5 = 82 HR; similarly we obtain 15.26 × 2.6 = 40 SB. In 1996, Bagwell's numbers would have been the equivalent of hitting 2.22 × 2.4 = 5 HR and stealing 20.17 × 2.0 = 40 bases in 1908.

Note that these numbers have not been adjusted for ballparks.

Demonstrating Sabermetrics

1. In 1998, Shawn Green had a season of 35 HR and 35 SB. Find his PSN.
When SB and HR are equal, the PSN is that common number, so Green's PSN is 35.00.

2. In 1998, Alex Rodriguez had the highest totals in a "40–40" season with 42 HR and 46 SB. While not a "40–40" season, Rickey Henderson combined 28 HR and 87 SB for the Yankees in 1986. Find their respective PSNs.

Rodriguez: $PSN = \dfrac{2 \times (42 \times 46)}{42 + 46} = \dfrac{3864}{88} = 43.91.$

Henderson: $PSN = \dfrac{2 \times (HR \times SB)}{HR + SB} = \dfrac{2 \times (28 \times 87)}{28 + 87} = \dfrac{4872}{115} = 42.37.$

3. Willie Mays hit 660 HR and stole 338 bases in his career. Find his career PSN.

$$PSN = \frac{2 \times (HR \times SB)}{HR + SB} = \frac{2 \times (660 \times 338)}{660 + 338} = \frac{446{,}160}{998} = 447.05.$$

4. The late Bobby Bonds was the first player to have more than two "30–30" seasons. In fact, as of the end of the 2008 season, he was tied for the most such seasons in a career with five. Bill James joked that he considered renaming the stat as the "Bobby Bonds number." Determine which of his "30–30" seasons had the best PSN given the data below.

Season	HR	SB	Season	HR	SB
1969	32	45	1977	37	41
1973	39	43	1978	31	43
1975	32	30			

Using $PSN = \dfrac{2 \times (HR \times SB)}{HR + SB}$, we obtain the following values:

Season	HR	SB	PSN
1969	32	45	37.40
1973	39	43	40.90
1975	32	30	31.07
1977	37	41	38.90
1978	31	43	36.02

So, Bobby Bonds' best "30–30" season was 1973, when his $PSN = 40.9$, which is a "virtual 40–40" season.

5. Tied for the most "30–30" seasons in a career is Barry Bonds, Bobby's son. Determine which of his "30–30" seasons had the best PSN.

Season	HR	SB		Season	HR	SB
1990	33	52		1996	42	40
1992	34	39		1997	40	37
1995	33	31				

Using $PSN = \dfrac{2 \times (HR \times SB)}{HR + SB}$, we obtain the following values:

Season	HR	SB	PSN
1990	33	52	40.38
1992	34	39	36.33
1995	33	31	31.97
1996	42	40	40.98
1997	40	37	38.44

Barry's best season was his "40–40," but we note that he also had a "virtual 40–40" in 1990.

6. The most "30–30" seasons by someone not named Bonds is Alfonso Soriano, with four as of the end of the 2008 season. In 2006, he had 46 *HR* and 41 *SB*. Find his *PSN*.

Soriano's $PSN = \dfrac{2 \times (HR \times SB)}{HR + SB} = \dfrac{2 \times (46 \times 41)}{46 + 41} = \dfrac{3772}{87} = 43.36.$

7. In 1908, Red Murray of the St. Louis Cardinals and "Turkey" Mike Donlin of the New York Giants had seasons that, in their time, combined power and speed.

Find their respective *PSNs*.

	HR	*SB*
Murray	7	48
Donlin	6	30

Using $PSN = \dfrac{2 \times (HR \times SB)}{HR + SB}$, we obtain the following values:

	HR	*SB*	*PSN*
Murray	7	48	
Donlin	6	30	

8. Using the expected *HR* value from 1908 (2.22), find the *DOD – HR* for Murray and Donlin.

Murray: $\dfrac{\text{Player } HR}{\text{Expected } HR} = \dfrac{7}{2.22} = 3.15$.

Donlin: $\dfrac{\text{Player } HR}{\text{Expected } HR} = \dfrac{6}{2.22} = 2.70$.

9. Using the expected *SB* value from 1908 (20.18), find the *DOD – SB* for Murray and Donlin. Then use the answer to Problem 8 to compute their overall Degrees of Difficulty.

Murray: $DOD - SB = \dfrac{\text{Player } SB}{\text{Expected } SB} = \dfrac{48}{20.17} = 2.38$, and his $DOD = DOD - HR + DOD - SB = 3.15 + 2.38 = 5.53$.

Donlin: $DOD - SB = \dfrac{\text{Player } SB}{\text{Expected } SB} = \dfrac{30}{20.17} = 1.49$, and his $DOD = DOD - HR + DOD - SB = 2.70 + 1.49 = 4.19$.

10. Using the Expected *HR* = 18.17 for 1996, determine the projected 1996 home runs for Murray and Donlin.

Murray: 18.17 × 3.15 = 57 *HR*.

Donlin: 18.17 × 2.70 = 49 *HR*.

11. Using the Expected *SB* = 15.26 for 1996, determine the projected 1996 stolen bases for Murray and Donlin.

Murray: 15.26 × 2.38 = 36 *SB*.

Donlin: 15.26 × 1.49 = 23 *SB*.

12. Ellis Burks of the Colorado Rockies had 40 *HR* and 32 *SB*. Find his *PSN*.

Burks $PSN = \dfrac{2 \times (HR \times SB)}{HR + SB} = \dfrac{2 \times (40 \times 32)}{40 + 32} = \dfrac{2560}{72} = 35.56$.

13. Determine Burks' *DOD* for 1996.

$$DOD = DOD - HR + DOD - SB = \frac{\text{Player } HR}{\text{Expected } HR} + \frac{\text{Player } SB}{\text{Expected } SB}$$

$$= \frac{40}{18.17} + \frac{32}{15.26} = 2.2 + 2.1 = 4.3.$$

14. Determine Barry Bonds' career *PSN*.

$$\text{Bonds' } PSN = \frac{2 \times (HR \times SB)}{HR + SB} = \frac{2 \times (762 \times 514)}{762 + 514} = \frac{783,336}{1276} = 613.90.$$

This is a virtual "600–600" career.

Practicing Sabermetrics

1. In 1956, New York Giants great Willie Mays had 40 stolen bases, the highest total in the National League since 1929. He coupled that with 36 home runs. Find his *PSN*.

[Answer: *PSN* = 37.89.]

2. In 1956, the National League had 8 teams which clubbed a total of 1219 home runs. There was no designated hitter that year. Find the Expected *HR*.

[Answer: Expected *HR* = 17.9.]

3. The 8 NL teams in '56 had a total of 372 stolen bases. Find the Expected *SB*.

[Answer: Expected *SB* = 5.5.]

4. Continuing with 1956, find Mays' *DOD – HR*.

[Answer: *DOD – HR* = 2.0.]

5. Determine Mays' *DOD – SB* in 1956.

[Answer: *DOD-HR* = 7.3.]

6. Find Mays' *DOD* for his "30–30" season in 1956.

[Answer: *DOD* = 9.3.]

7. Determine the equivalence of Mays' 1956 *HR* and *SB* in 1908.

[Answers: 4 *HR* and 147 *SB*.]

8. Using the result of Problem 2 and the fact the he had *DOD–HR* = 4.5, find Honus Wagner's equivalent *HR* for 1956.

[Answer: *HR* = 81.]

9. Using the result of Problem 3 and the fact the he had *DOD – SB* =2.6, find Honus Wagner's equivalent *SB* for 1956.

[Answer: *HR* = 14.]

10. In 1958, Mickey Mantle had 42 home runs and 18 stolen bases. Determine his *PSN*.

[Answer: *PSN* = 25.20.]

11. Given that players in the American League hit 1057 home runs and stole 353 bases in 1958, find the Expected *HR* and Expected *SB*.

[Answers: *HR* per slot = 15.5; *SB* per slot = 5.2.]

12. Using the information in Problems 10 and 11, find the *DOD – HR* for Mickey Mantle in 1958.

[Answer: *DOD – HR* = 2.7.]

13. Again using the information in Problems 10 and 11, find the *DOD – SB* and *DOD* for Mantle in 1958.

[Answers: *DOD – SB* = 3.5; *DOD* = 6.2.]

14. Determine the 1908 equivalence for Mantle's 1958 *HR* and *SB* totals.

[Answers: 6 *HR*; 71 *SB*.]

15. Determine the 1958 equivalence for Wagner's 1908 *HR* and *SB*.

[Answers: 70 *HR*; 14 *SB*.]

16. Find Babe Ruth's *PSN* for 1920, when he hit 54 *HR* and had *14 SB*.

[Answer: *PSN* = 22.24.]

The next three questions are just for fun: find Babe Ruth's *DOD – HR* for 1920, when he hit 54 home runs in an eight-team league that combined for 369 *HR* with no designated hitter.

[Answer: *DOD – HR* = 10.0.]

17. The National League in 2001 (the year in which Barry Bonds hit 73 *HR*) had 2952 total *HR*. Find the Expected *HR*.

[Answer: Expected *HR* = 21.7.]

18. To what would Ruth's 1920 *HR* be equivalent in 2001?

[Answer: 217 *HR*. That's right — 217.]

CHAPTER 18

Range Factor

Introduction

In baseball, the most difficult thing to measure is fielding. There is a certain amount of subjectivity as to what constitutes a "good play" and there are many times when the Official Scorers change a hit to an error or an error to a hit.

The three main components of fielding statistics are Putouts (PO), Assists (A) and Errors (E). The sum of these three give a measure called the Total Chances (TC). The most common metric used in fielding is called Fielding Percentage ($FPCT$), which is defined as:

$$FPCT = \frac{PO+A}{TC} = \frac{PO+A}{PO+A+E}.$$

This statistic is discussed in Chapter 3. We usually express this fraction in decimal form, carried out to three decimal places. If there are no errors ($E = 0$), then $FLD = 1.000$.

In this chapter we define a statistic known as the Range Factor (RF) and define it as:

$$RF = \frac{TC}{G} - \frac{E}{G} = \frac{PO+A+E}{G} - \frac{E}{G} = \frac{PO+A}{G},$$

where G is the number of games played. By convention, we will carry out the decimal part of RF to two places. As we can see from the formula, the RF is a very easy measure to compute. For example, National League all star Keith Hernandez is arguably considered to be the finest defensive first baseman of his era (and perhaps of any era). In his career, he played in 2021 games, had 17,909 putouts and was credited with 1682 assists. So his lifetime range factor is calculated to be

$$RF = \frac{PO+A}{G} = \frac{17,909+1682}{2021} = 9.69.$$

In other words, based on this measure, Hernandez successfully handled 9.69 chances per game.

A better and truer measure of *RF* would be obtained if we could replace *G* by *I*, where *I* is the number of innings played, following by multiplying this fraction by a factor of 9 (as we do for earned run average (*ERA*); see Chapter 3). In this instance,

$$RF_i = 9\left(\frac{PO + A}{I}\right).$$

Note that we have subscripted this measure with an *i*. This version of the formula is be particularly helpful in the cases where defensive specialists are inserted into the latter parts of games for an inning or two. However, with the exception of the position of pitcher, the innings played statistics for the remaining eight positional players are difficult to obtain.

Because of this, we will be forced to use the first *RF* definition for the positional players. By the way, the expression, *PO + A*, taken as a sum, is often referred to as successful chances.

Let's illustrate the *RF* with the following example. Lefthander Bobby Shantz won the American League Most Valuable Player Award in 1952 when he posted a 24–7 won-loss record with the Philadelphia Athletics. He pitched in 33 games while logging 279⅔ innings. He was credited with 29 putouts and 49 assists. Using the basic *RF* formula for Shantz, we calculate

$$RF = \frac{PO + A}{G} = \frac{29 + 49}{33} = 2.36.$$

On the other hand, using the modified metric, we have

$$RF_i = 9\left(\frac{PO + A}{I}\right) = 9\left(\frac{29 + 49}{279\frac{2}{3}}\right) = 2.51.$$

Note the difference of 2.51 − 2.36 = 0.15 between these two measures. If we multiply the difference by the number of games in which Shantz appeared (33), we obtain 4.95. That is, the *RF*ᵢ measure accounts for *nearly five more successful chances* handled by Shantz during the 1952 season.

Demonstrating Sabermetrics

1. Over his career, Bobby Shantz (see Introduction to this chapter) pitched in 538 games, hurled 1935⅔ innings, participated in 175 putouts and amassed 468 assists. Using both formulas, compute his lifetime range factor.

The original formula gives $RF = \dfrac{PO+A}{G} = \dfrac{175+468}{538} = 1.20$. Regarding RF_i, our result is $RF_i = 9\left(\dfrac{PO+A}{I}\right) = 9\left(\dfrac{175+468}{1935\frac{2}{3}}\right) = 2.99$. The discrepancy in these numbers can be partially explained by the fact that Shantz appeared in many games as a reliever, as opposed to a starter, toward the latter part of his career. This would tend to lower the basic RF statistic.

2. Many fans believe southpaw Jim Kaat belongs in the Hall of Fame. He pitched in 898 games, had a won–loss record of 283–237, hurled 4530⅓ innings and amassed an earned run average of 3.45. He also recorded 744 assists while being credited for 262 putouts. As a pitcher, he won sixteen Gold Gloves, second only to Greg Maddux. Find his range factor using both formulas.

The basic RF formula yields $RF = \dfrac{PO+A}{G} = \dfrac{262+744}{898} = 1.12$. Using the RF_i formula, we obtain $RF_i = 9\left(\dfrac{PO+A}{I}\right) = 9\left(\dfrac{262+744}{4530\frac{1}{3}}\right) = 2.00$. Again there is a discrepancy between the two factors. This is partly due to Kaat's not pitching nine innings in every outing. This example illustrates how the RF_i measure is more accurate than the basic RF measure.

3. Given the following information, determine which Hall of Fame second sacker had the higher RF statistic:

Player	PO	A	G
Rogers Hornsby	3206	5166	1561
Ryne Sandberg	3807	6363	1995

For "the Rajah," we have $RF = \dfrac{PO+A}{G} = \dfrac{3206+5166}{1561} = 5.36$; in the case of Ryno, $RF = \dfrac{PO+A}{G} = \dfrac{3807+6363}{1995} = 5.10$. Hornsby tops Sandberg.

4. The outfield trio comprised by left fielder Duffy Lewis, center fielder Tris Speaker and right fielder Harry Hooper has been called the greatest defensive group to ever play the game. Find the career RF for each of these players, given the information below.

Player	PO	A	G
Lewis	2657	210	1432
Speaker	6788	449	2698
Hooper	3981	344	2285

For Duffy Lewis, $RF = \dfrac{PO+A}{G} = \dfrac{2657+210}{1432} = 2.00$, with Tris Speaker,

$RF = \dfrac{PO+A}{G} = \dfrac{6788+449}{2698} = 2.68$ and with Harry Hooper, we find that

$RF = \dfrac{PO+A}{G} = \dfrac{3981+344}{2285} = 1.89$.

5. Consider the data from Problem 4 again. Find the average *RF* for the Lewis-Speaker-Hooper outfield.

Summing the *PO* provides 2657 + 6788 + 3981 = 13,426; totaling the *A* yields 210 + 449 + 344 = 1003; and adding the *G* gives 1432 + 2698 + 2295 = 6514. Therefore, the average *RF* is given by $RF = \dfrac{13426+1003}{6514} = 2.25$.

This value of 2.25 has no real significance other than "averaging out" the three outfielders in question. A more interesting statistic would be the combined *RF*, which is the sum of the three individual *RF*s. The higher the sum, the better the defensive unit. See the next two problems.

6. Find the combined career *RF* of the Lewis-Speaker-Hooper outfield.

Summing the individual *RF*s, we have 2.00 + 2.68 + 1.89 = 6.57. Based on this measure, the outfield successfully handled 6.57 chances per game.

7. Compare the results of Problem 6 with the combined *RF* of the famed Yankees' outfield of the 1930s and 1940s, comprised of Charlie Keller, Joe DiMaggio and Tommy Henrich, given the following lifetime totals for each Bronx Bomber.

Player	*PO*	*A*	*G*
Keller	2235	46	1019
DiMaggio	4516	153	1721
Henrich	2008	96	1017

Computing the *RF* for Keller, $RF = \dfrac{13426+1003}{6514} = 2.25$; for DiMaggio, $RF = \dfrac{4516+153}{1721} = 2.71$; and for Henrich, $RF = \dfrac{2008+96}{1017} = 2.07$. Summing these three *RF* values gives RF = 7.02, which betters the Lewis-Speaker-Hooper outfield.

8. Three outfielder known for their strong throwing arms were Roberto Clemente of the Pirates, Jesse Barfield of the Blue Jays and Yankees and Rocky Colavito of the Indians and Tigers. Given the data below, compute the *RF* for each player.

Player	PO	A	G
Barfield	2951	162	1387
Clemente	4697	269	2373
Colavito	3407	124	1787

For the Blue Jays' Barfield, $RF = \dfrac{PO + A}{G} = \dfrac{2951 + 162}{1387} = 2.24$;

for Clemente, $RF = \dfrac{PO + A}{G} = \dfrac{4697 + 269}{2373} = 2.10$;

and for Colavito, $RF = \dfrac{PO + A}{G} = \dfrac{3407 + 124}{1787} = 1.98$.

    9. In his Hall of Fame career, Babe Ruth played 2241 games in the outfield, amassing 4444 putouts and 204 assists. As a pitcher, he hurled 1221⅓ innings in 163 games while being credited for 95 putouts and 354 assists. Find his RF as and outfielder and his RF and RF_i as a pitcher.

Regarding Ruth as an outfielder, $RF = \dfrac{PO + A}{G} = \dfrac{4444 + 204}{2241} = 2.07$.

His basic RF as a pitcher yields $RF = \dfrac{PO + A}{G} = \dfrac{95 + 354}{163} = 2.75$,

while his modified value becomes $RF_i = 9\left(\dfrac{PO + A}{I}\right) = 9\left(\dfrac{95 + 354}{1221⅓}\right) = 3.31$.

    10. In 1956 Detroit outfielder Al Kaline had a $RF = 2.36$. If he played in 153 games and was credited with 343 putouts, how many assists did he have that year?

Starting with $RF = 2.36 = \dfrac{PO + A}{G} = \dfrac{343 + A}{153}$, we solve for A finding $A = 18$.

    11. On July 10, 1910, writer Franklin P. Adams published a classic poem in the *New York Evening Mail*. While it is sometimes known as "Baseball's Sad Lexicon," it is usually called the "Tinker to Evers to Chance" poem, which immortalized the double play combination of the Chicago Cubs. The lesser known Cub which rounded out this infield, was third baseman Harry Steinfeldt. Given the career position statistics for each player below, solve for w, x, y and z.

Player	PO	A	G	RF
Chance	w	615	997	10.53
Evers	3758	x	1735	5.12
Tinker	3758	5848	y	5.11
Steinfeldt	1774	2799	1386	z

To solve for w, use Chance's statistics to obtain $RF = 10.53 = \dfrac{w + 615}{997}$; this provides $w = 9885$. Using Ever's numbers, we see that $RF = 5.12 = \dfrac{3758 + x}{1735}$, which leads to x = 5124. Next, for y, Tinker's stats give $RF = 5.11 = \dfrac{3758 + 5848}{y}$, so that $y = 1743$. Finding Steinfeldt's z is straight forward, as $z = RF = \dfrac{1774 + 2799}{1386} = 3.30$.

Practicing Sabermetrics

1. Given the career numbers for six Hall of Fame center fielders: Richie Ashburn, Earle Combs, Mickey Mantle, Willie Mays, Duke Snider and Robin Yount. Rank the players according to their *RF* scores.

Player	PO	A	G
Ashburn	6089	178	2104
Combs	3449	69	1387
Mantle	4438	117	2019
Mays	7095	195	2842
Snider	4099	123	1918
Yount	3056	52	1150

[Answers: Ashburn (2.98); Yount (2.70); Mays (2.57); Combs (2.54); Mantle (2.26); Snider (2.20).]

2. In the 1964 World Series, the opposing third basemen were brothers Clete Boyer of the Yankees and Ken Boyer of the Cardinals. Which one of the brothers had a higher *RF* for that year, given the information that Clete played in 123 games at the hot corner, had 118 putouts and assisted in 278 plays, while Ken play in all 162 games at third base while accumulating 131 putouts and 337 assists?

[Answer: Clete had the higher *RF* that year with 3.22; brother Ken had an *RF* of 2.89.]

3. Referring to Problem 2, which Boyer brother had the higher lifetime *RF*, given the following table:

Player	PO	A	G
Clete Boyer	1470	3218	1439
Ken Boyer	1567	3652	1785

[Answer: Clete again had the higher career *RF* with 3.26; Ken had a lifetime *RF* of 2.92.]

4. Rank the following shortstops with respect to *RF*. Both Ozzie Smith and Honus Wagner are already in the Hall of Fame. All Star Derek Jeter's statistics are valid through the 2007 season.

Player	PO	A	G
Jeter	2732	4667	1825
Smith	4249	8375	2511
Wagner	4576	6041	1887

[Answer: Wagner (5.63); Smith (5.03); Jeter (4.05).]

5. Rank the five third basemen below according to *RF*. Alex Rodriguez's stats are valid through the 2007 season. All the other players are enshrined in the Hall of Fame.

Player	PO	A	G
George Brett	1372	3674	1692
Brooks Robinson	2697	6205	2870
Alex Rodriguez	417	1062	621
Mike Schmidt	1591	5045	2212
Pie Traynor	2289	3521	1863

[Answer: Traynor (3.12); Robinson (3.10); Schmidt (3.00); Brett (2.98); Rodriguez (2.38).]

6. In his career, All Star Alex Rodriguez played in 1272 games as a shortstop. He was credited with 2014 putouts, while assisting in 3604 plays. How does his *RF* compare with that of Hall of Famer Ernie Banks, who played in 1125 games as a shortstop, made 2087 putouts and amassed 3441 assists.

[Answer: Rodriguez's *RF* is 4.42; Banks' *RF* is 4.91.]

7. Given below are career statistics for three Hall of Fame catchers: Johnny Bench, Yogi Berra and Al Lopez. Also listed are the career statistics, through the 2007 season, of All Star backstop Ivan Rodriguez. Solve for the values of *w*, *x*, *y* and *z*.

Player	PO	A	G	RF
Bench	*w*	850	1742	5.80
Berra	8738	*x*	1699	5.61
Lopez	6644	1115	*y*	4.05
Rodriguez	12510	1039	2061	*z*

[Answers: w = 9246; x = 798; y = 1918; z = 6.57.]

8. In his Major League career, Hall of Famer Satchel Paige had a RF_i = 1.49 while totaling 17 putouts and 62 assists. How many innings did Paige total for his career?

[Answer: Paige totaled 476 innings.]

9. Many baseball experts consider Lefty Grove to be one of the greatest pitchers ever. Find the total number of plays in which he assisted if his career statistics show that he had 65 putouts, pitched in 3940⅔ innings and had a lifetime RF_i = 1.80.

[Answer: Grove had 722 assists in his career.]

10. Find the values of p, q, r, s and t in the following table which contains seasonal pitching data for five Hall of Fame hurlers:

Player	PO	A	G	IP	RF_i
Whitey Ford (1961)	45	12	39	p	1.81
Sandy Koufax (1963)	4	q	40	311	1.10
Bob Gibson (1965)	27	33	38	299	r
Juan Marichal (1968)	s	64	38	326	2.68
Jim Palmer (1970)	42	21	t	305	1.86

[Answers: p = 283; q = 34; r = 1.81; s = 33; t = 39.]

11. Given the information below, compute the individual RFs for each of the fifteen players comprising the follow infields (including the catching position): Brooklyn Dodgers of the 1950s, the Los Angeles Dodgers of the 1960s and the Los Angeles Dodgers of the 1970s. Which era Dodger team had the higher combined *RF* value?

1950s Dodgers	PO	A	G
Roy Campanella	6520	550	1183
Gil Hodges	15344	1281	1908
Jackie Robinson	1877	2047	748
Pee Wee Reese	4040	5891	2014
Billy Cox	668	1273	700

1960s Dodgers	PO	A	G
Johnny Roseboro	9291	675	1476
Wes Parker	9640	695	1108
Jim Lefebvre	1305	1612	613
Maury Wills	2550	4804	1555
Jim Gilliam	533	1265	761

1970s Dodgers	*PO*	*A*	*G*
Steve Yeager	6110	674	1230
Steve Garvey	18844	1026	2059
Davey Lopes	3142	3829	1418
Bill Russell	2536	5546	1746
Ron Cey	1500	4018	1989

[Answers: 1950s Dodgers: Campanella (5.98); Hodges (8.71); Robinson (5.25); Reese (4.93); Cox (2.77); 1950s Dodgers Combined (27.64);

1960s Dodgers: Roseboro (6.75); Parker (9.33); Lefebvre (4.76); Wills (4.73); Gilliam (2.36); 1960s Dodgers Combined (27.93);

1970s Dodgers: Yeager (5.52); Garvey (9.65); Lopes (4.92); Russell (4.63); Cey (2.77) 1970s Dodgers Combined (27.49).]

CHAPTER 19

Hoban Effectiveness Quotient

Introduction

A professor of mathematics (as well as dean) at Monmouth University in New Jersey, Michael Hoban, was looking to develop a simple additive formula to evaluate a player's sustained performance over time. He called his formula the Hoban Effectiveness Quotient for Offense (*HEQ-O*) and defined it as $HEQ\text{-}O = TB + R + RBI + SB + 0.5 \times BB$.

Hoban states that the formula is constructed in such a way so that an *HEQ-O* of 600 represents an outstanding year with the bat. When evaluating players' careers, he takes the average of the players' 10 best seasons of *HEQ-O*. In this way, he is measuring consistency of a player's level of achievement over time. The beauty of the formula lay in its simplicity; it is measure of how involved a player is in the offense or defense.

Consider Houston Astros great and former Seton Hall University standout Craig Biggio. In 1999, he was primarily a second baseman, putting up the following numbers:

R	RBI	SB	BB	TB
123	73	28	88	292

We calculate his *HEQ-O* to be $HEQ\text{-}O = TB + R + RBI + SB + 0.5 \times BB = 292 + 123 + 73 + 28 + 0.5 \times 88 = 560.0$.

His Astros teammate and infield partner, Jeff Bagwell, was a different kind of hitter. In the same season, Bagwell's numbers were

R	RBI	SB	BB	TB
143	126	30	149	332

which gives an $HEQ\text{-}O = TB + R + RBI + SB + 0.5 \times BB = 332 + 143 + 126 + 149 + 0.5 \times 149 = 705.5$.

A statistic such as $HEQ\text{-}O$ can put players like Biggio and Bagwell on a more equal plane, so that they can still be compared in a statistic that seems not to favor one type of hitter over another, as many offensive statistics tend to do. Biggio's game was more of a speedster's type, while Bagwell was a prototypical power-hitting first baseman.

While the $HEQ\text{-}O$ is not recommended as a measure to compare people from different seasons, it is still enlightening within a season. Suppose we want to introduce an element of relativity to the measure; let's say we want to come up with a way to see how well the player's $HEQ\text{-}O$ stacks up with the league's value. Continuing with the 1999 season, the National League in as a whole put up these numbers:

R	SB	BB	H	2B	3B	HR
12966	1959	9602	23880	4619	512	2893

The *RBI* numbers are not readily available for the league. Bear in mind that using runs scored (*R*) in place of *RBI* is not recommended, as there are many runs scored in a season for which no one receives credit for a run batted in. Therefore, we must look up each NL team's *RBI* total for 1999. Those numbers are provided here:

ARI	COL	SFG	CIN	NYM	ATL	PHI	HOU
865	863	828	820	814	791	797	784

MIL	STL	LAD	PIT	CHI	MON	SDP	FLA
777	STL	761	735	717	680	671	655

These sum up to a palindromic 12,321 *RBI* for the National league in 1999. It seems as though there are 35 to 45 runs per team not accounted for by *RBI*, so we could subtract 40 runs per team from the runs scored and get a decent estimate of *RBI* should the totals not be available. We also need to calculate the total bases, *TB*, which we obtain by $TB = H + 2B + (2 \times 3B) + (3 \times HR) = 23880 + 4619 + (2 \times 512) + (3 \times 2893) = 38,202$.

Putting this all together, the National League in 1999 had an $HEQ\text{-}O = TB + R + RBI + SB + 0.5 \times BB = 38202 + 12966 + 12321 + 1959 + 4601 = 70,249$. Then, using a technique presented in Chapter 17, we can estimate the $HEQ\text{-}O$ for any slot in the batting order by dividing by the number of teams in the league (16 for the NL in 1999) and then divide by the number of batting order slots (8.5 for this, a non–DH league, 9 otherwise).

Thus, we have $\dfrac{\left(\dfrac{70249}{16}\right)}{8.5} = 516.5$ per batting order slot. Recalling that

Jeff Bagwell had an *HEQ-O* = 705.5, his *relative HEQ-O* = $\dfrac{705.5}{516.5} = 1.37$, or 37 percent better than the average player. For Craig Biggio, his *relative HEQ-O* = $\dfrac{560}{516.5} = 1.08$, or 8 percent better than the average player.

Obviously, relativity works both ways. The late Ken Caminiti, on the downside of his career, put up the following offensive numbers in 1999:

R	RBI	SB	BB	TB
45	56	6	46	130

in 73 games as the Astros' third baseman that year. His *HEQ-O* = *TB* + *R* + *RBI* + *SB* + 0.5 × *BB* = 130 + 45 + 56 + 6 + 23 = 260. His *relative HEQ-O* = $\dfrac{260}{516.5}$, which rounds to about 0.50, or 50 percent of an average player in 1999.

HEQ-Defense

The defensive formula for HEQ is a bit more complicated, but it still is relatively easy to use. The fact is that, despite the disfavor into which fielding percentage has fallen among baseball researchers, there are not many ways to quantify defense.

Just like the *HEQ-O* formula, *HEQ-D* reflects the quantity of positive defensive plays. It includes a different weighted sum for each defensive position, involving *PO* (putouts), *A* (assists), *E* (errors) and *DP* (double plays). In addition, there is a Position Multiplication Factor (*PMF*) that adjusts the numbers in such a way that a season of 400 is considered outstanding. Pitchers are not measured using this statistic.

Here are the *HEQ-D* formulas by position:

C: (*PO* + 3 *A* + 2 *DP* – 2 *E*) – 0.445

[Note: 0.445 is the *PMF*, and *PO* are capped at 800.]

1B: (0.25 *PO* + 3 *A* + *DP* – 2 *E*) – 0.51

[Note: 0.51 is the *PMF*.]

2B, 3B, SS: $(PO + A + DP - 2\ E) - PMF$
[Note: $PMF_{2B} = 0.46$, $PMF_{SS} = 0.548$, and $PMF_{3B} = 0.888$.]

OF: $(PO + 4\ A + 4\ DP - 2\ E) - 1$
[Note: There is no *PMF* for OF.]

As an example, in 1999, Craig Biggio was almost exclusively a second baseman. His defensive stats at 2B were:

PO	A	E	DP	PMF
359	430	12	117	0.46

Therefore, his *HEQ-D* for 1999 is $HEQ\text{-}D = (PO + A + DP - 2\ E) - 0.46 = (359 + 430 + 117 - (2 \times 12)) - 0.46 = 405.7$, which is considered a fine defensive season.

In Hoban's analysis, the *HEQ-O* and *HEQ-D* are added together to obtain *HEQ-T,* or total *HEQ*. A player's 10 best *HEQ-T* are averaged to obtain the *PCT* (Player Career Total). Ten seasons are chosen because Hall of Fame candidates need to have played for 10 years. A *PCT* of 830 seems to be the boundary line for Hall of Fame induction. We will examine Don Mattingly's Hall of Fame credentials using this metric in the Practicing Sabermetrics section at the end of this chapter.

Biggio in 1999 had $HEQ\text{-}T = HEQ\text{-}O + HEQ\text{-}D = 560 + 405.7 = 965.7$, an excellent season, but just shy of the 1000 threshold for excellence. Meanwhile, Jeff Bagwell played first base fro the Astros. His 1999 numbers were:

PO	A	E	DP	PMF
1336	107	8	141	0.51

We remark that the *HEQ-D* formula displays the conventional wisdom that *PO* for the first baseman mostly come about because of routine throws from other infielders. In fact, only one-fourth of the *PO* are counted. Bagwell's *HEQ-D* is $HEQ\text{-}D = (0.25\ PO + 3\ A + DP - 2\ E) - 0.51 = (0.25 \times 1336 + 3 \times 107 + 141 - 2 \times 8) - 0.51 = 397.8$, giving him an excellent all-around $HEQ\text{-}T = HEQ\text{-}O + HEQ\text{-}D = 705.5 + 397.8 = 1103.3$.

In 1991, Biggio was a catcher. His defensive stats line for that season reads:

PO	A	E	DP	PMF
889	64	10	10	0.445

and noting that Hoban caps catchers' putouts at 800, because catchers are credited with a *PO* whenever they hold onto the third strike in a strikeout. His *HEQ-D* for that year is $HEQ\text{-}D = (PO + 3\,A + 2\,DP - 2\,E) - 0.445 = (800 + 3 \times 64 + 2 \times 10 - 2 \times 10) \times 0.445 = 441.4$.

However, by 2003, Biggio was primarily a centerfielder for Houston. In 150 games that year, he had the following statistics:

PO	A	E	DP	PMF
326	9	1	1	1*

*There is no PMF for outfielders. His *HEQ-D* for 2003 was $HEQ\text{-}D = (PO + 4\,A + 4\,DP - 2\,E) = (326 + 4 \times 9 + 4 \times 1 - 2 \times 1) = 364.0$.

Demonstrating Sabermetrics

1. Using his stat line, calculate Willie Mays' *HEQ-O* for 1962.

Year	R	RBI	SB	BB	TB
1962	130	141	18	78	382

$HEQ\text{-}O = TB + R + RBI + SB + 0.5 \times BB = 382 + 130 + 141 + 18 + 0.5 \times 78 = 710$.

2. Using his stat line, calculate Maury Wills' *HEQ-O* for 1962.

Year	R	RBI	SB	BB	TB
1962	130	48	104	51	259

$HEQ\text{-}O = TB + R + RBI + SB + 0.5 \times BB = 259 + 130 + 48 + 104 + 0.5 \times 51 = 566.5$.

3. Using his stat line, calculate Willie Mays' *HEQ-D* for 1962. He played in the Giants' outfield.

PO	A	E	DP	PMF
425	6	4	1	1*

*There is no PMF for outfielders.

$HEQ\text{-}D = PO + 4\,A + 4\,DP - 2\,E = 425 + 4 \times 6 + 4 \times 1 - 2 \times 4 = 445$.

4. Using his stat line, calculate Maury Wills' *HEQ-D* for 1962. He played shortstop.

PO	A	E	DP	PMF
295	493	36	86	0.548

HEQ-D = $(PO + A + DP - 2\ E) - 0.548$ = $(295 + 493 + 86 - (2 \times 36))$ $- 0.548$ = 439.5.

5. Compute Mays' and Wills' *HEQ-T* for 1962.

Wills HEQ-T = $566.5 + 439.5 = 1006$.

Mays HEQ-T = $710 + 445 = 1155$.

As discussed in Chapter 13, Wills won the MVP Award that year, and Mays finished a close second. Both had outstanding seasons by the *HEQ* measure.

6. Using his stat line, calculate Mike Piazza's *HEQ-O* for 1999.

Year	R	RBI	SB	BB	TB
1999	100	124	2	51	307

HEQ-O = $TB + R + RBI + SB + 0.5 \times BB$ = $307 + 100 + 124 + 2 + 0.5 \times 51 = 558.5$.

7. Using the data in the Introduction section of this chapter, find Mike Piazza's *relative HEQ-O*

Relative HEQ-O = $\dfrac{558.5}{516.5}$ = 1.08, or 8 percent better than the average player.

8. Using his stat line, calculate Mike Piazza's *HEQ-D* for 1999. He played as catcher.

PO	A	E	DP	PMF
953	47	11	5	0.445

HEQ-D = $(PO + 3\ A + 2\ DP - 2\ E) \times 0.445$ = $(800 + 3 \times 47 + 2 \times 5 - 2 \times 11) \times 0.445$ = 413.4.

9. Compute Piazza's *HEQ-T* for 1999.

HEQ-T = $558.5 + 413.4 = 971.9$.

10. Discussions of defense at third base begin and end with Baltimore Orioles Hall of Famer Brooks Robinson. Find his *HEQ-D* for 1967 given his numbers:

PO	A	E	DP	PMF
147	405	11	37	0.888

$$HEQ\text{-}D = (PO + A + DP - 2\ E) \times P \times 0.888 = (147 + 405 + 37 - 2 \times 11)$$
$$\times\ 0.888 = 503.5.$$

Practicing Sabermetrics

In this section, we will examine the case for Don Mattingly as a Hall of Fame candidate. We will calculate his *HEQ-T* for the twelve seasons in which he had more than 300 *AB*. Then, we will select the 10 best and compute his *PCT*. There are fewer numbered problems in this section than usual, but each problem requires multiple calculations.

Here are the seasonal numbers for Mattingly:

Year	R	RBI	SB	BB	TB	PO	A	E	DP
1984	91	110	1	41	324	1107	124	5	135
1985	107	145	2	56	370	1318	87	7	154
1986	117	113	0	53	388	1377	100	6	132
1987	93	115	1	51	318	1239	91	5	122
1988	94	88	1	41	277	1250	99	9	131
1989	79	113	3	51	301	1274	87	7	143
1990	40	42	1	28	132	800	78	3	81
1991	64	68	2	46	231	1119	77	5	135
1992	89	86	3	39	266	1209	116	4	129
1993	78	86	0	61	236	1258	84	3	123
1994	62	51	0	60	153	919	68	2	95
1995	59	49	0	40	189	996	81	7	90

1. Compute Mattingly's *HEQ-O* and *HEQ-D* for the 1984–1995 seasons. He was a first baseman.

[Answers:]

Year	HEQ-O	HEQ-D
1984	546.5	394.6
1985	652.0	372.6
1986	644.5	389.8
1987	552.5	354.3
1988	480.5	368.5
1989	521.5	361.3
1990	129.0	259.6
1991	388.0	324.2
1992	463.5	393.3
1993	430.5	348.6
1994	296.0	267.6
1995	317.0	289.7

2. Find Mattingly's *HEQ-T* for those seasons.

[Answers:]

Year	HEQ-O	HEQ-D	HEQ-T
1984	546.5	394.6	941.1
1985	652.0	372.6	1024.6
1986	644.5	389.8	1034.3
1987	552.5	354.3	906.8
1988	480.5	368.5	849.0
1989	521.5	361.3	882.8
1990	129.0	259.6	388.6
1991	388.0	324.2	712.2
1992	463.5	393.3	856.8
1993	430.5	348.6	779.1
1994	296.0	267.6	563.6
1995	317.0	289.7	606.7

3. Select Mattingly's 10 highest seasons of *HEQ-T*.

[Answers:]

Year	R	RBI	SB	BB	TB	PO
1986	117	113	0	53	388	1377
1985	107	145	2	56	370	1318
1984	91	110	1	41	324	1107
1987	93	115	1	51	318	1239
1989	79	113	3	51	301	1274
1992	89	86	3	39	266	1209
1988	94	88	1	41	277	1250
1993	78	86	0	61	236	1258
1991	64	68	2	46	231	1119
1995	59	49	0	40	189	996

Year	A	E	DP	HEQ-O	HEQ-D	HEQ-T
1986	100	6	132	644.5	389.8	1034.3
1985	87	7	154	652.0	372.6	1024.6
1984	124	5	135	546.5	394.6	941.1
1987	91	5	122	552.5	354.3	906.8
1989	87	7	143	521.5	361.3	882.8
1992	116	4	129	463.5	393.3	856.8
1988	99	9	131	480.5	368.5	849.0
1993	84	3	123	430.5	348.6	779.1
1991	77	5	135	388.0	324.2	712.2
1995	81	7	90	317.0	289.7	606.7

4. Find the average *HEQ-T* for these 10 seasons. Does he meet the 830 threshold?

[Answer: $PCT = \dfrac{8593.4}{10} = 859.3$, so he exceeds the criterion of *PCT* greater than 830 for the Hall of Fame.]

CHAPTER 20

Equivalence Coefficient

Introduction

The *Equivalence Coefficient* (*EC*) is an instrument which can be used in both predicting results and in attempting to answer questions like "What might have been if...?" For example, Red Sox outfielder Ted Williams had a career which spanned from 1939 through 1960. Yet, because of military duty, both in World War II and the Korean Conflict, he lost nearly five years of playing time. Dodger lefthander Sandy Koufax's career was cut short by a chronic problem with his pitching arm. Both players are in the Hall of Fame, but we can ponder as to what their records might have been, had they been able to have careers which were uninterrupted.

The equivalence coefficient for cumulative hitting statistics, such as home runs (*HR*), is given by the formula

$$EC = 1 + \frac{\Delta AB}{AB}(k),$$

where *AB* is the number of career at-bats, ΔAB is the number of additional at-bats, and *k* is a special factor, sometimes called a *kicker*. This factor reflects the assumption that the batter may have been "better" (*k* > 1), "as good as" (*k* = 1) or "worse" (*k* < 1) for these additional at-bats. We usually, though not always, express the kicker to the nearest hundredth.

The number *EC*, which we define as the *equivalence coefficient*, is multiplied by the actual cumulative total (for example, 521 career home runs for Ted Williams) to give a predicted new home run total, based on the additional number of at-bats and the value of the kicker. We generally compute the *EC* to four decimal places. We usually assume a number for the ΔAB figure, based on the career of the player and how it was impacted by injuries or other factors.

A word of caution, though. This approach only works for *cumulative* measures. If we wanted to predict statistics dealing with *averages*, we would have to determine each constituent term, and then apply the definition. For example, if we wanted to predict batting average, we would determine the new number of hits and divide that number by the new at-bat total. In other words, a player's career batting average is not the average of his seasonal averages, unless he happens to have the exact same number of at bats in each season.

The equivalence coefficient metric for pitchers' earned-run average (*ERA*) is given by,

$$ERA = (9)\frac{ER + \Delta ER}{IP + \Delta IP(k)},$$

where *ER* is the number of earned runs allowed, ΔER is the additional number of earned runs allowed, *IP* is the number of innings pitched, ΔIP is the additional number of innings pitched, and *k* is, as before, a kicker. As was the case with the cumulative hitting statistics above, this kicker reflects the assumption that the pitcher may have been "better" (*k* > *1*), "as good" (*k* = *1*) or "worse" (*k* < *1*) for these additional innings pitched. We note that this formula yields the predicted *ERA*; no further mathematical manipulations are needed. Here, too, we assume the ΔIP figure, based on the length of the pitcher's career. We obtain the ΔER number by using an interpolation approach (see the Demonstrating Sabermetrics section, Problem 10).

Demonstrating Sabermetrics

1. Hall of Famer Ted Williams had 7706 at-bats (*AB*) in his career. Find his equivalence coefficient if we assume that he would have had 2500 additional at-bats, and he would have been 3 percent better for those at-bats.

Since, we have *AB* = 7706, ΔAB = 2500, *k* = 1.03, we have

$$EC = 1 + \frac{\Delta AB}{AB}(k) = 1 + \frac{2500}{7706}(1.03) = 1.3342.$$

2. Use the results in Problem 1 to predict Ted Williams' career home run (*HR*) total.

Since Williams hit 521 career home runs, his predicted total is 521 × 1.3342 = 695.

3. Based on the assumptions in Problem 1, what would Ted Williams' lifetime batting average (*BA*) of .344 become, given the fact that he accumulated 2654 hits (*H*) in his career?

His at-bat total would be 7706 + 2500 = 10206. His predicted hit total becomes 2654 (1.3342) = 3541. Therefore, since

$$BA = \frac{H}{AB} = \frac{3541}{10206} = .347.$$

4. Ted Williams' lifetime slugging percentage (*SLG*) of .634 is the second highest ever, trailing only Hall of Famer Babe Ruth's career mark of .690. Given that Williams accumulated 4884 total bases (*TB*), predict his slugging percentage based on the assumptions above.

Slugging percentage is defined as the number of total bases accumulated (*TB*) divided by *AB*. Therefore, since $SLG = \dfrac{TB}{AB} = \dfrac{TB}{10206}$, we have to determine his career total base number. Using the equivalence coefficient, we find that $TB = 4884\,(1.3342) = 6516$. Hence, $SLG = \dfrac{6516}{10206} = .638$.

5. Find the kicker needed for Ted Williams to have an equivalence coefficient of 1.4000, given $\Delta AB = 2500$.

Since $EC = 1 + \dfrac{\Delta AB}{AB}(k) = 1 + \dfrac{2500}{7706}(k) = 1.4000$ implies that $k = 1.23$. This means that Williams would have been 23 percent better.

6. Babe Ruth slugged 714 home runs in 8398 at-bats. Given a new career at-bat total of 10,000, predict his career home run figure if he played at a 3 percent decrease for the additional at-bats.

The kicker is 0.97 because we are assuming that Ruth would have been on a 3 percent decline. The additional number of at-bats, ΔAB is 10000 – 8398 = 1602. Therefore, the $EC = 1 + \dfrac{1602}{8398}(0.97) = 1.1852$. Hence, Ruth's predicted *HR* total is 714 (1.1852) = 846.

7. In his career, Babe Ruth drove in 2217 runs (*RBI*). How many *RBI* would he have totaled, based on the *EC* determined in Problem 6?

Since the *EC* = 1.1852, Ruth would have amassed 2217 (1.1852) = 2628 RBI.

8. Slugger Jimmie Foxx clubbed 534 home runs in 8134 at-bats. Find the value of the kicker which would have enabled him to reach 700 home runs with 2000 additional at-bats.

We want to solve the equation $700 = 534\left(1 + \dfrac{\Delta AB}{AB}(k)\right) = 534\left(1 + \dfrac{2000}{8134}(k)\right)$. This implies that $k = 1.26$.

9. Hall of Fame outfielder Ralph Kiner hit 369 career home runs in 5205 at-bats. Find the value of k which would be required for Kiner to raise his career *HR* total to 500, given an additional 1000 at-bats.

Since $EC = 1 + \dfrac{\Delta AB}{AB}(k)$, with $\Delta AB = 1000$, we want to find k such that $500 = 369\left(1 + \dfrac{1000}{5205}(k)\right)$. Solving for k yields $k = 1.85$.

10. During his pitching days, Babe Ruth hurled 1221⅓ innings (*IP*) in his career, while surrendering 309 earned runs (*ER*), giving him an earned run average (*ERA*) of 2.28. Recall that $ERA = \dfrac{9(ER)}{IP}$. If we assume Ruth had pitched an additional 1500 innings (Δ*IP*), and was a 4 percent better pitcher for these additional innings, predict his career earned-run average.

Since Δ*IP* = 1500, we obtain Δ*ER* as follows: $\dfrac{ER}{IP} = \dfrac{ER + \Delta ER}{IP + \Delta IP}$. This implies $\dfrac{309}{1221\frac{1}{3}} = \dfrac{309 + \Delta ER}{1221\frac{1}{3} + 1500}$, which gives us Δ*ER* = 380 (rounded off to the the nearest run). Note that this approach which enables one to determine the additional number of earned runs is called *interpolation*. Therefore, because Ruth's kicker is 1.04, his predicted *ERA* is lowered to

$$(9)\frac{ER + \Delta ER}{IP + \Delta IP(k)} = (9)\frac{309 + 380}{1221\frac{1}{3}. + 1500(1.04)} = 2.23.$$

11. Given the following totals for Hall of Fame pitchers, predict their earned run averages if they pitched 1000 additional innings and were assumed to be 2.5 percent better.

Dizzy Dean: *IP* = 1967⅓, *ER* = 661, *ERA* = 3.02, *k* = 1.025
Sandy Koufax: *IP* = 2324⅓, *ER* = 713, *ERA* = 2.76, *k* = 1.025

We must compute Δ*ER* for both pitchers. Following the technique used in Problem 9, we find that Δ*ER* = 336 for Dean, while Δ*ER* = 307, where both figures are rounded off to the nearest run. Therefore, Dean's predicted *ERA* becomes $(9)\dfrac{661 + 336}{1967\frac{1}{3} + 1000(1.025)} = 3.00$, and the corresponding figure for Koufax is $(9)\dfrac{713 + 307}{2324\frac{1}{3} + 1000(1.025)} = 2.74$.

12. Using the information from Problem 10, what would be the value of Sandy Koufax's kicker to reduce lifetime his earned run average to 2.65?

Since $ERA = (9)\dfrac{ER + \Delta ER}{IP + \Delta IP(k)}$, we substitute our values to get $2.65 = (9)\dfrac{713 + 307}{2324\frac{1}{3} + 1000(k)}$, which yields *k* = 1.14. This means that Koufax would have had to be 14 percent better for the 1000 additional innings pitched.

13. All Star Pete Rose batted 14,053 times and accumulated 4256 hits, giving him a lifetime batting average of .303. Using the *EC*, project Rose's hit total and his batting average, assuming 800 additional at-bats and performing at a decreased rate of 6 percent.

The value of the kicker, *k*, is 0.94. Since *AB* = 14,053 and Δ*AB* = 800, the equivalence coefficient becomes $EC = 1 + \dfrac{\Delta AB}{AB}(k) = 1 + \dfrac{800}{14,053}(0.94) =$ 1.0535. So the projected number of career hits for Rose is (1.0535) (14,053) = 4484 and the projected batting average is $\dfrac{4484}{14053 + 800} = .302$.

Practicing Sabermetrics

1. Compute the equivalence coefficient (to four decimal places) for the following players, with the given assumptions.

Player	AB	H	HR	ΔAB	k
Lou Gehrig	8001	2721	493	2000	0.98
Hank Greenberg	5193	1628	331	3500	1.02
Joe Jackson	4981	1772	54	4000	1.03
Don Mattingly	7003	2153	222	2500	0.96
Dale Murphy	7960	2111	398	2000	0.94

[Answers: Gehrig (1.2450); Greenberg (1.6875); Jackson (1.8271); Mattingly (1.3427); Murphy (1.2362).]

2. Using the answers to Problem 1, project the number of hits (*H*) for each player.

[Answers: Gehrig (3388); Greenberg (2747); Jackson (3238); Mattingly (2891); Murphy (2610).]

3. Referring to Problems 1 and 2, project the batting averages (*BA*) for each player.

[Answers: Gehrig (.339); Greenberg (.316); Jackson (.360); Mattingly (.304); Murphy (.262).]

4. Given the information in Problem 1, find the value of the kicker for the following situations:
    a. Lou Gehrig would hit 650 *HR*;
    b. Hank Greenberg would hit 650 *HR*;
    c. Joe Jackson would hit 150 *HR*;
    d. Don Mattingly would hit 300 *HR*;
    e. Dale Murphy would hit 525 *HR*.

[Answers: Gehrig (1.2740); Greenberg (1.4300); Jackson (2.2139); Mattingly (0.9842); Murphy (1.2700).]

5. Consider the following statistics (through 2007) for All Stars Albert Pujols and Alex Rodriguez, with the respective assumptions:

	AB	*HR*	*TB*	*ΔAB*	*k*
Pujols	4054	282	2541	5000	1.02
Rodriguez	7350	518	4251	2700	0.99

Find the *EC* for each player and use it to predict their *TB*, *SLG* and *HR* totals.

[Answers: Pujols: *EC* = 2.2580, *TB* = 5738, *SLG* = .634, *HR* = 637;
Rodriguez: *EC* = 1.3637, *TB* = 5797, *SLG* = .577, *HR* = 706.]

6. Predict the additional earned runs (*ΔER*) and career earned run average (*ERA*) for the following pitchers, with the given assumptions.

	IP	*ER*	*ΔIP*	*k*
Don Drysdale	3432	1124	800	0.97
Whitey Ford	3170⅓	967	1000	1.02
Ron Guidry	2392	874	1500	1.03
Juan Marichal	3507⅓	1126	500	0.96
Carl Mays	3021⅓	979	1000	0.98

[Answers: Drysdale: *ΔER* = 262 and *ERA* = 2.91
Ford: *ΔER* = 305 and *ERA* = 2.73
Guidry: *ΔER* = 548 and *ERA* = 3.25
Marichal: *ΔER* = 161 and *ERA* = 2.9
Mays: *ΔER* = 324 and *ERA* = 2.93.]

7. Find values of *k* in Problem 6 which would reduce Ford's *ERA* to 2.65 and Guidry's *ERA* to 3.15.

[Answers: Ford: *k* = 1.15; Guidry: *k* = 1.11.]

8. Consider Don Drysdale's *IP* and *ER* statistics from Problem 4. Assuming that *ΔER* = 300 and *k* = 1.05, what would his *ΔIP* have to be to arrive at an *ERA* to 2.75?

[Answer: Drysdale would have had to pitch another 1170 innings.]

9. Consider Carl Mays' *IP* and *ER* statistics from Problem 6. Assuming that *ΔER* = 200 and *ΔIP* = 700, find a value for *k* which would yield a career *ERA* of 2.75.

[Answer: *k* = 1.19.]

10. Al Kaline, of the Detroit Tigers, walloped a total of 399 home runs in 10,116 at-bats. Find the number of addition at-bats which Kaline would need to attain 500 career home runs if we assume a kicker value of $k = 0.88$.

[Answer: Kaline would need a figure of $\Delta AB = 2910$.]

11. First baseman Willie McCovey slugged 521 home runs in 8197 at-bats. How many additional home runs would he have accumulated, given 2000 more AB and a value of k equal to 0.93?

[Answer: McCovey would have hit an additional 118 home runs.]

12. The career leader for doubles ($2B$) is centerfielder Tris Speaker with 792. Given that Speaker batted 10,195 times, project his additional number of doubles with 2000 more ABs, and a kicker of $k = 0.93$.

[Answer: Speaker would have had an additional 144 doubles.]

13. Given the information in Problem 12, determine the value of the kicker for Speaker to have reached 1000 doubles in his career.

[Answer: $k = 1.06$.]

14. Hall of Fame outfielder Sam Crawford is the career leader for triples ($3B$) with 309, which he accumulated in 9570 at-bats. Project his additional number of triples with 2000 more ABs, and a kicker of $k = 0.97$.

[Answer: Crawford would have had an additional 63 triples.]

15. Given the information in the Problem 14, determine the value of the kicker for Crawford to have reached 400 triples in his career.

[Answer: $k = 1.41$.]

16. Of all Major League pitchers who have logged at least 1000 innings and have at least 100 decisions (wins plus losses), Hall of Famer "Big Ed" Walsh holds the record for the lowest ERA with a mark of 1.82. Fellow Hall of Famer Addie Joss is in second place with an ERA of 1.89. Joss gave up 488 ER in 2327 IP. If we assume that Joss would have pitched an additional 1000 innings, find the additional number of earned runs (ΔER) which Joss would have allowed and the value of the kicker which would have lowered Joss' ERA to 1.81, putting him in first place on the all time ERA list.

[Answer: Joss would have allowed an additional 210 earned runs; $k = 1.14$.]

CHAPTER 21

Predicting with the
Use of Regression

Introduction

In this chapter, we will develop a regression model to predict the future based on past performances. As a basic example, consider two variables, x, and y, that represent two quantities, say batting average and salary, respectively. If the salary is based solely on batting average, plus perhaps a constant, we could use a linear relationship, such as $y = \beta_0 = \beta_1 x$. The slope β_1 and y-intercept β_0 determine a straight line. In this example, the batting average (x) is the independent variable, and the salary (y), is the dependent variable. Given a set of values for x, we could predict values for y in a linear fashion. In the context of our example, if we know the player's batting average, we multiply it by a constant β_1 (the slope), add another constant β_0 (the intercept), and determine the salary. This is known as a simple linear regression model.

Using the Method of Least Squares, we develop a trend line (the best fit of the data to a line). The principle behind the least squares method tells us that the vertical deviation of a point from a line is equal to the y-value of the point minus the y-value of the line for a given x-value. In other words, it is equal to $y - (\beta_0 + \beta_1 x)$. This difference is calculated for all (x_i, y_i) pairs of the data, and then each vertical deviation is squared and summed. The point estimates of β_1 and β_0 are called the least squares estimates and are those values which minimize the sum of the squared difference between y and $(\beta_0 + \beta_1 x)$.

Many modeling or numerical analysis textbooks go into great detail on the Method of Least Squares. For our purposes, we will simply state that in a linear model, with m data points (x_i, y_i), in order to minimize $\sum_{i=1}^{m}(y_i - \beta_0 - \beta_1 x_i)^2$, the partial derivatives of this expression with respect to β_0 and β_1 must be zero. The two resulting equations can be rearranged to yield:

$$\beta_0 = \frac{\sum x_i^2 \sum y_i - \sum x_i y_i \sum x_i}{m \sum x_i^2 - \left(\sum x_i\right)^2} \quad \text{and} \quad \beta_1 = \frac{m \sum x_i y_i - \sum x_i \sum y_i}{m \sum x_i^2 - \left(\sum x_i\right)^2}.$$

As an example, consider the 2007 American League East starting second basemen. Below we list those second basemen who played the most games for their respective teams in 2007, followed by their batting averages, and their 2007 salaries. Brian Roberts was the every day second baseman for the Baltimore Orioles, batting 0.290. Based solely on the batting averages of his peers, what should Roberts' salary have been?

Player	Team	2007 Average	2007 Salary
Dustin Pedroia	Red Sox	0.317	$380,000
Robinson Cano	Yankees	0.306	$490,800
Aaron Hill	Blue Jays	0.291	$395,000
B.J. Upton	Devil Rays	0.300	$386,900

The first step in developing a regression analysis that involves just two variables is to try to develop a trend for the data. We can create a scatter plot of the observed data with the independent variable, batting average, on the x-axis, and the dependent variable, salary, on the y-axis.

An initial look at the chart seems to reveal no pattern. Is there a trend?

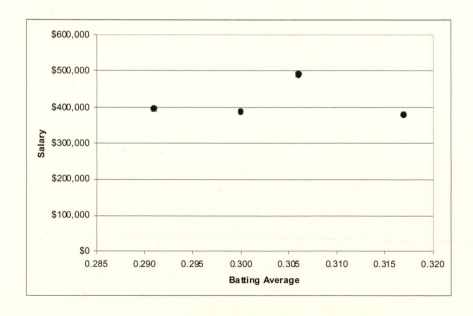

Using the Method of Least Squares outlined above, $\beta_0 \approx 357,618$ and $\beta_1 \approx 183,503$, so the equation for the trend line is given by $y = 183,053x + 357,618$. In this case, $m = 4$, and the x_i values are the batting averages and the y_i values are the associated salaries.

How good is this trend line? In truth, for this model it's not very good at all. The equation basically states that a ballplayer would be paid over $350,000 if he never had an at-bat, or if his batting average remained at 0.000. Substituting in Brian Roberts' batting average of 0.290, he should have made $410,703. His actual 2007 salary was almost ten times that, at $4,200,000. Obviously, there are many more factors which go into determining a professional ballplayer's salary. Also, we tried to make a prediction using only four other data points. In practice, a few data points will generally not yield a high correlation between the trend line and the actual data.

Rather than try to find one variable which can accurately predict another, let's discuss a model which takes as its input several independent variables (x_i) and then predicts one dependent variable y. We will add up the independent variables (multiplied by different coefficients) and then create a model. Looking back at Chapter 8, the Linear Weights formula for runs involves a regression of several variables (namely, hits, doubles, triples, and home runs). Recall that Lindsey determined that Runs = $(0.41 \times 1B) + (0.82 \times 2B) + (1.06 \times 3B) + (1.42 \times HR)$. Thorn and Palmer improved on the formula to add *HBP*, *BB*, *SB*, and *CS*; they also incorporated league batting factors. How did they do it? There are several statistical packages available (Minitab, for example), which determine the weights (coefficients) for the inputted independent variables (1*B*, 2*B*, 3*B*, and *HR*).

Instead of runs produced, perhaps runs batted in can be predicted by using home runs, triples, and doubles. We assign a variable to each independent variable and our general additive multiple regression model becomes

$$y = \beta_0 + \beta_1 x_1 + \beta_2 x_2 + \beta_3 x_3 + \varepsilon,$$

where x_1 corresponds to the number of doubles in a season, x_2 corresponds to triples, and x_3 are home runs. One might believe that a high number of extra-base hits correlates to a high number of *RBI*s. Let's see if it's true. There is still some error (ε) associated with this method. All of the independent variables appear linearly in this expression. This is the simplest multiple regression model. The dependent variable y is a linear function and we get a deviation from the expression by some amount known as the error. Notice that there is no interaction among the independent variables. Other multiple regression models exist which offer no interaction or complete interaction among the variables. For example,

$$y = \beta_0 + \beta_1 x_1 + \beta_2 x_2 + \beta_3 x_1^2 + \beta_4 x_2^2 + \varepsilon$$

is a model which is now nonlinear but has no interaction between x_1 and x_2. On the other hand,

$$y = \beta_0 + \beta_1 x_1 + \beta_2 x_2 + \beta_3 x_1 x_2 + \varepsilon$$

shows interaction between x_1 and x_2 and is thus nonlinear (we could also add a term which has x_1^2 or x_2^2, if desirable). Further, the powers of each variable need not be integers. Nonlinear multiple regression models can be very complicated and we will not explore them further in this discussion. Again, we reiterate that many statistical programs can be employed to determine the coefficients of the (linear or nonlinear) multivariable models.

As an example of the simple multiple regression model, there have only been fifteen times when a major league player has had 100 or more extra-base hits in a season. The first to do it was Babe Ruth in 1921, and his record of 119 extra-base hits in a single season still stands. Amazingly, four occurrences sprung out of the 2001 season. Just below this extraordinary listing of players are eight occurrences of 99 extra-base hits, including twice by Babe Ruth. Carlos Delgado is also one of the "not-quite-100" extra base hit players. Suppose we wished to calculate how many *RBIs* Carlos Delgado should have had in 2004, given his extra-base hit data. Let's compare his statistics to those 15 best extra-base hit seasons. In the following table, we list the players, listed in order of the most extra-base hits.

Player	*Year*	*H*	*2B*	*3B*	*HR*	*XBH*	*RBI*
Babe Ruth	1921	204	44	16	59	119	171
Lou Gehrig	1927	218	52	18	47	117	175
Chuck Klein	1930	250	59	8	40	107	170
Barry Bonds	2001	156	32	2	73	107	137
Todd Helton	2001	197	54	2	49	105	146
Chuck Klein	1932	226	50	15	38	103	137
H Greenberg	1937	200	49	14	40	103	183
Stan Musial	1948	230	46	18	39	103	131
Albert Belle	1995	173	52	1	50	103	126
Todd Helton	2000	216	59	2	42	103	147
Sammy Sosa	2001	189	34	5	64	103	160
Rogers Hornsby	1922	250	46	14	42	102	152
Lou Gehrig	1930	220	42	17	41	100	174
Jimmie Foxx	1932	213	33	9	58	100	169
Luis Gonzalez	2001	198	36	7	57	100	142
Carlos Delgado	2000	196	57	1	41	99	137

In trying to predict the number of runs batted in, we use Minitab to determine that the intercept, β_0, should equal 74.509, and the other three coefficients are as follows: $\beta_1 = 0.612$, $\beta_2 = 1.765$, and $\beta_3 = 0.704$. Putting this all together, the prediction for runs batted in becomes

$$RBIs = 74.509 + 0.612 \times 2B + 1.765 \times 3B + 0.704 \times HR.$$

If we substitute Babe Ruth's 1921 totals into the equation, we find that he should have had $74.509 + 0.612 \times 44 + 1.765 \times 16 + 0.704 \times 59 = 171$ RBIs, which is exactly his actual 1921 total of 171. Todd Helton's 2001 season also predicts an RBI total of 146, his actual amount. What about Carlos Delgado? Based upon this multiple regression, his predicted RBI total should have been 140, which is within 2.1 percent of his actual total of 137.

Another technique that is useful in a variety of scenarios involves power models. Suppose we want to fit an equation of the form $y = Ax^B$, where A and B are constant parameters. Take the natural logarithm of each side of the above equation to obtain

$$\ln(y) = \ln(A) + B\ln(x).$$

This is now the equation of a line. Transform the data points (x_i, y_i), using the natural logarithm, into a linear fit and use the Method of Least Squares to determine the slope and intercept (B and $\ln(A)$, respectively). Then transform back to the power equation.

As an example, let's fit a power model to some batting data. In 2007, Albert Pujols led the NL in on-base percentage with a mark of .469. The following table lists five batters who had high *OBP*, with the number of walks each drew.

Player	*Team*	*BB*	*OBP*
Albert Pujols	STL	91	0.469
Lance Berkman	HOU	81	0.434
Matt Holliday	COL	68	0.419
Brad Hawpe	COL	68	0.394
Ryan Theriot	CHC	64	0.392

Let's determine the relationship, if any, of walks to *OBP*. Initially we will assume a model where

$$OBP = a\,(BB)^b,$$

where a and b are constants. How do we determine their values? Taking the natural log of each side of this equation, we find that $\ln(OBP) = \ln(a) + b\ln(BB)$. We take the natural log of the data pairs, let $Y = \ln(OBP)$, $X =$

$\ln(BB)$, $\beta_0 = \ln(a)$, and $\beta_1 = b$. As before, we use the Method of Least Squares, and with m data points (X_i, Y_i), we minimize $\sum_{i=1}^{m}(Y_i - \beta_0 - \beta_1 X_i)^2$. The two resulting equations can be rearranged to yield:

$$\beta_0 = \frac{\sum X_i^2 \sum Y_i - \sum X_i Y_i \sum X_i}{m\sum X_i^2 - \left(\sum X_i\right)^2} \quad \text{and} \quad \beta_1 = \frac{m\sum X_i Y_i - \sum X_i \sum Y_i}{m\sum X_i^2 - \left(\sum X_i\right)^2}.$$

Once they are determined (in this case $\beta_0 = 2.9318$ and $\beta_1 + 0.4814$), we need to transform back to the power model. Start with $Y = \beta_0 + \beta_1 X$. Exponentiating yields $e^Y = e^{\beta_0 + \beta_1 X} = e^{\beta_0} e^{\beta_1 X}$. Substituting in the values for X and Y, we find that

$$\begin{aligned} e^{\ln(OBP)} = OBP &= e^{\beta_0} e^{\beta_1 \ln(BB)} \\ &= e^{\beta_0} e^{\ln(BB)^{\beta_1}} \\ &= e^{\beta_0}(BB)^{\beta_1}. \end{aligned}$$

Therefore, the model becomes $OBP = e^{-2.9318}(BB)^{0.4814}$, or $OBP = 0.0533$ $(BB)^{04804}$. If a batter had 70 walks in 2007, we would expect his OBP to be about 0.410.

Demonstrating Sabermetrics

1. In 1937, Joe DiMaggio had 35 doubles, 15 triples, and 46 home runs. Using the formula for RBIs for the 100-extra-base hit club, calculate how many runs *Joltin' Joe* should have driven in.

Using $RBIs$ 74.509 + 0.612 × 2B + 1.765 × 3B + 0.704 × HR, we substitute in DiMaggio's values and find that he should have batted in 154.79, or 155, runs. His actual RBI total for 1937 was 167. DiMaggio only had 96 extra-base hits, so we might expect a small error.

2. In 1974, the Oakland Athletics beat the Los Angeles Dodgers in the World Series, 4 games to 1. Four of the games were decided by a 3 to 2 score. Let's assume that the time of the game is a function of the number of pitches thrown by both teams. Interestingly, as the Series progressed, the games were shorter in time. Given the table of data below, develop a power model for the time of game (in minutes), based on the number of pitches.

1974 WS	Pitches	Time	1974 WS	Pitches	Time
Game 1	287	163	Game 4	238	137
Game 2	266	160	Game 5	224	143
Game 3	247	155			

Let x be the number of pitches and y be the time of game. We take the natural logarithm of all values ($X = \ln(x)$ and $Y = \ln(y)$) and then sum them.

$$\sum X = 27.6363, \quad \sum Y = 25.0952, \quad \sum XY = 138.7320, \quad \text{and} \quad \sum X^2 = 152.7902.$$

We can then determine that $\beta_0 = \dfrac{\sum X_i^2 \sum Y_i - \sum X_i Y_i \sum X_i}{m \sum X_i^2 - \left(\sum X_i\right)^2} = 1.3875$ (with

$m = 5$) and $\beta_1 = \dfrac{m \sum X_i Y_i - \sum X_i \sum Y_i}{m \sum X_i^2 - \left(\sum X_i\right)^2} = 0.6570$. Exponentiating β_0 gives

4.0046, so the power model becomes Time = 4.0046 (Pitches)$^{0.687}$.

3. Suppose we want to model the number of runs scored per game (R/G) using only a team's on-base percentage (OBP). The table below gives the 2007 season totals for the National League, sorted by OBP. Determine a power model.

2007 Team	OBP	R/G	2007 Team	OBP	R/G
PHI	5.51	0.354	SDP	4.55	0.322
COL	5.28	0.354	LAD	4.54	0.337
ATL	5.00	0.339	STL	4.48	0.337
NYM	4.96	0.342	PIT	4.47	0.325
MIL	4.94	0.329	HOU	4.46	0.330
FLA	4.88	0.336	ARI	4.40	0.321
CIN	4.83	0.335	SFG	4.22	0.322
CHC	4.64	0.333	WSN	4.15	0.325

Let x be OBP and y be R/G. We take the natural logarithm of all values ($X = \ln(x)$ and $Y = \ln(y)$) and then sum them as in Problem 2 above. We can

then determine that $\beta_0 = \dfrac{\sum X_i^2 \sum Y_i - \sum X_i Y_i \sum X_i}{m \sum X_i^2 - \left(\sum X_i\right)^2} = -1.6074$ (with $m =$

16) and $\beta_1 = \dfrac{m \sum X_i Y_i - \sum X_i \sum Y_i}{m \sum X_i^2 - \left(\sum X_i\right)^2} = 0.3296$. Exponentiating β_0 gives

0.2004, so the power model becomes $R/G = 0.2004\,(OBP)^{0.3296}$.

4. Let's model a power hitter's home run rate, as a function of his age. In this case, the home run rate is defined as the number of cumulative home runs divided by the number of cumulative at-bats. If a batter's HRR is 0.05, for instance, that would mean he hits a homer every 20 at-bats. In the table below, we show the cumulative home run rate for Manny Ramirez, as a function of his cumulative at-bats (through the 2007 season). We will ignore the first two rows of the data, as Manny was not yet a starter in those seasons.

Determine a linear model to predict Manny's HRR as a function of at-bats (age > 22).

Age	AB	Cum AB	HR	Cum HR	HRR
21	53	53	2	2	0.0377
22	290	343	17	19	0.0554
23	484	827	31	50	0.0605
24	550	1377	33	83	0.0603
25	561	1938	26	109	0.0562
26	571	2509	45	154	0.0614
27	522	3031	44	198	0.0653
28	439	3470	38	236	0.0680
29	529	3999	41	277	0.0693
30	436	4435	33	310	0.0699
31	569	5004	37	347	0.0693
32	568	5572	43	390	0.0700
33	554	6126	45	435	0.0710
34	449	6575	35	470	0.0715
35	483	7058	20	490	0.0694

Let x be the number of cumulative at-bats and y be the cumulative *HRR*. We sum the columns for x and y and can then determine that

$$\beta_0 = \frac{\sum x_i^2 \sum y_i - \sum x_i y_i \sum x_i}{m \sum x_i^2 - \left(\sum x_i\right)^2} = 5.7661 \text{ and } \beta_1 = \frac{m \sum x_i y_i - \sum x_i \sum y_i}{m \sum x_i^2 - \left(\sum x_i\right)^2}$$

$= 0.000217$. This gives a linear model of $HRR = 0.000217 \, AB + 5.7661$.

You see that the slope of the model is very small. Almost all great sluggers have a cumulative home run rate which levels off as they age (there have been a few exceptions). For more information, see the paper by Costa, Huber, and Saccoman, listed in the References.

Practicing Sabermetrics

1. In 1980, the Philadelphia Phillies beat the Kansas City Royals in the World Series, 4 games to 2. Game 3 went 10 innings. Let's assume that the time of the game is a function of the number of pitches thrown by both teams. Given the table of data below, develop a power model for the time of game (in minutes), based on the number of pitches.

1980 WS	Pitches	Time		1980 WS	Pitches	Time
Game 1	292	181		Game 4	231	157
Game 2	301	181		Game 5	240	180
Game 3	298	199		Game 6	281	180

[Answer: Times = 6.8284 (pitcher)$^{0.5813}$.]

2. Suppose we want to model the number of runs allowed per game (R/G) using only the total of hits plus walks allowed (($H+BB)/G$) as the independent variable. The table below gives the 2007 season totals for the National League. Determine both a linear model and a power model.

2007 Team	(H+BB)/G	R/G
SDP	11.5	4.09
CHC	11.8	4.26
ATL	12.2	4.52
ARI	12.3	4.52
SFG	12.6	4.44
LAD	12.1	4.49
NYM	12.2	4.63
COL	12.3	4.65
MIL	12.4	4.79
WSN	12.9	4.83
STL	12.4	5.12
HOU	12.8	5.02
PHI	13.0	5.07
PIT	13.2	5.22
CIN	12.9	5.27
FLA	14.1	5.50

[Answer: Linear: $R/G = 0.569 ((H + BB)/G) - 2.3616$.
Power: $R/G = 0.1022 ((H + BB)/G)^{1.5196}$.]

CHAPTER 22

Higher Mathematics
Used in Sabermetrics

Introduction

At times, the traditional statistics may not help us gain insight into a situation in baseball. Even more recent measures, such as Linear Weights, Runs Created, and Win Shares, may not suffice, as they are simply algebraic manipulations of the traditional stats. In Chapter 21, we studied prediction using regression, which gives us an approximation based on simple linear models. In this chapter, we will use calculus to attempt a deeper understanding of the physics behind the game of baseball. In another light, often we wish to simply study the applications of calculus to baseball. If you haven't studied calculus before, don't worry; as we try to offer solution techniques to simple problems, we will explain our methods.

Related Rates

A typical problem in differential calculus is as follows: A baseball diamond is a square where each side measures 90 feet. Suppose that a right-handed batter hits the ball and runs toward first base. Once he crosses home plate, the batter's speed remains constant at 23 feet per second. Let's answer a basic question. At what rate is his distance from second base changing when he is halfway to first base?

To answer this problem, we will use some geometry. Define the distance down the first base line that the batter is from home plate to be x. Then the distance from the batter to first base is $90 - x$. Let y be the distance from the batter to second base. Since the bases form a square and the base paths are at right angles, we will use the Pythagorean Theorem. The batter's position, first base, and second base form a right triangle, with the distance from second base to the batter as the hypotenuse and the distances from the batter to first and from first to second as the sides (draw yourself a picture). Therefore,

$$y^2 = (90 - x)^2 + 90^2.$$

Differentiating both sides of this equation with respect to t, we find that

$$2y\frac{dy}{dt} = 2(90 - x)\left(-\frac{dx}{dt}\right);$$

we use the chain rule, since both x and y are functions of t. When the batter is halfway to first base, $x = 45$. Further, when $x = 45$, $y =$

$\sqrt{45^2 + 90^2} = 45\sqrt{5} \approx 100.62$ feet. We are given that the batter's speed is 23

feet per second. Speed is the magnitude of velocity and velocity is the rate of change of distance with respect to time. In terms of our variables, speed is

$\frac{dx}{dt}$, which allows us to write the batter's speed with the expression $\frac{dx}{dt} =$

23. We are trying to find $\frac{dy}{dt}$, so, substituting in the known values, we see

that

$$2\left(45\sqrt{5}\right)\frac{dy}{dt} = 2(90 - 45)(- 23),$$

or, $\frac{dy}{dt} \approx -10.3$, which means that the distance from the batter to second

base is decreasing at a rate of 10.3 feet per second. Many calculus text books offer similar related rates problems, in the context of a baseball diamond.

Momentum and Force

The momentum of an object can be defined as the product of the object's mass and velocity. Define the momentum of a baseball as p, the mass m, and the velocity v. Therefore, by definition, $p = mv$. The baseball, which has a mass of 5 ounces, travels with an external force $F(t)$ acting on it, caused by the pitcher. We will assume that this force is a continuous function of time. From Newton's Second Law, we know that force is equal to the mass of the object times its acceleration, or $F = ma$. The ball will exhibit a change in momentum over a certain time interval. This change in momentum can be calculated as the accumulation of force over the interval. If the interval is $[t_1,$

$t_2]$, then the change in momentum, $\Delta p = \int_{t_1}^{t_2} F(t)\, dt = mv_2 - mv_1$. If we wish to

determine an average momentum over the interval, we would divide Δp by $t_2 - t_1$.

Many pitchers in baseball now throw the ball over 90 miles per hour. Many hitters can generate a high bat speed when impact is made with the ball. Most ball-bat collisions will therefore last for just a small fraction of a second; realistically, this is on the order of one-thousandth of a second. Consider an example. It's late in a close game and Randy Johnson is facing Gary Sheffield, who hits the ball as hard as anyone in the game. *The Big Unit* throws a 95 mile per hour heater to *Sheff*, who lines the ball directly back to Johnson on the mound. The ball is in contact with the bat for only 0.001 seconds, and Sheffield sends it back to the mound at 120 miles per hour, due to his tremendous bat speed. Determine the average momentum on the baseball.

To answer the problem, we note that the mass of the ball does not change, but its velocity does. Let v_1 miles per hour, which is $139\frac{1}{3}$ feet per second. Let $v_2 = -120$ miles per hour (opposite direction), which is exactly 176 feet per second. The mass of the ball needs to be converted to slugs (in the English system of measurement), so we divide the weight in pounds (one pound equals 16 ounces) by the gravitational constant ($g = 32$ feet per second squared), or $m = \dfrac{5/16}{32}$ slugs. The change in momentum is

$$\Delta p = mv_1 - mv_2 = m(v_1 - v_2) = \frac{5}{512}\left(139\tfrac{1}{3} - (-176)\right) \approx 3.08$$

slug feet per second. This change in momentum also equals the integral of the force. Knowing Δp, we can now divide by the time interval, 0.001 seconds, giving an average momentum or force of 3080 pounds.

Differential Equations

Often we are interested in a ball's time of travel, once it leaves the bat. When a fly ball is hit to an outfielder with a runner on third base, the sacrifice fly situation emerges. How much time does it take for the outfielder to throw the ball to the next base (in this case, from the outfield to home plate)?

Knowing the velocity at which the fielder throws the ball, we can calculate distance or time needed, if we know the rate at which the ball's velocity is decreasing due to air resistance, or drag. In this situation, we will assume the outfielder throws the ball on a straight line and ignore any vertical motion. So, the rate of change of velocity is proportional to the ball's velocity by the coefficient of drag. Symbolically, we write

$$\frac{dv}{dt} = -k\,v,$$

where k is the resistance due to drag.

This is a differential equation in v, the velocity. We solve this type of differential equation using a technique known as separation of variables. Dividing both sides of the equation by v and multiplying both sides by dt yields

$$\int \frac{dv}{v} = -\int k \, dt.$$

Integrating, we find that $\ln(v) = -kt = a$, where a is a constant of integration. Exponentiating both sides and solving for the velocity, we find that

$$v = ce^{-kt}$$

(we set $e^a = c$ another constant). Given an initial condition, we can solve for the unknown constant c and therefore for the velocity at any time t. This velocity can then be integrated to yield the distance traveled, as $s(t) = \int_0^t v(x) \, dx$.

[In this integral, x is a dummy variable.] Knowing the distance $s(t)$ allows us to find t, the time it takes the ball to travel from the outfield to home.

Here's the situation: It's October 18, 2003, and Game 1 of the World Series. Yankees pitcher David Wells is facing Marlins catcher Ivan Rodriguez with Luis Castillo on first, Juan Samuel on third, and no one out in the top of the first inning. *Pudge* hits Wells' first offering, a fly ball to Yankees center fielder Bernie Williams that's deep enough to bring home Samuel for a sacrifice fly and an early lead. [This is really what happened!] Let's assume that Rodriguez's fly ball travels 350 feet to straight-away center. Bernie Williams is not known for having a cannon for an arm, but let's assume that he does challenge Samuel at the plate by throwing the ball to Yankees catcher Jorge Posada with an initial speed of 110 feet per second. Further assume a drag coefficient of $k = 0.1$. How close is the play, and is Samuel safe, assuming he can run from third base to home in 3.75 seconds?

Well, you could look up the outcome of the play, but let's confirm it. The differential equation becomes $\frac{dv}{dt} = -0.1v$, and $v(0) = 110$. The solution, as noted above, is $v = ce^{-0.1t}$. Using the initial condition, substitute 0 for t in the solution and solve for c. $v(0) = 110 = ce^{-(0.1)(0)} = c$, so $v = 110e^{-0.1t}$. How long does it take the ball to travel 350 feet? Integrating the velocity and solving for t yields

$$s(t) = 350 = \int_0^t 110e^{-0.1x} \, dx = -1100(e^{-0.1t} - 1),$$

or $t = \dfrac{\ln\left(\dfrac{750}{1100}\right)}{-0.1} \approx 3.83$ seconds. Juan Samuel just barely beats the throw from Williams to Posada.

How Far did Mantle's Ball Travel?

Finally, we offer a solution to one of the greatest stories of the past 45 years. Only one time in the history of Yankee Stadium did a ball come close to leaving the park (literally). We analyze the situation and provide a solution for how far Mickey Mantle's mammoth drive in 1963 would have gone, had it not clipped the upper façade of Yankee Stadium in right field. One captioned photograph estimates that the ball traveled 374 feet to the façade. Is this true?

"Mantle's Homer Subdues A's" was the headline for a game played on May 22, 1963, when the New York Yankees hosted the Kansas City Athletics in a night game at Yankee Stadium, before a crowd of 9,727. According to John Drebinger of *The New York Times*, "Mickey Mantle belted one of the most powerful home run drives of his spectacular career." In the next paragraph, Drebinger continues, "First up in the last of the 11th with a score deadlocked at 7-all and a count of two balls and two strikes, the famed Switcher leaned into one of Carl [note: Fischer's first name was Bill] Fischer's fast ones and sent the ball soaring. It crashed against the upper façade of the right-field stand, which towers 108 feet above the playing field." The actual distances measured were a height of 108 feet, 1 inch, above the ground, and a straight-line (hypotenuse) distance of 374 feet.

How far would Mantle's mighty smash have traveled, had it not smacked the upper façade? Estimates range from near to far; however, a good estimate is just over 500 feet. It certainly would not have sailed 600 feet without the façade in the way.

Here are the facts bearing on the problem. The Yankees and Athletics were playing a night game on May 23. The game lasted three hours and thirteen minutes. That puts Mantle's at-bat somewhere in the 11:15 P.M. timeframe. According to *The New York Times* May 23 weather records, the temperature at 11 P.M. was 61 degrees, with 39 percent humidity, winds blowing from the west at 8 miles per hour, and a steady barometer of 30.05 inches. More on the weather later. Let's assume Mantle hit the ball when it was two feet off the ground, so that it rose 106 feet, 1 inch. If he crushed the ball straight into the façade, it would have left Mantle's bat at an angle of 15.84 degrees, which is very rare for batted balls. According to Robert K. Adair's

The Physics of Baseball, the optimum angle for batted balls is about 35 degrees, though balls projected at 30° to 40° could travel almost as far. If the ball was hit at an angle greater than 17°, it certainly could not have been rising when it struck the façade. Mickey Mantle was known to have an upper-cut-type swing when batting left-handed, which might increase the angle at which the ball traveled, relative to the ground.

Let's incorporate the speed at which the ball was hit. Fischer threw a fastball at Mickey. Assuming Fischer threw it at about 90 miles per hour, at an angle of 17 degrees, in the absence of air resistance (drag), the ball would have to leave the bat at over 540 miles per hour to intersect at a point 374 feet away and 108.0833 feet off the ground on a straight line. A more realistic angle might be 25 degrees. Again, in the absence of drag, a ball leaving home plate at 25 degrees would have to have a speed of about 138 miles per hour. Mickey claimed that night that "it was the hardest ball I ever hit." At an angle of 23 degrees, and in the absence of air resistance, the ball would have left home plate at a speed of about 156 miles per hour and taken just under two seconds to hit the façade. Toss in air resistance, and the time takes longer, but the ball doesn't travel as far. As the angle of trajectory increases, the "muzzle velocity" of the of the ball off the bat decreases. According to Professor Adair, Sterling Professor of Physics at Yale University, a 75 miles per hour swing will send the ball off at about 115 miles per hour, which might be taken as a maximum speed. If Mantle indeed crushed the ball as hard as he could, the speed coming off the bat might be higher. However, there would still be drag. The effect of drag would mean that the ball would not travel as a symmetric parabola, implying the same distance traveled after the façade as before, if it was at the apex of its trajectory. Rather, drag requires that the ball's trajectory is shortened on its way down.

So, back to the weather, a ball travels about 6 feet farther for every inch the barometer drops (it was steady and normal). Humidity has little effect on the ball, making it travel farther on a humid days by a few inches (humidity was low). A cooler evening causes the air to be denser and the ball to not travel as far. The wind was blowing to dead center (from the west) at approximately 8 miles per hour. It is unknown whether the New York City winds were the same in Yankee Stadium, but let's assume they were. Winds are usually measured a few meters off the ground, so winds at a higher point (where the ball was sailing) could have been higher. A ball traveling down right field line is about 45 degrees from center field, so the wind has a component of 8 $\times \sqrt{2} / 2 = 4\sqrt{2} \approx 5.66$ miles per hour. According to Adair, a 5.6 miles per hour tail wind would add about 17 feet to a 400 foot fly ball.

In his book, Adair has charted trajectories of baseballs projected at different angles off the bat and different velocities. He also states that the average ball hit at 35 degrees stays in the air for about 5 seconds. Finally, an uncertainty in the exact coefficient of drag can translate into and uncertainty in the distance traveled. If the drag coefficient changes by 10 percent, a 400-foot home run might actually go 414 feet or 386 feet.

How far, then, would the mammoth blast have gone? Let's assume Mickey Mantle hit the ball at 130 miles per hour. The baseball goes through a distance of 400 feet when the altitude is about 110 feet. Using the Pythagorean theorem, Mantle's ground distance to the façade was about 358 feet. Factoring drag into a 130 miles per hour curve until it reaches the ground, we calculate that the ball would travel past 500 feet, *if* the speed and angle were optimal. Then factor in the wind. So, a guess over 520 feet would be "in the ballpark." If the initial velocity of the ball is lower, or the angle is decreased, the range will be lower.

For the sake of legend, a maximum predicted distance for Mantle's mammoth drive would be 536 feet, one foot for every one of Mickey's career home runs.

There are plenty of theories on the internet as to how far the ball might have traveled. Our approach uses the most accepted methods, to include trajectories due to drag and weather. The partial differential equations governing the flight are complicated to solve; therefore, we recommend using accepted charts, as those found in Professor Adair's book.

Demonstrating Sabermetrics

1. A baseball diamond is a square where each side measures 90 feet. Suppose that a batter hits the ball and runs toward first base. Once out of the batter's box, his speed remains constant at 25 feet per second. At what rate is his distance from third base changing when he is 30 feet from first base?

Define the distance down the first base line that the batter is from home plate to be x. Let z be the distance from the batter to third base. Since the bases form a square and the base paths are at right angles, we will use the Pythagorean Theorem. The batter's position, home plate, and third base form a right triangle, with the distance from third base to the batter as the hypotenuse and the distances from the batter to first and from third to home as the sides (draw yourself a picture). Therefore,

$$z^2 = x^2 + 90^2.$$

Differentiating both sides of this equation with respect to t, we find that

$$2z\frac{dz}{dt} = 2x\frac{dx}{dt},$$

using the chain rule. We can divide both sides by 2. When the batter is 30 feet from first base, $x = 60$, which means that $z = \sqrt{60^2 + 90^2} = 30\sqrt{13} \approx$ 108.17 feet. We are given that the batter's speed is 25 feet per second. We are trying to find $\frac{dz}{dt}$, so, substituting in the known values, we see that

$$30\sqrt{13}\frac{dz}{dt} = 60 \times 25,$$

or, $\frac{dz}{dt} \approx 13.9$, which means that the distance from the batter to third base is increasing at a rate of 13.9 feet per second.

2. It's October 18, 2003, and still Game 1 of the World Series. Yankees pitcher David Wells is facing Marlins catcher Ivan Rodriguez with Luis Castillo on first, Juan Samuel on third, and no one out in the top of the first inning. "Pudge" hits Wells' first offering, a fly ball to Yankees center fielder Bernie Williams that's deep enough to bring home Samuel for a sacrifice fly and an early lead. Let's assume that Rodriguez's fly ball travels 350 feet to straight-away center. Yankees shortstop Derek Jeter moves into the short outfield to relay Bernie Williams' throw home to catcher Jorge Posada. Bernie still throws the ball with an initial speed of 110 feet per second. However, he only throws it 200 feet, as the Yankee captain races out to become the cut-off man. Jeter catches it, whirls around (this takes a quarter of a second) , and fires a bullet to Posada with a speed of 130 feet per second. Assume a drag coefficient of $k = 0.1$ for both throws. How long does it take the ball to get home? Does Jeter throw out Samuel at the plate, considering it takes the speedy Juan 3.5 seconds to run from third base to home?

The differential equation is still $\frac{dv}{dt} = -0.1v$, and $v(0) = 100$. The solution, as noted above, is $v = ce^{-0.1t}$. Using the initial condition, as in the Introduction, we find that $v = 110e^{-0.1t}$. How long does it take the ball to travel 200 feet? Integrating the velocity and solving for t yields

$$s(t) = 200 = \int_0^t 110e^{-0.1x}\, dx = -1100(e^{-0.1t} - 1),$$

or $t = \dfrac{\ln\left(\dfrac{900}{1100}\right)}{-0.1} \approx 2.00$ seconds. By the time Jeter throws the ball, 2.25 seconds have elapsed. Now, we solve a new differential equation for Jeter, since the distance is now only 150 feet and the velocity is 130 feet per second. Jeter's velocity is modeled by $v = 130e^{-0.1t}$. Solving for t yields

$$s(t) = 150 = \int_0^t 130e^{-0.1x} \, dx = -1300(e^{-0.1t} - 1),$$

or $t = \dfrac{\ln\left(\dfrac{1150}{1300}\right)}{-0.1} \approx 1.23$ seconds, for a total of 3.48 seconds, and Juan Samuel is OUT (theoretically...).

Practicing Sabermetrics

1. A good base stealer likes to get at least a ten to twelve foot lead from first base. Suppose he has a ten foot lead when he takes off for second base, a half a second before the pitcher releases a fastball towards the plate. The radar gun clocks the pitch at 90 miles per hour (equivalent to 132 feet per second). The catcher is up on his feet and takes another half second to catch and throw the ball towards second base, at a speed of 120 feet per second. The shortstop takes another half second to catch the ball and apply the tag. Given a drag coefficient of 0.12 (for both the pitcher and catcher) and a good throw to the bag, how much time does the runner have to get to second base?

[Answer: Approximately 3.10 seconds. The runner has to run 80 feet, while the ball travels 60.5 feet to home plate and then $90\sqrt{2} \approx 127.3$ feet from home to second base. There is a total of 1.5 seconds of time when the ball is not being thrown.]

2. Given the situation in Problem 1, suppose it takes 1.13 seconds for the ball to reach second base after leaving the catcher's hand. What is the momentum of the ball when it reaches second base?

[Answer: The ball's velocity at second is 104.8 feet per second, giving a momentum of 1.02 slug feet per second.]

CHAPTER 23

Potpourri

Lists are fun. Let's have some fun using sabermetrics.

Each one of the authors is going to choose his All-Time All-Star Team and his All-Time Favorite Franchise Team. He will also rate his top ten position players and top ten pitchers. While the selections are based on sabermetrical analyses, years of reading about the game, as well as watching it in person and on television, there is also a certain amount of *subjectivity* in our choices (see the Capsule Comments after each selection).

Costa's All-Time All-Star Team

1B	Lou Gehrig		RF	Babe Ruth
2B	Rogers Hornsby		C	Yogi Berra
SS	Honus Wagner		RHP	Walter Johnson
3B	Mike Schmidt		LHP	Lefty Grove
LF	Ted Williams		MGR	Connie Mack
CF	Willie Mays			

Capsule Comments: Hornsby's .358 lifetime batting average rates him above Joe Morgan or any other second baseman. Brooks Robinson or George Brett or Pie Trainor over Mike Schmidt? Maybe. Cobb over Williams? Maybe. DiMaggio over Mays? Maybe. Bench or Piazza over Berra? Maybe.

Costa's All-Time Yankee Team

1B	Lou Gehrig		RF	Babe Ruth
2B	Tony Lazzeri		C	Yogi Berra
SS	Derek Jeter		RHP	Red Ruffing
3B	Graig Nettles		LHP	Whitey Ford
LF	Mickey Mantle		MGR	Joe McCarthy
CF	Joe DiMaggio			

Capsule Comments: Mantle had to be on the team, even though he usually played center field. Dickey over Berra? Perhaps. Reynolds or Raschi over Ruffing? Ruffing was much more durable.

Costa's Top Ten Position Players

1. Babe Ruth
2. Willie Mays
3. Ty Cobb
4. Honus Wagner
5. Lou Gehrig
6. Ted Williams
7. Mickey Mantle
8. Joe DiMaggio
9. Albert Pujols
10. Henry Aaron

Capsule Comments: Permute positions 2 through 10 any way you wish, it is difficult not to put Ruth on top due to his dominance, not to mention his greatness as a pitcher.

Costa's Top Ten Pitchers

1. Walter Johnson
2. Lefty Grove
3. Grover Cleveland Alexander
4. Christy Mathewson
5. Warren Spahn
6. Whitey Ford
7. Sandy Koufax
8. Tom Seaver
9. Pedro Martinez
10. Bob Gibson

Capsule Comments: No Cy Young? No Greg Maddux? No Nolan Ryan? I had only ten slots.

Huber's All-Time All-Star Team

1B	Lou Gehrig	RF	Babe Ruth
2B	Rogers Hornsby	C	Yogi Berra
SS	Honus Wagner	RHP	Walter Johnson
3B	Brooks Robinson	LHP	Warren Spahn
LF	Ted Williams	MGR	Connie Mack
CF	Willie Mays		

Capsule Comments: I used *OPS*, *AVG*, and Runs Created to add weight to my selections. Todd Helton and Albert Pujols rank just behind Lou Gehrig. I'm guessing Pujols will be a better all-around hitter by the time he retires. Ivan Rodriguez compares very favorably to Yogi, but I've met Mr. Berra, too, and I am in awe of his accomplishments. Where to put Ty Cobb, Stan Musial and Frank Robinson? For sentimental reasons, I chose B. Robby over Schmidt.

Huber's All-Time Orioles Team

1B	Eddie Murray		RF	Frank Robinson
2B	Bobby Grich		C	Gus Triandos
SS	Cal Ripken, Jr.		RHP	Jim Palmer
3B	Brooks Robinson		LHP	Dave McNally
LF	Al Bumbry		MGR	Earl Weaver
CF	Paul Blair			

Capsule Comments: Davey Johnson was probably a better slugger, but Bobby Grich was a slightly better fielder, making more All-Star games than Davey. Roberto Alomar wasn't with the team that long. If I could have picked a DH, I'd have chosen Boog Powell or Ken Singleton. In left field, Bumbry beats out Don Baylor and Don Buford. Mark Belanger was a perennial Gold Glove winner at shortstop, but, c'mon, it's Cal Ripken!

Huber's Top Ten Position Players

1. Babe Ruth	6. Ted Williams
2. Willie Mays	7. Stan Musial
3. Ty Cobb	8. Lou Gehrig
4. Rogers Hornsby	9. Tris Speaker
5. Frank Robinson	10. Henry Aaron

Capsule Comments: I used *OPS, AVG*, and Runs Created to add weight to my selections. Hank Greenberg was close, and Albert Pujols and Manny Ramirez are the two dominant active hitters, although I'm not a fan of Manny's fielding. This list is dominated by outfielders.

Huber's Top Ten Pitchers

1. Walter Johnson	6. Tom Seaver
2. Christy Mathewson	7. Greg Maddux
3. Warren Spahn	8. Jim Palmer
4. Bob Gibson	9. Grover Cleveland Alexander
5. Sandy Koufax	10. Steve Carlton

Capsule Comments: I weighed *ERA*, shutouts, and *WHIP* heavily in my choices. I had the fortune of meeting Warren Spahn in 2003, which forced me to study his impressive career. Did you know that Christy Mathewson was a pitching coach at West Point before the 1908 season started? He got his arm in shape, en route to winning 37 games for the Giants that year. Greg Maddux is a great athlete; he can pitch, hit ("Chicks Dig the Long Ball") and field. Jim Palmer had eight 20-win seasons. I would have loved to have seen Walter Johnson in action. *Lefty* Carlton edges out Cy Young for putting up great numbers on not-so-great teams.

Saccoman's All-Time All-Star Team

1B	Lou Gehrig		RF	Babe Ruth
B	Joe Morgan		C	Yogi Berra
SS	Honus Wagner		RHP	Walter Johnson
3B	Mike Schmidt		LHP	Lefty Grove
LF	Ty Cobb		MGR	Leo Durocher
CF	Willie Mays			

Capsule Comments: I am partial to players good at all aspects of the game, which explains the omission of Rogers Hornsby and Ted Williams. In fact, if Joe DiMaggio were a first baseman, and as great defensively there as he were in center, he may have replaced the Iron Horse on my list. I select Durocher, because if my life depended on one game, and I could convince Leo that his life was on the line too, he would find a way to win.

Saccoman's All-Time Met Team

1B	Keith Hernandez		RF	Darryl Strawberry
2B	Edgardo Alfonzo		C	Mike Piazza
SS	Jose Reyes		RHP	Tom Seaver
3B	David Wright		LHP	Jerry Koosman
LF	Cleon Jones		MGR	Gil Hodges
CF	Tommie Agee			

Capsule Comments: The Mets have only been around since 1962, so these players fall nicely into place. Jerry Koosman started six postseason games in his career, and the Mets won all of them, pushing him ahead of Al Leiter. Traditionalists would rather see Harrelson instead of Reyes and Carter or Grote instead of Piazza. I go back to the day I was listening to the late, great Bob Murphy, announce a game, and he gave a voice to something I had suspected myself, "Ladies and gentlemen ... [Mike Piazza] is the finest hitter to ever wear a Mets uniform." Mr. Hodges' job in 1969 ranks as the greatest managerial feat in Mets history, and his shameful exclusion from the Baseball Hall of Fame (as of this writing) remains a mystery. Davey Johnson merits strong consideration, as does Bobby Valentine, as of this writing, the only manager to bring the Mets to back-to-back postseason appearances.

Saccoman's Top Ten Position Players

1. Babe Ruth
2. Willie Mays
3. Honus Wagner
4. Ty Cobb
5. Lou Gehrig
6. Ted Williams
7. Stan Musial
8. Henry Aaron
9. Alex Rodriguez
10. Oscar Charleston

Capsule Comments: I have let Win Shares inform (but not dominate) my selections. Barry Bonds would be number 11. Oscar Charleston was likely the finest player in the history of the Negro Leagues, and it is conceivable that he should rank even higher. Hornsby, Mantle, DiMaggio, Tris Speaker, and Rickey Henderson would be next. Then, some pitchers.

Saccoman's Top Ten Pitchers

1. Walter Johnson
2. Lefty Grove
3. Tom Seaver
4. Sandy Koufax
5. Christy Mathewson
6. Warren Spahn
7. Greg Maddux
8. Cy Young
9. Grover Cleveland Alexander
10. Mariano Rivera

Capsule Comments: If I had one game to win, I would want Bob Gibson on the mound. However, he does not quite make my top 10 overall. I did put Mariano Rivera there; although he has not pitched nearly as many innings as the others, his situations are highly leveraged, and his postseason performance has been extraordinarily clutch.

Appendix A: Abbreviations and Formulas

General

G = Games Played

Batting

AB = At-bats

H = Hits

BB = Bases on Balls (Walks)

IBB = Intentional *BB*

HBP = Hit by Pitch

R = Runs Scored (sometimes seen as *RS*)

RA = Runs Scored Against

RBI = Runs Batted In

SF = Sacrifice Flies

SH = Sacrifice Hits (Bunts)

1B = Singles

2B = Doubles

3B = Triples

HR = Home Runs

$GIDP$ = Grounded Into Double Play

BA = Batting Average = $\dfrac{H}{AB}$

OBA = On Base Average = $\dfrac{H + BB + HP}{AB + BB + HP}$

OBP = On Base Percentage = $\dfrac{H + BB + HP}{AB + BB + HP + SF}$

$TB = 1(1B) + 2(2B) + 3(3B) + 4(HR) = H + 2B + 2(3B) + 3(HR)$

SLG = Slugging Average = $\dfrac{TB}{AB}$

OPS = On Base Average Plus Slugging Average = $OBA + SLG$

$SLOB$ = On Base Average Times Slugging Average = $OBA \times SLG$

ISO = Isolated Power = $SLG - BA$

$PwrA$ = Power Average = $\dfrac{H + HR}{AB}$

$PwrF$ = Power Factor = $\dfrac{SLG}{BA} = \dfrac{TB}{H}$

TPQ = Total Power Quotient = $\dfrac{HR + TB + RBI}{AB}$

EC = Equivalence Coefficient (for batting) = $1 + \dfrac{\Delta AB}{AB}(k)$

BR = Batting Runs = $0.47\,H + 0.38\,2B + 0.55\,3B + 0.93\,HR + 0.33\,(BB + HBP) - ABF\,(AB - H)$, where ABF is found in Appendix B by season.

Runs Created = $\dfrac{(H + BB) \times TB}{AB + BB} = \dfrac{A \times B}{C}$, where $A = H + BB$, $B = TB$, $C = AB + BB$.

The HDG–21 formula for Runs Created has $RC = \dfrac{A \times B}{C}$ with:
  A = H + BB + HBP $-$ GIDP
  B = 1.02 (TB) + 0.26 (BB + HBP) + 0.05 (SB) + 0.5 (SH) $-$ 0.03 (SO)
  C = AB + BB + HBP + SH.

The HDG–23 formula for Runs Created has $RC = \dfrac{A \times B}{C}$ with:
  A = H + BB+ HBP $-$ CS $-$ GIDP
  B = TB + 0.29(BB + HBP $-$ IBB) + 0.64(SB) + 0.53(SF + SH) $-$ 0.03(K)
  C = AB + BB + HBP + SH + SF

$OUTS = AB - H + SH + GIDP$

$MR\text{-}O$ = Marginal Runs for Offense = $R - (0.5 \times R_{LGAVG})$

$MR\text{-}D$ = Marginal Runs for Defense = $(1.5 \times R_{LGAVG}) - RA_{TEAM}$

WS = Win Shares = $\dfrac{RC - \left(\dfrac{OUTS}{12}\right)}{3}$

$WS/27$ = Win Shares per Game (per 27 outs)

Pythagorean Record = $\dfrac{(RS)^x}{(RS)^x + (RA)^x}$, where x is a value close to 2 (varies by season)

PF = Park Factor = $\left(\dfrac{\left(\dfrac{R\,(\text{Home}) + RA\,(\text{Home})}{\text{Games (Home)}}\right)}{\left(\dfrac{R\,(\text{Road}) + RA\,(\text{Road})}{\text{Games (Away)}}\right)}\right).$

TA = Total Average = $\dfrac{(TB + BB + HBP + SB)}{(AB - H)}.$

BOP = Base-Out Percentage = $\dfrac{(TB + BB + HBP + SB + SH + SF)}{(AB - H + SH + SF + CS + GIDP)}.$

PSN = Power Speed Number = $\dfrac{2 \times (HR \times SB)}{HR + SB}$

Degree of Difficulty (HR) = $DOD - HR$ = $\dfrac{\text{Player } HR}{\text{Expected } HR}.$

Degree of Difficulty (SB) = $DOD - SB$ = $\dfrac{\text{Player } SB}{\text{Expected } SB}.$

Hoban Effectiveness Quotient for Offense $(HEQ\text{-}O)$ = $TB + R + RBI + SB + 0.5\ BB.$

Base Running

SB = Stolen Bases

CS = Caught Stealing

OOB = Outs on Base

PSN = Power Speed Number = $\dfrac{HR + SB}{2(HR)(SB)}$

BSR = Base Stealing Runs = $0.3\ SB\ (\ 0.6\ CS$

Pitching

IP = Innings Pitched

W = Wins

L = Losses

$WPCT$ = Winning Percentage = $\dfrac{W}{W+L}$

ER = Earned Runs Allowed

ERA = Earned Run Average = $\dfrac{9(ER)}{IP}$

K = Strikeouts

BB = Bases on Balls (allowed)

HBP = Hit by Pitch

SV = Saves

$WHIP = \dfrac{BB+H}{IP}$

WPR = Weighted Pitcher's Rating $= = \left(\dfrac{W}{W+L} - \dfrac{W_t}{W_t+L_t} \right)(IP).$

EC = Equivalence Coefficient (for ERA) = $(9)\dfrac{ER+\Delta ER}{IP+\Delta IP(k)}$

Pitching Runs ($PR1$) = Innings Pitched $\times \dfrac{\text{League } ERA}{9}$ – Earned Runs

Pitching Runs ($PR2$) = $\dfrac{\text{Innings Pitched} \times (\text{League } ERA - \text{Pitcher's } ERA)}{9}$

ERC = Component ERA = $\dfrac{A \times B}{C}$, where

$A = H + BB + HBP$

$B = \{[(H-HR) \times 1.255] + [4 \times HR]\} \times 0.89 + \{[BB-IBB] \times 0.56\} + [HBP \times 0.56]$

$C = BFP$ (i.e., batters faced by the pitcher)

$WS/9$ = Win Shares per Game (9 innings) = $\dfrac{WS}{\left(\dfrac{IP}{9}\right)}$

Fielding

A = Assists

PO = Putouts

E = Errors

TC = Total Chances = $A + E + PO$

$FPCT$ = Fielding Average = Fielding Percentage = $\dfrac{PO+A}{TC}$

RF = Range Factor (per game) = $\dfrac{PO+A}{G}$

RF_i = Range Factor (per inning) = $\dfrac{9(PO+A)}{I}$, where I is the number of innings played.

FR = Fielding Runs

Hoban Effectiveness Quotient for Defense (HEQ-D) by position:

    C: $(PO + 3\,A + 2\,DP - 2\,E) \times 0.445$
        [Note: 0.445 is the *PMF*, and *PO* are capped at 800.]
    1B: $(0.25\,PO + 3\,A + DP - 2\,E) \times 0.51$
        [Note: 0.51 is the *PMF*.]
    2B, 3B, SS: $(PO + A + DP - 2\,E) \times PMF$
        [Note: $PMF_{2B} = 0.46$, $PMF_{SS} = 0.548$, and $PMF_{3B} = 0.888$.]
    OF: $(PO + 4\,A + 4\,DP - 2\,E) \times 1$
        [Note: There is no *PMF* for OF.]

Appendix B: League Traditional Statistics and ABF Values

National League

NL Year	R/G	AB	H	2B	3B	HR	BB	BA	OBP	SLG	HBP	N L ABF
1901	4.63	38967	10398	1397	550	227	2685	0.267	0.321	0.348	418	**0.243**
1902	3.98	38146	9866	1170	414	98	2620	0.259	0.313	0.319	372	**0.226**
1903	4.78	38005	10223	1485	543	151	3103	0.269	0.331	0.349	407	**0.251**
1904	3.91	41010	10225	1369	544	175	2969	0.249	0.306	0.322	393	**0.224**
1905	4.11	41219	10515	1327	641	182	3207	0.255	0.315	0.332	421	**0.233**
1906	3.57	39649	9693	1258	489	126	3367	0.244	0.310	0.310	378	**0.222**
1907	3.40	39337	9566	1148	504	141	3277	0.243	0.308	0.309	377	**0.220**
1908	3.33	40078	9577	1244	502	151	3057	0.239	0.299	0.306	383	**0.214**
1909	3.66	40649	9907	1386	503	151	3574	0.244	0.310	0.314	323	**0.224**
1910	4.03	40615	10384	1516	592	214	4024	0.256	0.328	0.338	367	**0.246**
1911	4.42	41107	10675	1642	682	316	4279	0.26	0.335	0.356	380	**0.258**
1912	4.62	41153	11214	1762	683	287	3889	0.272	0.340	0.369	329	**0.266**
1913	4.15	41301	10812	1594	645	310	3530	0.262	0.325	0.354	321	**0.249**
1914	3.84	40846	10254	1510	543	267	3600	0.251	0.317	0.334	341	**0.237**
1915	3.62	40888	10140	1555	572	225	3266	0.248	0.309	0.331	350	**0.230**
1916	3.45	41090	10138	1455	589	239	3015	0.247	0.303	0.328	322	**0.225**
1917	3.53	41385	10316	1432	605	202	3054	0.249	0.305	0.328	273	**0.226**
1918	3.62	33780	8583	1119	475	139	2541	0.254	0.311	0.328	224	**0.229**
1919	3.65	37284	9603	1315	517	207	2615	0.258	0.311	0.337	252	**0.233**
1920	3.97	42197	11376	1604	644	261	3016	0.27	0.322	0.357	262	**0.248**
1921	4.59	42376	12266	1839	670	460	2906	0.289	0.338	0.397	233	**0.276**
1922	5.00	43050	12579	1911	662	530	3455	0.292	0.348	0.404	263	**0.286**
1923	4.85	43216	12348	1912	588	538	3494	0.286	0.343	0.395	264	**0.278**
1924	4.54	42445	12009	1881	622	499	3216	0.283	0.337	0.392	229	**0.273**
1925	5.06	42859	12495	2120	614	636	3460	0.292	0.348	0.414	228	**0.291**
1926	4.54	42009	11755	1948	589	439	3473	0.28	0.338	0.386	229	**0.272**
1927	4.58	42344	11935	1888	540	483	3413	0.282	0.339	0.386	216	**0.272**

NL

N L

Year	R/G	AB	H	2B	3B	HR	BB	BA	OBP	SLG	HBP	**ABF**
1928	4.70	42336	11901	2021	518	610	3848	0.281	0.344	0.397	225	**0.281**
1929	5.36	43030	12668	2253	569	754	3961	0.294	0.357	0.426	215	**0.303**
1930	5.68	43693	13260	2386	625	892	3691	0.303	0.360	0.448	202	**0.315**
1931	4.48	42941	11883	2188	532	493	3502	0.277	0.334	0.387	193	**0.270**
1932	4.60	43763	12091	2293	502	651	3141	0.276	0.328	0.396	197	**0.270**
1933	3.97	42559	11332	1854	422	460	2979	0.266	0.317	0.362	202	**0.248**
1934	4.68	42982	11996	2108	433	656	3247	0.279	0.333	0.394	198	**0.272**
1935	4.71	43438	12041	2053	462	662	3284	0.277	0.331	0.391	210	**0.270**
1936	4.71	43891	12206	2071	431	606	3565	0.278	0.335	0.386	219	**0.271**
1937	4.51	42660	11591	1922	458	624	3667	0.272	0.332	0.382	158	**0.266**
1938	4.42	42513	11358	1913	450	611	3708	0.267	0.329	0.376	184	**0.262**
1939	4.44	42285	11505	2032	418	649	3824	0.272	0.335	0.386	205	**0.271**
1940	4.39	42986	11328	1934	416	688	3779	0.264	0.326	0.376	207	**0.260**
1941	4.23	42729	11039	1892	359	597	4149	0.258	0.326	0.361	164	**0.255**
1942	3.90	41769	10391	1680	323	538	4076	0.249	0.318	0.343	174	**0.242**
1943	3.94	42491	10945	1739	388	432	4048	0.258	0.324	0.347	154	**0.247**
1944	4.25	42918	11191	1882	395	575	3984	0.261	0.326	0.363	176	**0.255**
1945	4.46	42823	11343	1823	336	577	4150	0.265	0.333	0.364	207	**0.260**
1946	3.96	42094	10762	1752	382	562	4399	0.256	0.329	0.355	173	**0.254**
1947	4.57	42434	11264	1860	392	886	4477	0.265	0.338	0.39	185	**0.275**
1948	4.43	42256	11022	1840	384	845	4406	0.261	0.333	0.383	163	**0.268**
1949	4.54	42711	11207	1865	370	935	4405	0.262	0.334	0.389	199	**0.272**
1950	4.66	42416	11085	1885	370	1100	4537	0.261	0.336	0.401	220	**0.278**
1951	4.46	42704	11088	1746	367	1024	4362	0.26	0.331	0.39	222	**0.270**
1952	4.17	41878	10582	1672	338	907	4147	0.253	0.323	0.374	235	**0.258**
1953	4.75	42639	11342	1777	414	1197	4220	0.266	0.335	0.411	224	**0.282**
1954	4.56	42027	11142	1816	403	1114	4414	0.265	0.335	0.407	229	**0.282**
1955	4.53	41773	10808	1677	362	1263	4240	0.259	0.328	0.407	236	**0.277**
1956	4.25	41849	10716	1659	372	1219	3982	0.256	0.321	0.401	200	**0.269**
1957	4.38	42919	11162	1733	365	1178	3866	0.26	0.322	0.400	237	**0.269**
1958	4.40	42143	11026	1769	365	1183	4065	0.262	0.328	0.405	247	**0.276**
1959	4.40	42330	11015	1788	324	1159	3974	0.26	0.325	0.400	232	**0.271**
1960	4.24	42176	10745	1722	384	1042	3937	0.255	0.319	0.388	220	**0.263**
1961	4.52	42128	11029	1749	350	1196	3995	0.262	0.327	0.405	254	**0.275**
1962	4.48	55449	14453	2075	453	1449	5265	0.261	0.327	0.393	373	**0.269**
1963	3.81	54803	13434	1984	439	1215	4560	0.245	0.306	0.364	372	**0.243**
1964	4.01	55284	14032	2161	427	1211	4394	0.254	0.311	0.374	327	**0.251**
1965	4.03	55377	13794	2122	422	1318	4730	0.249	0.311	0.374	404	**0.251**
1966	4.09	55385	14202	2099	412	1378	4404	0.256	0.313	0.384	363	**0.256**
1967	3.84	55026	13698	2133	427	1102	4672	0.249	0.310	0.363	354	**0.246**
1968	3.43	54913	13351	1995	359	891	4275	0.243	0.300	0.341	352	**0.231**
1969	4.05	65751	16461	2455	471	1470	6397	0.25	0.319	0.369	443	**0.255**
1970	4.52	66465	17151	2743	554	1683	6919	0.258	0.329	0.392	393	**0.271**
1971	3.91	65903	16590	2505	457	1379	6059	0.252	0.316	0.366	395	**0.252**
1972	3.91	63116	15683	2392	430	1359	5985	0.248	0.315	0.365	358	**0.250**
1973	4.15	66087	16817	2600	386	1550	6453	0.254	0.322	0.376	358	**0.260**

NL												**N L**
Year	R/G	AB	H	2B	3B	HR	BB	BA	OBP	SLG	HBP	**ABF**
1974	4.15	66212	16907	2642	447	1280	6828	0.255	0.326	0.367	360	**0.259**
1975	4.13	66102	17002	2781	458	1233	6730	0.257	0.327	0.369	367	**0.260**
1976	3.98	65814	16778	2652	499	1113	6263	0.255	0.320	0.361	310	**0.252**
1977	4.40	66700	17465	3033	526	1631	6487	0.262	0.328	0.396	330	**0.273**
1978	3.99	65156	16556	2861	482	1276	6279	0.254	0.320	0.372	330	**0.257**
1979	4.22	66088	17229	2886	518	1427	6188	0.261	0.325	0.385	332	**0.265**
1980	4.03	66272	17186	2856	523	1243	5969	0.259	0.320	0.374	257	**0.258**
1981	3.91	43654	11141	1881	354	719	4107	0.255	0.319	0.364	185	**0.253**
1982	4.09	66263	17085	2823	445	1299	5964	0.258	0.319	0.373	305	**0.257**
1983	4.10	65717	16781	2753	484	1398	6424	0.255	0.322	0.376	292	**0.260**
1984	4.06	65919	16842	2770	451	1278	6149	0.255	0.319	0.369	249	**0.255**
1985	4.07	65818	16596	2861	437	1424	6373	0.252	0.319	0.374	280	**0.257**
1986	4.18	65730	16643	2991	387	1523	6560	0.253	0.322	0.38	312	**0.262**
1987	4.52	66276	17275	3126	435	1824	6577	0.261	0.328	0.404	349	**0.276**
1988	3.88	65563	16277	2828	415	1279	5793	0.248	0.310	0.363	368	**0.247**
1989	3.94	65817	16215	2903	411	1365	6251	0.246	0.312	0.365	318	**0.250**
1990	4.20	65968	16917	2967	405	1521	6221	0.256	0.321	0.383	352	**0.263**
1991	4.10	65365	16363	2819	441	1430	6254	0.25	0.317	0.373	367	**0.255**
1992	3.88	65748	16538	2967	459	1262	5978	0.252	0.315	0.368	395	**0.253**
1993	4.49	77489	20427	3588	513	1956	7104	0.264	0.327	0.399	567	**0.273**
1994	4.62	55068	14695	2784	377	1532	5193	0.267	0.333	0.415	451	**0.284**
1995	4.63	69049	18184	3367	418	1917	6668	0.263	0.331	0.408	624	**0.280**
1996	4.68	77711	20398	3782	434	2220	7501	0.262	0.330	0.408	683	**0.280**
1997	4.60	77203	20300	3907	485	2163	7704	0.263	0.333	0.410	773	**0.283**
1998	4.60	88700	23213	4493	491	2565	8710	0.262	0.331	0.410	824	**0.281**
1999	5.00	89010	23880	4619	512	2893	9602	0.268	0.342	0.429	799	**0.298**
2000	5.00	88743	23594	4633	532	3005	9735	0.266	0.342	0.432	898	**0.298**
2001	4.70	88100	23027	4613	488	2952	8567	0.261	0.331	0.425	969	**0.288**
2002	4.45	87794	22753	4482	488	2595	8921	0.259	0.331	0.410	895	**0.282**
2003	4.61	88426	23126	4657	491	2708	8666	0.262	0.332	0.417	967	**0.285**
2004	4.64	88622	23271	4687	494	2846	8736	0.263	0.333	0.423	944	**0.288**
2005	4.45	88120	23058	4754	468	2580	8396	0.262	0.330	0.414	980	**0.283**
2006	4.76	88844	23501	4834	561	2840	8600	0.265	0.334	0.427	1030	**0.291**
2007	4.71	89488	23796	4898	505	2705	8576	0.266	0.334	0.423	934	**0.289**
2008	4.54	88595	23071	4729	478	2608	8816	0.260	0.331	0.413	879	**0.283**

American League

AL												**A L**
Year	R/G	AB	H	2B	3B	HR	BB	BA	OBP	SLG	HBP	**ABF**
1901	5.35	38138	10559	1534	688	228	2780	0.277	0.333	0.371	412	**0.261**
1902	4.89	38005	10451	1661	569	258	2815	0.275	0.331	0.369	340	**0.259**
1903	4.10	37434	9553	1549	618	184	2266	0.255	0.303	0.344	322	**0.231**

AL   **A L**

Year	R/G	AB	H	2B	3B	HR	BB	BA	OBP	SLG	HBP	**ABF**
1904	3.54	41479	10138	1482	610	156	2611	0.244	0.295	0.321	384	**0.217**
1905	3.69	40622	9783	1531	479	156	2982	0.241	0.299	0.314	397	**0.217**
1906	3.67	40413	10051	1374	515	137	2802	0.249	0.303	0.318	350	**0.221**
1907	3.66	40965	10132	1325	455	104	2824	0.247	0.302	0.309	362	**0.216**
1908	3.44	40601	9702	1279	499	116	2803	0.239	0.294	0.304	388	**0.210**
1909	3.44	39972	9747	1272	499	109	2931	0.244	0.303	0.309	441	**0.217**
1910	3.64	40925	9948	1299	567	147	3395	0.243	0.308	0.313	424	**0.222**
1911	4.61	41154	11239	1623	641	198	3559	0.273	0.338	0.358	464	**0.260**
1912	4.44	40887	10826	1591	671	156	3794	0.265	0.333	0.348	388	**0.252**
1913	3.93	39911	10209	1476	621	159	3743	0.256	0.325	0.336	381	**0.243**
1914	3.65	40743	10085	1435	598	148	3920	0.248	0.319	0.323	348	**0.234**
1915	3.96	40304	10005	1409	617	160	4217	0.248	0.325	0.326	378	**0.239**
1916	3.68	40837	10147	1540	552	144	4062	0.248	0.321	0.324	318	**0.236**
1917	3.65	40670	10075	1477	533	133	3856	0.248	0.318	0.320	306	**0.232**
1918	3.64	33535	8502	1204	410	96	3207	0.254	0.323	0.322	237	**0.236**
1919	4.09	37387	10021	1607	531	240	3367	0.268	0.333	0.359	279	**0.257**
1920	4.76	41986	11902	2007	620	369	3809	0.283	0.347	0.387	299	**0.279**
1921	5.12	42829	12525	2140	694	477	3965	0.292	0.356	0.408	318	**0.295**
1922	4.75	42281	12041	2032	585	525	3797	0.285	0.348	0.398	335	**0.285**
1923	4.78	42068	11876	2010	553	442	4092	0.283	0.351	0.388	341	**0.282**
1924	4.98	42280	12253	2197	551	397	4136	0.290	0.358	0.397	324	**0.291**
1925	5.20	42595	12418	2218	557	533	4289	0.292	0.360	0.408	267	**0.298**
1926	4.73	41762	11750	2195	568	424	4232	0.281	0.351	0.392	255	**0.285**
1927	4.92	42117	12024	2261	610	439	4018	0.286	0.352	0.399	266	**0.288**
1928	4.76	42117	11831	2200	620	483	3828	0.281	0.344	0.397	229	**0.282**
1929	5.01	42181	11976	2229	599	595	4054	0.284	0.349	0.407	192	**0.290**
1930	5.41	42882	12338	2375	656	673	3975	0.288	0.351	0.421	206	**0.297**
1931	5.14	43670	12154	2323	538	576	4168	0.278	0.344	0.396	188	**0.281**
1932	5.23	43430	12017	2287	570	707	4405	0.277	0.346	0.404	170	**0.286**
1933	5.00	42674	11637	2090	545	607	4370	0.273	0.342	0.390	149	**0.278**
1934	5.13	42932	11968	2205	449	688	4615	0.279	0.351	0.399	144	**0.288**
1935	5.09	42999	12033	2212	525	663	4544	0.280	0.351	0.402	172	**0.289**
1936	5.67	43747	12657	2400	548	758	4847	0.289	0.363	0.421	194	**0.307**
1937	5.23	43303	12178	2294	539	806	4773	0.281	0.355	0.415	164	**0.298**
1938	5.37	42500	11935	2133	485	864	4924	0.281	0.358	0.415	164	**0.300**
1939	5.21	42594	11866	2107	498	796	4657	0.279	0.352	0.407	148	**0.292**
1940	4.97	43017	11674	2167	513	883	4497	0.271	0.342	0.407	151	**0.285**
1941	4.74	43125	11492	2066	508	734	4742	0.266	0.341	0.389	148	**0.277**
1942	4.26	41955	10785	1797	400	533	4318	0.257	0.329	0.357	165	**0.255**
1943	3.89	42213	10522	1728	369	473	4325	0.249	0.322	0.341	173	**0.244**
1944	4.09	42748	11114	1771	413	459	3951	0.260	0.325	0.353	173	**0.250**
1945	3.90	41624	10634	1674	392	430	4145	0.255	0.325	0.346	154	**0.247**
1946	4.06	42239	10793	1827	401	653	4401	0.256	0.328	0.364	143	**0.257**
1947	4.14	42002	10739	1708	412	679	4745	0.256	0.333	0.364	132	**0.261**
1948	4.73	42155	11212	1846	450	710	5230	0.266	0.349	0.382	179	**0.280**
1949	4.67	41669	10961	1737	391	769	5627	0.263	0.353	0.379	176	**0.282**

AL Year	R/G	AB	H	2B	3B	HR	BB	BA	OBP	SLG	HBP	A L ABF
1950	5.04	42407	11474	1829	423	973	5418	0.271	0.356	0.402	216	**0.294**
1951	4.63	42361	11103	1836	349	839	4889	0.262	0.342	0.381	227	**0.274**
1952	4.18	42317	10690	1716	339	794	4631	0.253	0.330	0.365	247	**0.260**
1953	4.46	42358	11117	1816	331	879	4469	0.262	0.336	0.383	263	**0.271**
1954	4.19	41909	10766	1639	386	823	4619	0.257	0.331	0.373	212	**0.265**
1955	4.44	41817	10802	1574	338	961	4808	0.258	0.336	0.381	270	**0.272**
1956	4.66	42007	10937	1680	353	1075	5019	0.260	0.341	0.394	281	**0.281**
1957	4.23	41987	10703	1663	307	1024	4309	0.255	0.326	0.382	274	**0.265**
1958	4.17	41684	10595	1623	290	1057	4062	0.254	0.322	0.383	252	**0.263**
1959	4.36	41964	10621	1690	267	1091	4210	0.253	0.323	0.384	264	**0.264**
1960	4.39	41838	10689	1720	274	1086	4447	0.255	0.328	0.388	268	**0.269**
1961	4.53	54904	14037	2226	404	1534	5902	0.256	0.329	0.395	319	**0.273**
1962	4.44	55239	14068	2238	400	1552	5671	0.255	0.325	0.394	336	**0.270**
1963	4.08	55011	13609	2114	352	1489	5031	0.247	0.312	0.380	342	**0.255**
1964	4.06	55180	13637	2109	333	1551	5227	0.247	0.315	0.382	367	**0.257**
1965	3.94	54362	13158	2077	365	1370	5306	0.242	0.311	0.369	316	**0.250**
1966	3.89	54082	13005	2021	408	1365	4927	0.240	0.306	0.369	319	**0.246**
1967	3.70	54179	12766	1949	365	1197	4993	0.236	0.303	0.351	397	**0.237**
1968	3.41	53709	12359	1874	338	1104	4881	0.230	0.297	0.339	426	**0.229**
1969	4.09	65536	16120	2385	378	1649	7032	0.246	0.321	0.369	439	**0.257**
1970	4.17	65675	16404	2492	373	1746	6808	0.250	0.322	0.379	432	**0.261**
1971	3.87	64641	15957	2426	351	1484	6477	0.247	0.317	0.364	426	**0.252**
1972	3.47	61712	14751	2260	316	1175	5742	0.239	0.306	0.343	393	**0.236**
1973	4.28	66276	17193	2624	404	1552	6647	0.259	0.328	0.381	397	**0.266**
1974	4.10	66044	17062	2564	400	1369	6135	0.258	0.323	0.371	414	**0.258**
1975	4.30	65371	16861	2662	429	1465	6672	0.258	0.328	0.379	394	**0.265**
1976	4.01	65711	16820	2588	467	1122	6128	0.256	0.320	0.361	374	**0.252**
1977	4.53	77274	20572	3408	644	2013	7270	0.266	0.330	0.405	461	**0.278**
1978	4.20	76411	19952	3325	538	1680	7287	0.261	0.326	0.385	442	**0.267**
1979	4.67	76704	20682	3529	548	2006	7413	0.270	0.334	0.408	422	**0.282**
1980	4.51	77888	20958	3489	553	1844	7221	0.269	0.331	0.399	400	**0.276**
1981	4.07	50813	13016	2119	305	1062	4761	0.256	0.321	0.373	279	**0.258**
1982	4.48	77886	20566	3493	519	2080	7338	0.264	0.328	0.402	372	**0.275**
1983	4.48	77821	20662	3710	549	1903	7094	0.266	0.328	0.401	425	**0.274**
1984	4.42	77910	20539	3443	534	1980	7171	0.264	0.326	0.398	419	**0.272**
1985	4.56	77257	20182	3562	528	2178	7465	0.261	0.327	0.406	419	**0.276**
1986	4.61	77376	20237	3520	468	2290	7667	0.262	0.330	0.408	500	**0.279**
1987	4.90	77819	20620	3667	461	2634	7812	0.265	0.333	0.425	493	**0.289**
1988	4.36	77005	19967	3558	425	1901	7191	0.259	0.324	0.391	550	**0.268**
1989	4.29	77004	20078	3404	457	1718	7277	0.261	0.326	0.384	483	**0.266**
1990	4.30	76800	19900	3559	460	1796	7631	0.259	0.327	0.388	509	**0.269**
1991	4.49	77603	20195	3680	453	1953	7730	0.260	0.329	0.395	538	**0.273**
1992	4.32	77147	20006	3596	386	1776	7704	0.259	0.328	0.385	585	**0.269**
1993	4.71	77506	20661	3861	427	2074	8006	0.267	0.337	0.408	633	**0.285**
1994	5.23	55198	15048	2939	325	1774	5938	0.273	0.345	0.434	425	**0.302**
1995	5.06	69522	18791	3591	406	2164	7572	0.270	0.344	0.427	595	**0.298**

AL   **A L**

Year	R/G	AB	H	2B	3B	HR	BB	BA	OBP	SLG	HBP	**ABF**
1996	5.39	79090	21922	4205	421	2742	8592	0.277	0.350	0.445	721	**0.311**
1997	4.93	78235	21171	4097	398	2477	7962	0.271	0.340	0.428	676	**0.296**
1998	5.01	78416	21276	4248	408	2499	7737	0.271	0.340	0.432	763	**0.297**
1999	5.18	78126	21447	4121	419	2635	8289	0.275	0.347	0.439	780	**0.306**
2000	5.30	78547	21652	4269	420	2688	8503	0.276	0.349	0.443	674	**0.309**
2001	4.86	78134	20852	4200	440	2506	7239	0.267	0.334	0.428	921	**0.291**
2002	4.81	77788	20519	4218	433	2464	7325	0.264	0.331	0.424	851	**0.288**
2003	4.86	78311	20931	4170	443	2499	7223	0.267	0.333	0.428	882	**0.290**
2004	5.01	78731	21251	4232	404	2605	7486	0.270	0.338	0.433	896	**0.296**
2005	4.76	78215	20933	4109	420	2437	6811	0.268	0.330	0.424	817	**0.287**
2006	4.97	78497	21572	4301	391	2546	7247	0.275	0.339	0.437	787	**0.299**
2007	4.90	78294	21181	4299	433	2252	7503	0.271	0.338	0.423	821	**0.299**
2008	4.78	78119	20901	4285	408	2270	7521	0.268	0.336	0.420	793	**0.299**

Appendix C:
Technological Notes

Ten to fifteen years ago, researchers would open *Total Baseball* or *The Baseball Encyclopedia* and search through hundreds of pages to collect data and study players. Fortunately, now the data is available on the Internet, using sites such as baseball-reference.com or retrosheet.org. Gathering data has been very efficient and easy. In this appendix we show how to capture data from the Internet and use a spreadsheet to manipulate the numbers. As an example, suppose we wish to calculate the Total Power Quotient (*TPQ*) for Babe Ruth and compare it to that of Albert Pujols. We start by accessing the internet and going to Babe Ruth's homepage on baseball-reference.com. It should look like this:

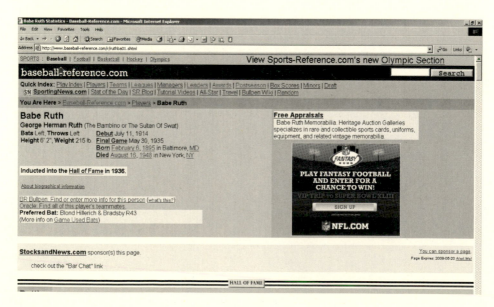

You can see the web address on the Address line. Scrolling down the page, we wish to copy all of Ruth's Batting data.

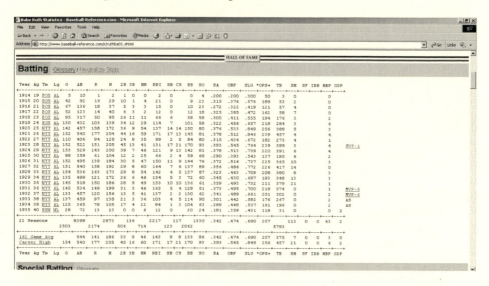

Place the cursor to the left of "Year" and click the left mouse button, holding it down while you highlight all of the data.

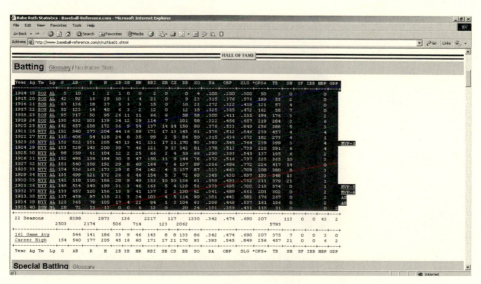

Copy the data onto your clipboard ("Edit — Copy," or CTRL C).
Now, open up your spreadsheet program (we will show Microsoft Excel).

Paste the data into the spreadsheet ("Edit — Paste," or CTRL V, or use the paste icon on the toolbar). It should look like the following:

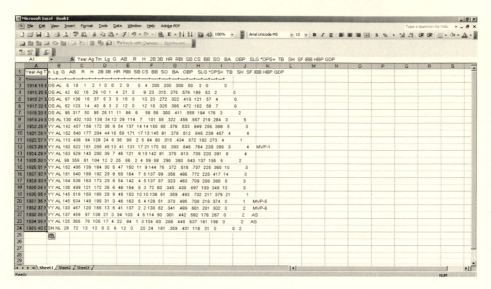

Notice that the first column is highlighted, but things aren't lined up as you had hoped. Don't worry. Click "Data — Text to Columns," and you should see the following (your data is being neatly converted from a database into a spreadsheet organized with column breaks:

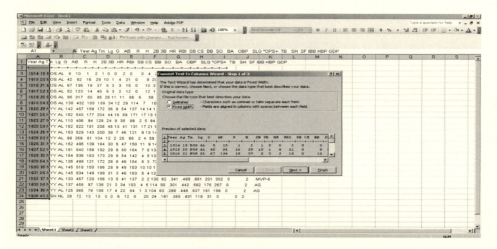

Click "Next" twice, and you should see the following screen, explaining how data is converted:

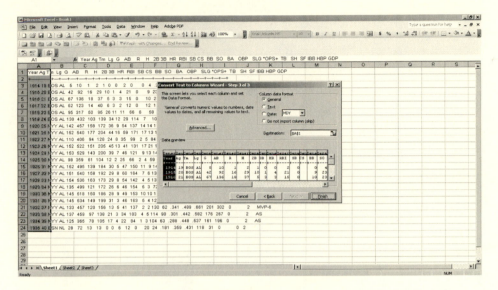

Click "Finish" and the data has been neatly sorted into columns under each header:

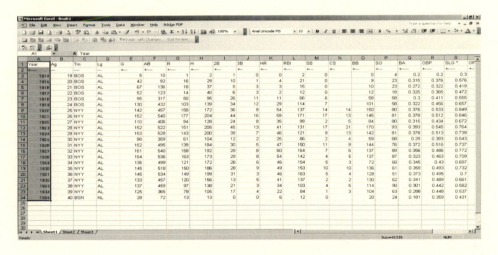

You should notice a few things here. The data is now sorted by column, but sometimes you cannot see it all, or it is not centered. Click the box to the left of column "A" and above Row "1" and then the "Center" icon:

This centers the data in each cell. You may notice that some of the numbers are taken to different decimal values (see cells Q7 or S20). In 1918, Ruth batted .300, so the spreadsheet lists it as 0.3. In 1931, he slugged 0.700. Simply highlight the columns in questions (columns Q, R, & S) and format the data to list 3 decimals by clicking "Format — Cells — Number — 3 decimal places" as shown below. Click "OK."

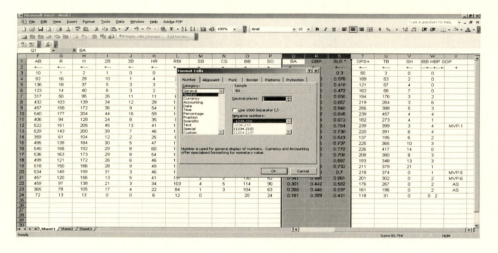

Now you are ready to manipulate the data. We know that

$$TPQ = \frac{HR + TB + RBI}{AB}.$$

Perhaps you wish to delete all the rest of the data, except for columns A (Year), F (*AB*), K (*HR*), L (*RBI*), and U (*TB*). Simply highlight each of those columns and then click "Edit — Delete." You should be left with the following:

Year	AB	HR	RBI	TB
1914	10	0	2	3
1915	92	4	21	53
1916	136	3	15	57
1917	123	2	12	58
1918	317	11	66	176
1919	432	29	114	284
1920	457	54	137	388
1921	540	59	171	457
1922	406	35	99	273
1923	522	41	131	399
1924	529	46	121	391
1925	359	25	66	195
1926	495	47	150	365
1927	540	60	164	417
1928	536	54	142	380
1929	499	46	154	348
1930	518	49	153	379
1931	534	46	163	374
1932	457	41	137	302
1933	459	34	103	267
1934	365	22	84	196
1935	72	6	12	31

Click on cell F3, next to the 3 total bases for 1914. We are now ready to enter the formula for *TPQ*. For 1914, the *TPQ* was $(0 + 3 + 2)/10$, or 0.5000. Excel requires an equal sign ("=") to initiate a formula, so type "= (" and then click cell C3 then "+" then cell E3 then "+" then cell F3 then ") /" then cell B3. You should be able to see the formula in the command line.

STDEV   =(C3+D3+E3)/B3

Year	AB	HR	RBI	TB	F
1914	10	0	2		=(C3+D3+E3)/B3
1915	92	4	21	53	
1916	136	3	15	57	
1917	123	2	12	58	
1918	317	11	66	176	
1919	432	29	114	284	
1920	457	54	137	388	
1921	540	59	171	457	
1922	406	35	99	273	
1923	522	41	131	399	
1924	529	46	121	391	
1925	359	25	66	195	
1926	495	47	150	365	
1927	540	60	164	417	
1928	536	54	142	380	
1929	499	46	154	348	
1930	518	49	153	379	
1931	534	46	163	374	
1932	457	41	137	302	
1933	459	34	103	267	
1934	365	22	84	196	
1935	72	6	12	31	

Press the "Enter" key and the formula is enacted. You should see a value of "0.5." You can set the decimal places to 4 as described above. Now, instead of retyping this formula into every cell in column F, we simply highlight cell F3 and place the mouse cursor over the lower right-hand corner of cell F3 until a bolded plus sign appears. Click the right mouse button and drag the mouse down through cell F24. Release the right button and you should see

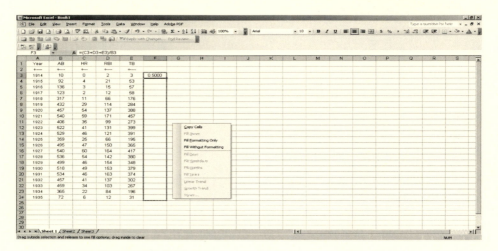

Click the "Fill Without Formatting" and the formula is fitted into each cell in column F.

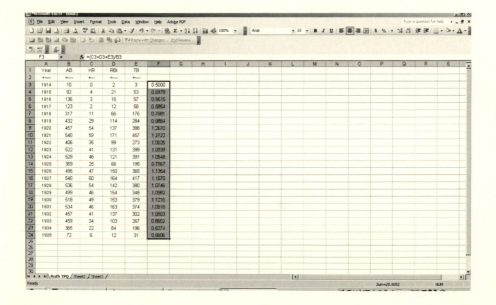

You can rename the worksheet as "Ruth TPQ" by right-clicking on the "Sheet 1" and clicking "Rename" and typing in the desired sheet name.

Do the same for Pujols. You can either add his data into the same worksheet, under Ruth, or into a new worksheet (Sheet 2):

	Year Ag Tm Lg	AB	HR	RBI	TB	
1	Year Ag Tm Lg	AB	HR	RBI	TB	
2	+	+	+	+	+	
3	2001 21 STL NL	590	37	130	360	0.8932
4	2002 22 STL NL	590	34	127	331	0.8339
5	2003 23 STL NL	591	43	124	394	0.9492
6	2004 24 STL NL	592	46	123	389	0.9426
7	2005 25 STL NL	591	41	117	360	0.8765
8	2006 26 STL NL	535	49	137	359	1.0187
9	2007 27 STL NL	565	32	103	321	0.8071
10	2008 28 STL NL	338	21	65	208	0.8698

Notice that the "Year — Age — Team — League" data is all in column A. Sometimes that happens from the database. You can always retype them into separate columns, but in this example, it doesn't affect our calculations. We see that Pujols' highest season *TPQ* was 2006 with a value of 1.0187. Ruth's was 1921 with a value of 1.2722.

Suppose you wanted to find the seasonal average *TPQ* for Albert Pujols. Noting that his *AB* have been fairly consistent from season to season, you can highlight the TPQ values and then use the "Average" function, which is built-in to Excel, with the sigma icon on the toolbar. Highlight the data plus at least one blank cell below it and then click the sigma icon, selecting "Average." The extra cell is needed to put the desired average into.

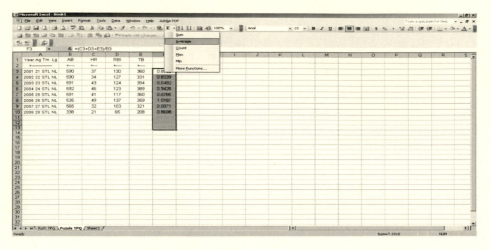

A more accurate method would be to sum all of the columns and then find Pujols' *TPQ* using his total data. In this instance, we find that both values are very similar (using the data through the 2008 All Star Break). His career *TPQ* is 0.8996 and his seasonal average *TPQ* is 0.8990. This is a great example of consistency.

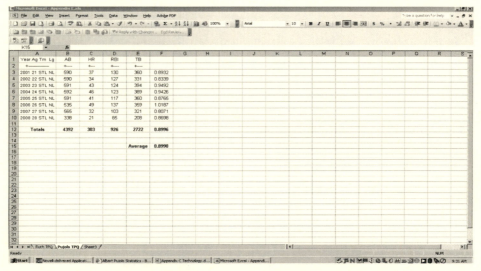

Copying data from the Internet into a spreadsheet greatly simplifies the manipulation and reduces the tediousness of the calculations. You can then save the spreadsheet for later use. You can add as many worksheets as necessary for your calculations.

Appendix D:
Sabermetrics in the Classroom

At the end of our previous book, *Understanding Sabermetrics*, we included a module or primer which dealt with the *teaching* of sabermetrics; that is, courses taught in the classrooms of colleges and universities. We specifically referenced two courses: MATH 1011, a one-credit course offered at Seton Hall University, and MA 488, a three-credit course given at the United States Military Academy.

Because we believe that there exists a kind of "cross-curriculum" richness in such courses, it has been our hope that other educators would offer similar courses at their institutions. We are aware of statistics courses involving baseball (or vice versa) which are given at Bowling Green State University and Quinnipiac University, to name but two such instances. We hope many more colleges and universities will follow their lead.

And not only that; we believe that sabermetrics can be taught on the high school level. Perhaps not in the form of full-blown courses, but certainly as *parts* of courses.

And we do not stop there. Why can't this be extended to the elementary levels of education? Surely, many youngsters suffering from "math anxiety" would feel more at ease when numbers are applied to the understanding of the national pastime. What do you think?

Before we sign off, we ask that you feel free to contact us if you have any comments or suggestions, or if we can be of any assistance whatsoever. Our e-mail addresses are given below:

gabriel.costa@usma.edu
huber@muhlenberg.edu
saccomjt@shu.edu

Sources

Print Sources

Adair, R. *The Physics of Baseball*. New York: HarperCollins, 1994.

Albert, J. "Exploring Baseball Hitting Data: What About Those Breakdown Statistics?" *Journal of the American Statistical Association* 89 (1994): 1066–1074.

Costa, G., M. Huber and J. Saccoman. "Cumulative Home Run Frequency and the Recent Home Run Explosion." *The Baseball Research Journal* 34 (2005): 37–41.

_____. *Understanding Sabermetrics: An Introduction to the Science of Baseball Statistics*. Jefferson, NC: McFarland, 2008.

Gillette, G., and P. Palmer, eds. *The 2006 ESPN Baseball Encyclopedia*. New York: Sterling, 2006.

Hoban, M. *Baseball's Complete Players: Ratings of Total-Season Performance for the Greatest Players of the 20th Century*. Jefferson, NC: McFarland, 2000.

Huber, M. *West Point's Field of Dreams: Major League Baseball at Doubleday Field*. Quechee, VT: Vermont Heritage, 2004.

James, B. *The Bill James Baseball Abstract*. New York: Ballantine, various years.

_____. *The Bill James Historical Baseball Abstract*. New York: Villard, 1988.

_____, J. Dewan, N. Munro and D. Zminda, eds. *STATS All-Time Baseball Sourcebook*. Skokie, IL: STATS, 1998.

James, B., and J. Henzler. *Win Shares*. Morton Grove, IL: STATS, 2002.

Lindsey, G. "An Investigation of Strategies in Baseball." *Operations Research* 11 (1963): 447–501.

Lowry, P. *Green Cathedrals: The Ultimate Celebrations of All 273 Major League and Negro League Ballparks Past and Present*. New York: Addison-Wesley, 1993.

Schwartz, A. *The Numbers Game*. New York: St. Martin's, 2004.

Siwoff, S. *The Book of Baseball Records*. New York: Seymour Siwoff, 2004.

Spatz, L., ed. *The SABR Baseball List & Record Book*. New York: Scribner, 2007.

Thorn, J., and P. Palmer. *The Hidden Game of Baseball*. Garden City, NY: Doubleday, 1985.

_____, eds. *Total Baseball*. 2d ed. New York: Warner, 1991.

Online Sources

http://espn.go.com/mlb

http://hardballtimes.com

http://www.baseball-reference.com

http://www.mlb.com

http://www.popaward.com/htdocs/index.htm

http://www.retrosheet.org

About the Authors

Gabriel B. Costa is a Roman Catholic priest, ordained for service in 1979 for the Archdiocese of Newark, New Jersey. He is on an extended academic leave from Seton Hall University and presently is professor of mathematical sciences at the United States Military Academy at West Point, New York, where he also functions as an associate chaplain. He is a member of the Society for American Baseball Research (SABR) and has published significant baseball research in *The Baseball Research Journal, Elysian Fields Quarterly* and other journals. He co-founded the first sabermetrics courses at Seton Hall University (1988) and the United States Military Academy (1996). He has been a New York Yankees fan since he was 10 years old in 1958.

Michael R. Huber is an associate professor of mathematics at Muhlenberg College in Allentown, Pennsylvania. He was a co-teacher of the sabermetrics course at the United States Military Academy with Gabe Costa from 1996 to 2006. He is a SABR member, has published his baseball research in *The Baseball Research Journal,* the *Journal of Statistics Education,* and *Base Ball: A Journal of the Early Game* and is the author of *West Point's Field of Dreams: Major League Baseball at Doubleday Field* (Vermont Heritage, 2004). He has also contributed to SABR's Bio Project, including the special edition dedicated to the 1970 Baltimore Orioles. He has been rooting for the Orioles since 1968 and enjoys attending college and minor league baseball games with his family.

John T. Saccoman is a professor of mathematics and computer science at Seton Hall University in South Orange, New Jersey. He still team-teaches the earliest known sabermetrics course there with Gabe Costa. He is a charter member of the Elysian Fields (New Jersey) Chapter of SABR, and his significant baseball research has appeared in numerous SABR publications, including *Deadball Stars of the National League, Deadball Stars of the American League,* the *Fenway Project,* and *The Baseball Research Journal.* He has contributed biographies of Gil Hodges and Willie Mays, among others, to the SABR Bio Project. John resides in northern New Jersey with his son and fellow Mets fan, Ryan, and Bosox-loving wife, Mary.

Index